Generalization notation

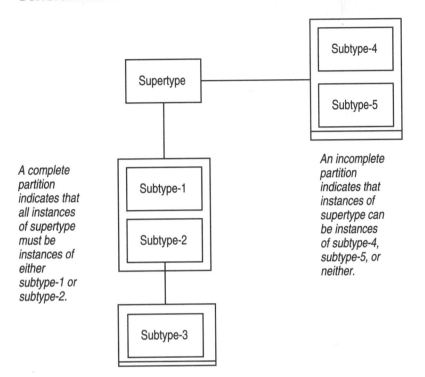

A complete partition indicates that all instances of supertype must be instances of either subtype-1 or subtype-2.

An incomplete partition indicates that instances of supertype can be instances of subtype-4, subtype-5, or neither.

Notation for semantic statements

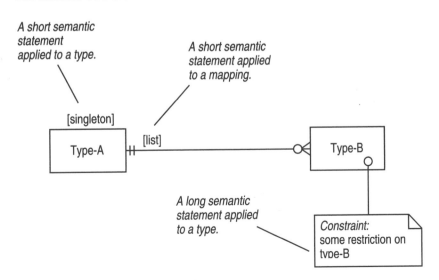

A short semantic statement applied to a type.

A short semantic statement applied to a mapping.

A long semantic statement applied to a type.

Analysis Patterns:
Reusable Object Models

The Addison-Wesley Series in Object-Oriented Software Engineering
Grady Booch, Series Editor

Grady Booch, *Object Solutions: Managing the Object-Oriented Project*
0-8053-0594-7

Grady Booch, *Object-Oriented Analysis and Design with Applications,* Second Edition
0-8053-5340-2

Grady Booch and Doug Bryan, *Software Engineering with ADA,* Third Edition
0-8053-0608-0

Dave Collins, *Designing Object-Oriented User Interfaces*
0-8053-5350-X

Martin Fowler, *Analysis Patterns: Reusable Object Models*
0-201-89542-0

Wilf LaLonde, *Discovering Smalltalk*
0-8053-2720-7

Ira Pohl, *Object-Oriented Programming Using C++*
0-8053-5382-8 (Second Edition available fall 1996)

David N. Smith, *IBM Smalltalk: The Language*
0-8053-0908-X

Daniel Tkach and Richard Puttick, *Object Technology in Application Development.*
Second Edition
0-8054-9833-2

Daniel Tkach, Walter Fang, and Andrew So, *Visual Modeling Technique:*
Object Technology using Visual Programming
0-8053-2574-3

Lockheed Martin Advanced Concepts Center and Rational Software Corporation,
Succeeding with the Booch and OMT Methods: A Practical Approach
0-805-32279-5

New for Fall 1996
David Bellin and Susan Suchman Simone, *The CRC Card Book*
0-201-89535-8

Robert Hathaway, *Object-Technology FAQ*
0-201-89541-2

Thomas Mowbray and William Ruh, *Introduction to CORBA*
0-201-89540-4

Analysis Patterns:
Reusable Object Models

Martin Fowler

 ADDISON-WESLEY

An imprint of Addison Wesley Longman, Inc.

Menlo Park, California • Reading, Massachusetts • Harlow, England
Berkeley, California • Don Mills, Ontario • Sydney • Bonn • Amsterdam • Tokyo • Mexico City

Senior Acquisitions Editor: J. Carter Shanklin
Editorial Assistant: Angela Buening
Senior Production Editor: Teri Hyde
Copy Editor: Barbara Conway
Proofreader: Holly McLean-Aldis
Indexer: Nancy Kopper
Compositor: Proctor-Willenbacher
Art House: London Road Design
Cover Design: Yvo Riezebos

The publisher offers discounts on this book when ordered in quantity for special sales. For more information please contact:
Corporate & Professional Publishing Group
Addison-Wesley Publishing Company
One Jacob Way
Reading, Massachusetts 01867

Library of Congress Cataloging-in-Publication Data

Fowler, Martin.
    Analysis patterns : reusable object models / Martin Fowler.
        p.   cm.
    Includes index.
    ISBN 0-201-89542-0
    1. Object-oriented methods (Computer science)   2. System analysis.
    I. Title.
    QA76.9.035F69   1997
    005.1'2--dc20   96-42988
                                                         CIP
ISBN   0-201-89542-0
3 4 5 6 7 8   MA   00 99 98 97
3rd Printing September, 1997

Addison Wesley Longman, Inc
2725 Sand Hill Road
Menlo Park, CA 94025

Foreword

When the "Gang of Four" was writing *Design Patterns*, we knew that there were lots of software patterns other than object-oriented design patterns. By the time we were through with the book, we had seen distributed programming patterns, user interface patterns, and even patterns of organizing software development groups. However, we hadn't seen any patterns that were clearly object-oriented analysis patterns. Peter Coad's patterns were the closest, but they were a lot like our patterns and it seemed to us that pure analysis patterns should differ more.

I found what I was looking for when I read a draft of Martin Fowler's book, *Analysis Patterns*. Its patterns contain a lot of domain knowledge yet can be used in all kinds of business software. Like the design patterns, they are abstract enough to help your software ride over the bumps of requirement changes but concrete enough to be understandable. They are not the most obvious solutions to modeling problems, yet they rang true to me. I had seen many of these solutions before, and they had worked.

I'm a designer more than a modeler, and I don't have a lot of experience in most of the domains that Martin Fowler describes. Though I felt the patterns were good, I couldn't have a lot of confidence in my feelings. Since I read the book, I have been trying out the patterns on projects and using them in teaching. They work! My confidence grew further when I ran across David Hay's book, *Data Model Patterns*, and realized that, despite their different backgrounds and vocabularies, they saw many of the same patterns. Patterns are supposed to describe reality, not invent a new one, and Martin Fowler accurately described the patterns in object-oriented models of business software. You can have confidence in the patterns he described.

This is not a book of principles that you must learn to apply before they can help you, though Martin describes many modeling principles. It is not a book that you have to read through and practice before it can do you any good. It is a book full of practical patterns that you can use right away. Look for the chapters that match the kind of problem you are working on now, and you will find lots of ideas that will help you. You can read the book chapter by chapter, and each chapter will give you new ideas.

To make the most of this book, you need to know two things. First, many of the patterns are more powerful than they might appear at first. Patterns like Accountability can be applied in nearly any project. Don't read only the chapters that obviously apply to your project, but learn as many patterns as you can, and try them out to see whether they apply. Second, make sure your coworkers read the book. One of the biggest advantages of patterns is that they help us communicate better. You will find that your team meetings will run more smoothly when you have a common vocabulary. This book will make documentation more consistent and easier to understand. Plus, it will make your coworkers better analysts, and it is more fun to work with people who do a good job!

— Ralph Johnson

Foreword

When I look at a software development project, I look for experience. Does the development team have experience doing relevant work? Can they apply their experience to the objects they build? Unfortunately, the answer to these questions is often no.

A growing number of us in the object-oriented development community feel we have misplaced our collective attention for some time. We no longer need to focus on tools, techniques, notations or even code. We already have in our hands the machinery to build great programs. When we fail, we fail because we lack experience.

Martin Fowler has found a way to give us what we need: experience in book form.

He has done for domain objects what Eric Gamma et al. did for implementation objects in their landmark work *Design Patterns: Elements of Reusable Object-Oriented Software*. Martin uses the familiar terminology of our nascent community but in a different way. He uses the word *pattern*, for example, not because he's duplicating or extending Gamma's book (or any of the other new titles bursting onto the market). He calls his written form of experience patterns simply because that is what they are. In his work as a consultant in object modeling information systems, he repeatedly found solutions to recurring problems, and discovered the pattern form in the process.

Martin Fowler easily could have written a book on object-oriented analysis. Luckily, he didn't. Instead we have a book cataloging the result of analysis. Each chapter reports the conclusion of his (and his colleagues') analytic efforts applied to common business problems. The domains addressed vary from medical record keeping to financial derivative trading, with several stops in between. Which chapters apply to you? Amazingly, they all do. Martin places each problem in a context and then offers a solution for that context. You will see familiar aspects in every context. You will recognize the problems. You will appreciate the results. And there it is: experience.

Finally, Martin writes in a personal style, relaying his thoughts and judgments. We feel his respect for his clients and colleagues from whom, he admits, most insights arise. We watch him keep his distance from the vagaries of implementation while still preserving implementability—a tightrope walk that defies direct explanation. As we see into the mind of an expert analyst, we gain a lesson in the how-to of analysis that adds to our own store of experience.

—*Ward Cunningham*
Cunningham & Cunningham, Inc.

Contents

Preface

Not long ago, no books were available on object-oriented analysis and design. Now there are so many that it is impossible for any practitioner to keep up with them all. Most of these books concentrate on teaching a notation, suggesting a simple process for modeling, and illustrating it with a few simple examples. *Analysis Patterns: Reusable Object Models* is a different kind of book. Instead of focusing on the process—how to do modeling—it concentrates on the result of the process—the models themselves.

I am a consultant in object modeling for information systems. Clients ask me to train staff on modeling and to provide mentoring on projects. Much of my skill comes from a knowledge of modeling techniques and how to use them. More important, however, is my experience in actually creating many models and regularly seeing problems repeat themselves. Frequently I find that many aspects of a project revisit problems I have faced before. That experience allows me to reuse models I have built before, improve them, and adapt them to new demands.

Over the last few years, more and more people have also become aware of this phenomenon. We have realized that the typical methodology books, though valuable, only present the first step in a learning process that must also capture the actual things that are built. This realization has flowered into the *patterns* movement. This is a varied group of people, representing many different interests and opinions yet sharing the goal of propagating useful patterns of software systems.

As a result of the diversity of this patterns community, we have had difficulty in defining the term *pattern*. We all think we can recognize a pattern when we see it, we think most of us would agree in most cases, but we cannot come up with a single definition. Here is my definition: A *pattern is an idea that has been useful in one practical context and will probably be useful in others.*

I like to leave the definition quite loose because I wish to stay as close to the underlying motivation of patterns, without adding too many restrictive amendments. A pattern can have many forms, and each form adds specializations that are useful for that kind of pattern. (Section 1.2 discusses the current state of the patterns world and where this book fits in.)

This book is about patterns in analysis, patterns that reflect conceptual structures of business processes rather than actual software implementations. Most of the chapters discuss patterns for various business domains. Such patterns are hard to classify into traditional vertical areas (manufacturing, finance, health care, and so on) because they are often useful in several areas. These patterns are important because they help us to understand how people perceive the world. It is valuable to base a computer system's design on this perception and, indeed, to change that perception—which is where business process reengineering (BPR) comes in.

Conceptual patterns cannot exist in isolation, however. Conceptual models are only useful to software engineers if they can see how to implement them. In this book I present patterns that can be used to turn conceptual models into software, and I discuss how that software fits into an architecture for a large information system. I also discuss specific implementation tips with the patterns.

I wrote this book because this was the book that I wanted to read when I started out. Modelers will find ideas in this book to help them begin working in a new domain. The patterns contain useful models, the reasoning behind their designs, and when they should and should not be applied. With this information a modeler can adapt the models to fit a specific problem.

The patterns in this book can also be used in reviewing models—to see what might have been left out and to suggest some alternatives that may lead to improvement. When I review a project, I usually compare what I see with the patterns I have learned from previous work. I have found that being aware of patterns in my work helps me to apply my past experiences more easily. Patterns like this also uncover modeling issues that go beyond what can be covered in a simple text book. By discussing why we model things the way we do, we gain a greater understanding of how to improve our modeling, even if we don't use the patterns directly.

Structure of this Book

This book is divided into two sections. The first section covers analysis patterns, which are patterns from conceptual business models. They provide key abstractions from domains such as trading, measurement, accounting, and organizational relationships. The patterns are conceptual because they represent the way people think about the business, rather than the way a computer system is designed. The chapters in this section stress alternative patterns that can be used, and the strengths and weaknesses of those alternatives. Although each pattern will clearly be useful to those working in the same domain, the basic pattern is often useful in other domains.

The second section focuses on support patterns, which help you use analysis patterns. Support patterns show how analysis patterns fit into an information systems architecture, how the constructs of conceptual models turn into software interfaces and implementations, and how certain advanced modeling constructs relate to simpler structures.

To describe these patterns, I need a notation. The appendix provides a brief discussion of the notation I use and what the symbols mean. I do not use a single method but prefer to mix techniques from different methods. The appendix is not designed to be a tutorial on techniques, but it should provide an outline and refresh your memory. It also tells you where to find a tutorial on the techniques I use.

Each section is divided into chapters. Each chapter on analysis patterns contains patterns that are related by a loose notion of subject area, influenced by the projects that spawned them. This organization reflects the fact that any pattern must come from a practical context. Each pattern appears in its own subsection within a chapter. I do not use any of the formal headings for patterns that are used by some patterns authors (see Section 1.2.2). I describe each pattern in a form that is as close to the original project form as is reasonable, with a minimum of abstraction. I add examples to show the use of the pattern within its original domain and also to suggest how the pattern might be used in other domains. One of the greatest difficulties of patterns is abstracting them into other domains; I follow the principle that this should be left to the reader (see Section 1.2.3).

This book is thus a catalog, rather than a book to be read from cover to cover. I have tried to write each chapter in such a way that it can be read independently from the other chapters. (This is not always possible, however. Whenever a chapter requires that another chapter be read first, I say so in the chapter introduction.) Each chapter has an introduction that explains the general subject area of the chapter, summarizes the patterns in the chapter, and says what projects the patterns originated from.

How to Read this Book

I suggest reading all of Chapter 1 first and then reading each chapter introduction. Then feel free to delve into the chapters in any order you like. If you are not familiar with the approach I take to modeling, or the notation and concepts I use, read the appendix. The Table of Patterns gives a brief summary of what each pattern is about, so you can use that to help you explore or to find a pattern when you come back to the book at a later time. It is important to stress that each pattern in this book is useful outside the domain that gave it birth. Thus I encourage you to look into chapters that you might think are outside your field of interest. For example, I found that models of observation and measurement designed for health care proved to be very useful for corporate financial analysis.

Who Should Read this Book

This book can be useful to a range of readers, although different readers will learn different things from it and may need some different preparations.

I expect my biggest audience to be *analysts and designers* of object-oriented (OO) computer systems, particularly those working at the analysis end. Such readers should have made at least some use of an OO analysis and design method. This book does not provide any introduction to this subject, so I would suggest first reading a book on OO analysis and design if you are new to this field. I must stress that the patterns in this book are conceptual in nature, and I use a very conceptual approach to modeling. This leads to some stylistic differences from those texts that use a more implementation-based approach to modeling.

A small, but very important, audience consists of those people who act as *domain experts for a modeling project*. Such readers do not require a knowledge of computers but do need to know about conceptual modeling. One of the main reasons I use conceptual models in this book is to make things easier for this group of readers. The modeling project here may be analysis for computer system development or BPR. I have taught many professionals (including doctors, financial traders, accountants, nurses, and payroll supervisors) this kind of modeling and have found that a software background is neither an advantage nor a disadvantage to conceptual modeling. The business model patterns are as much about business modeling as they are about computer systems analysis (see Section 1.4). Any such reader should take a course on OO analysis that stresses the conceptual aspect. (Odell's book [1] is particularly valuable in this respect.)

I hope many *programmers* will delve between these covers, although some programmers may take exception to the lack of code and the conceptual slant. For these readers I suggest you take particular note of Chapter 14, which should help to explain the relationship between the conceptual models and the resulting software.

This is an object-oriented book, and I do not hesitate in proclaiming my belief that the object-oriented approach is the superior way to develop software. These models, however, are primarily conceptual models, and many *data modelers* have had a long tradition of using conceptual (or logical) models. Data modelers should find many of the patterns useful, particularly if they use more advanced semantic techniques. The object-oriented features of the models will reveal many of the differences between object-oriented and traditional approaches. I would encourage such readers to use this book in conjunction with an OO analysis book that stresses the conceptual side of modeling and the links between OO and semantic data modeling.

Managers will find the book useful as a starting point for development activity. Starting from a pattern can help to clarify goals, and project planning can take advantage of the broad ground that patterns map out.

I have not aimed this book at *students*. I've written it more for the professional software engineer. I hope, however, that some students will take a look. When I was learning analysis and design, I found it difficult because there were few good examples I could learn from, examples that came out of the world outside the university. Just as looking at good code can teach you a lot about programming, looking at good models can teach you a lot about analysis and design.

A Living Book

Every author I know shares a frustration: Once a book is published it is fixed. The book spreads its advice around the community, yet the author has little way of expressing changes. I know how much I keep learning, and I am sure this learning will modify my ideas. I want these changes to be passed on to my readers.

With this book, Addison-Wesley will provide a web site <http://www.aw.com/cp/fowler.html> which will be used to pass on further materials to keep this book alive. At this stage I am not sure exactly what it will contain, but I expect the following:

- any new things I learn about the patterns in the book.
- answers to questions about the book
- useful commentary from others about the patterns
- new analysis patterns by myself, and by others
- when the Unified Modeling Notation appears (or whatever it is called by then) I will redraw all the diagrams in the book in the new notation and put them on the site.

This site will be a complement to the book, so keep an eye on it and use it to let me know how to improve and develop the ideas between these pages.

Acknowledgments

Any author is indebted to many others who help. For this book this is particularly true since so many of the patterns were built with the help of my clients, colleagues, and friends. I would like to give my sincere thanks to the following, both named and implied.

First and foremost, Jim Odell has been an essential part of my career. He has taught me much about developing information systems and has been a constant source of inspiration, helpful advice, and strange humor. I can safely say that without his support this book would not have happened.

The team at Coopers & Lybrand in London helped with much of the early work and helped pass many evenings at Smithfield's.

John Edwards formed many of my early ideas about conceptual modeling and its role in software development, as well as introducing me to many interesting ideas, including those of Christopher Alexander.

John Hope urged me to think of the domain first and technology second, as well as casting a helpful spell at several key points in my career.

Tom Cairns and Mark Thursz, doctors at St. Mary's Hospital in London, worked with me in developing the health care models that form the basis of Chapters 2, 3, and 8. They are proof that a computer background is not necessary to be a top-class conceptual modeler. Mark also was a willing source for health care examples with impressive-sounding medical terminology.

The health care projects also involved many software and health care professionals from St. Mary's, the Hospital for Sick Children (HSC), St. Thomas's Hospital, and the University of Wales. Anne Casey, a nurse at HSC, and Hazim Timimi, an analyst, helped put together the final Cosmos model. Gerry Gold set up this work and made sure it kept going.

Brad Kain has had a great impact on my thinking on reuse and components, as well as undertaking the important task of showing me the nightlife of Boston.

Applying the health care models to corporate finance in Chapter 4 was the experience that, for me, proved the usefulness of analysis patterns across different domains. Lynne Halpin and Craig Lockwood led the MBFW team at Xerox, and Vivek Salgar got our conceptual ideas into the brutal reality of C++.

David Creager, Steve Shepherd, and their team at Citibank worked with me in developing the models from which I drew the financial patterns in Chapters 9–11. They also further developed many of the architectural ideas of Chapter 12 from their health care origins, and taught me much about the frenetic life in The City.

Fred Peel set up and maintained my work at Citibank, when not scaring me with his driving. Daniel Poon and Hazim Timimi from Valbecc got many of my fuzzy ideas into detailed specifications.

The accounting patterns in Chapter 6 have had a long gestation. Tom Daly, Peter Swettenham, Tom Hadfield, and their respective teams developed models that gave birth to the patterns in this book. Rich Garzaniti got my accounting terminology sorted out. Kent Beck did much to improve my Smalltalk.

Chapter 14 was written with the help of James Odell.

I have been very much a latecomer to the patterns community, getting to know it well only after most of this book was written. It is a very open and friendly group that has done much to encourage my work. Kent Beck, Ward Cunningham, and Jim Coplein encouraged me to get involved with the community and to develop my ideas as patterns. Ralph Johnson provided particularly helpful comments on the first draft of this book.

I have had first-class comments from my many reviewers whom I would like to name: Dave Collins, Ward Cunningham (Cunningham & Cunningham, Inc.), Henry A. Etlinger (Department of Computer Science, RIT), Donald G. Firesmith (Knowledge Systems Corporation), Erich Gamma, Adele Goldberg, Tom Hadfield (TesserAct Technology), Lynne Halpin (Netscape Communications), Brian Henderson-Sellers, Neil Hunt (Pure Software), Ralph E. Johnson (University of Illinois at Urbana-Champaign), Jean-Pierre Kuilboer (University of Massachusetts, Boston), Patrick D. Logan (Intel Corporation), James Odell, Charles Richter (Objective Engineering, Inc.), Douglas C. Schmidt (Washington University), and Dan Tasker. I will mention that Don Firesmith went above the call of duty in tracking down problems that needed to be fixed.

As this is my first book, I'm particularly grateful to those at Addison-Wesley who helped me through the process. Carter Shanklin directed affairs and assembled a formidable panel of reviewers with much assistance from Angela Buenning. Teri Hyde coordinated the book production on a painfully tight schedule and Barbara Conway rescued my prose from its usual erratic state, and ruthlessly eliminated my native accent.

References

1. Martin, J., and J. Odell. *Object-Oriented Methods: A Foundation.* Englewood Cliffs, NJ: Prentice-Hall, 1995.

Introduction

1.1 Conceptual Models

Most books on object modeling talk about analysis and design. There is little agreement on where the boundary between these two activities lies. An important principle in object development is designing software so that its structure reflects that of the problem. One result of this principle is that the models produced from both analysis and design end up deliberately similar, leading many people to think that there is no difference.

I believe a difference between analysis and design still exists, but it is increasingly becoming one of emphasis. When doing analysis you are trying to understand the problem. To my mind this is not just listing requirements in use-cases [8]. Use-cases are a valuable, if not essential, part of system development, but capturing them is not the end of analysis. Analysis also involves looking behind the surface requirements to come up with a mental model of what is going on in the problem.

Consider someone who wants to write software to simulate a game of snooker. This problem could be evaluated in terms of use-cases that describe the surface features: "The player hits the white ball so it travels at a certain speed; it hits the red ball at a certain angle, and the red ball travels a certain distance and direction." You could film several hundred such incidents and measure ball speeds, angles, distances traveled. But these examples alone would probably not be enough to write a good simulation. To do the job well, you would need to look behind the surface to understand the laws of motion that relate mass, velocity, momentum, and the like. Understanding those laws would make it much easier to see how the software could be built.

The snooker ball problem is unusual because the laws are well known and have been well known for a long time. In many enterprises the equivalent foundations are not so well understood, and we have to make the effort to uncover them. To do this we create a conceptual model—a mental model that allows us to understand and simplify the problem. Some kind of conceptual model is a necessary part of software development, and even the most uncontrolled hacker does it. The difference is whether we think about conceptual modeling as a process in itself or as one aspect of the entire software design process.

It is important to remember that a conceptual model is a *human artifact.* The laws of motion that a developer uses to create something like the snooker simulation are not part of the real world; they represent a model of the real world, a model created by human beings. They are effective, in engineering terms, because they allow us to better understand what happens in the real world. Also, a developer can use more than one model; for the snooker simulation a Newtonian or Einsteinian model could be used. You could argue that the Einsteinian model would be more correct because it takes into account changes of mass due to the speed the balls are traveling and is thus more precise. The developer would almost certainly prefer the Newtonian model, however, because the speeds would be so low that they would make a negligible difference to the simulation but would involve a lot of extra complexity. This illustrates an important principle: There is no right or wrong model, merely one that is more useful for the job at hand.

Modeling Principle *Models are not right or wrong; they are more or less useful.*

The choice of model affects the flexibility and reusability of the resulting system. You might argue that the developer should use an Einsteinian model because the resulting software would be flexible enough to handle problems involving atomic collisions. But this is a dangerous path to go down. Building too much flexibility into a system can make it too complex, and this is bad engineering. Engineering demands a trade-off between the cost of building and maintaining an artifact and the features it will provide. To build software that is fit for a purpose, you have to develop a conceptual model that is appropriate to your needs. You need the simplest model you can get away with. Don't add flexibility you are unlikely to use.

The simplest model is not necessarily the first one you think of. Finding a simple solution takes a lot of time and effort, which can be frustrating. People often react to a simple model by saying "Oh yes, that's obvious" and thinking "So why did it take so long to come up with it?" But simple models are always worth the effort. Not only do they make things easier to build, but more importantly they make them easier to maintain and extend in the future. That's why it is worth replacing software that works with simpler software that also works.

How do you express a conceptual model? For many people the conceptual model is built into their software language. The advantage of a language is that you can execute a model to verify its correctness and to further explore it. This is no small advantage; I often use Smalltalk in my conceptual modeling. Another advantage is that you have to turn the model into a programming language eventually, so modeling in your target language saves the step of translation. (There are tools that can interpret or compile analysis and design models, thus reducing the problems associated with translation.)

The danger of using a language is that it is easy to get lost in the issues of using that language and lose sight of the problem you are trying to understand. (This is less of a problem with higher-level languages, such as Smalltalk. I know several gifted conceptual modelers who do their modeling in that language.) Modeling in a programming language also presents the danger of tying the models to that language. The model may use features of that language that are not available in other languages. This does not mean that the conceptual model cannot be moved to another language, but it can make the process more difficult.

To avoid these problems, many people use analysis and design techniques for conceptual modeling. These techniques can help people concentrate on conceptual rather than software design issues, and they can be easier to teach to domain experts. Analysis and design techniques use graphics to be more expressive. They may be rigorous, but they don't have to be. Techniques designed to be executable must be rigorous, but when analysis methods are used in conjunction with a programming language, they need not be as rigorous.

One of the main reasons I use analysis and design techniques is to involve domain experts. It is *essential* to have domain experts involved in conceptual modeling. I believe that effective models can only be built by those that really understand the domain—*full-time* workers in the domain, not software developers, no matter how long they have worked in the domain. If domain experts are to do conceptual modeling, they must be taught. I have taught OO analysis and design techniques to customer service supervisors, doctors, nurses, financial traders, and corporate financial analysts. I have found that an IT background is neither a help nor a hindrance to skill in modeling. The best modeler I know is a physician at a London hospital. As the professional analyst and modeler, I bring valuable skills to the process: I can provide rigor, I know how to use the techniques, and my outsider's view can challenge accepted wisdom. All this is not enough. However much work I do in health care computing, I will never know as much about health care as a doctor or nurse. Expert knowledge is central to a good analysis model.

Analysis techniques are intended to be independent of software technology. Ideally a conceptual modeling technique is totally independent of software technology, as are the laws of motion. This independence would prevent technology from hindering an understanding of the problem, and the resulting model would be equally useful for all kinds of software technology. In practice this purity does not occur. I try to develop very conceptual models that focus entirely on the problem, yet my techniques are object-oriented and hence reflect a software design approach. You can get a good sense of how software technology affects conceptual modeling by comparing the models in this book with those of David Hay [7]. We are both trying to build conceptual models, yet our results are different because he uses a relational technique and I use an object-oriented one. This is an inevitable result of the nature of software. Building software is building virtual machines. The languages in which we build software can both control the physical machine and express the needs of the problem. One of the reasons our languages change is because we find better ways to express the needs of a problem. These language changes thus influence the way we build conceptual models. Despite a few tricky areas (see Chapter 14), the resulting models are not difficult to turn into object-oriented software.

One caution I do need to raise now, however, is that conceptual models relate closely to software interfaces rather than software implementations. One of the important things about object-oriented software is that it separates interface from implementation. Unfortunately this distinction is too easily lost in practice because common languages do not make an explicit distinction between the two. The difference between a software component's interface (its type) and its implementation (its class) is extremely important. Many important delegation-based patterns in the "Gang of Four" book [6] rely on this distinction. When implementing these models, don't forget the difference.

Modeling Principle   *Conceptual models are linked to interfaces (types) not implementations (classes).*

1.2   The World of Patterns

In the last couple of years, patterns have become one of the hottest topics in the object community. They are rapidly becoming the leading-edge fad, generating a huge amount of interest and the usual hype. We are also seeing internal battles over what fits into the community, including many arguments about exactly what a pattern is. Certainly it is difficult to find any common definition of *pattern*.

The roots of the patterns movement come from various sources. In recent years an increasing number of people felt that the software world was not very good at describing and proliferating good design practice. Methodologies abounded, but they defined a language for describing designs rather than describing actual designs. There was (and still is) a dearth of technical papers describing useful designs based on practice, which could be used to educate and inspire. As Ralph Johnson and Ward Cunningham put it: *"Projects fail despite the latest technology for lack of ordinary solutions"* [4].

Patterns evolved from several initiatives. Kent Beck and Ward Cunningham, two of the pioneers of Smalltalk, came across the ideas of Christopher Alexander, who had developed a theory and collection of patterns in architecture. Bruce Anderson led workshops at OOPSLA in the early 1990s that investigated building a handbook for software architects. Jim Coplien's C++ book [3] described idioms useful in C++. A number of these people formed the Hillside Group to explore these ideas further.

A greater public knowledge of the movement was triggered by the publication of the seminal "Gang of Four" book [6] and the PLoP (Pattern Language of Programming) conference started by the Hillside group in 1994 [4].

I had had very little contact with this growing community. I had long wanted to read books that described conceptual models, because I felt such books would give me good ideas. I didn't feel I could write about such things until I had enough models to form a worthwhile book. I was interested in the patterns movement and I found many of their principles appealing, but I was put off by the impression of a cliquey group that was obsessed with the architect Christopher Alexander and had a very stylized form of pattern writing. In the last year I have had more contact and attended the second PLoP. The most noticeable aspect of the patterns community is that it is quite a diverse group. Yes, there are those who seem to regard Alexander's works as sacred text, with alternative interpretations to be argued over. There are also plenty of those who dismiss Alexander as irrelevant. There are those who seem to see a mystical virtue in patterns, and those who can't stand the "touchy-feely" aspect of patterns. There are those who see patterns as overturning analysis and design methods, those who see conceptual modeling as a waste of time, and those who have encouraged me to produce this book to show what analysis, or conceptual, patterns can be like.

The idea of software patterns is not confined to the object-oriented community; David Hay has written a valuable book on data model patterns [7]. The models follow relational data modeling style, but they are very conceptual models. This makes the models valuable even if you are using object technology.

1.2.1 Christopher Alexander

For many people, the word *pattern* has appeared in software almost entirely due to the work of Christopher Alexander, a professor of architecture at the University of California at Berkeley. Alexander developed a range of theories about patterns in architecture and published these in a series of books. His pattern language book [1], a catalog of patterns in architecture, is seen as the prototype to patterns books in software. His style of writing patterns is used, to some extent, by many pattern writers. His phrase "a quality without a name" is often quoted as an attribute that all good patterns should have.

Many people, however, would deny Alexander his central role as the inspiration for software patterns. Peter Coad points out that the notion of patterns is used by many writers in other fields, many of whom he thinks are better examples than Alexander. Many people question Alexander's standing in the architectural profession: His ideas are by no means universally accepted. The "Gang of Four" book has had much more influence in software patterns than Alexander's work, and three out of those four authors had not read Alexander before writing that book.

1.2.2 The Literary Form

One of the most distinctive features of pattern writing is the form in which it is often done. Frequently patterns are written in a very set format. There is, however, no single format, as a quick glance through PLoP papers will confirm. Many people follow the inspiration of Alexander's style. Others follow the format used by the "Gang of Four."

It is commonly said that a pattern, however it is written, has four essential parts: a statement of the *context* where the pattern is useful, the *problem* that the pattern addresses, the *forces* that play in forming a solution, and the *solution* that resolves those forces. This form appears with and without specific headings but underlies many published patterns. It is an important form because it supports the definition of a pattern as "a solution to a problem in context," a definition that fixes the bounds of the pattern to a single problem-solution pair.

To many people the use of a fixed format, whether that of the "Gang of Four" or the context-problem-forces-solution form, is one determiner of a pattern. Use of an accepted pattern form clearly marks the pattern as something different from the average piece of technical writing.

A fixed form carries its own disadvantages, however. In this book, for instance, I do not find that a problem-solution pair always makes a good unit for a pattern. Several patterns in this book show how a single problem can be solved in more than one way, depending on various trade-offs. Although this could always be expressed as separate patterns for each solution, the notion of discussing several solutions together strikes me as no less elegant than pattern practice. Of course, the contents of the pattern forms make a lot of sense—any technical writing usually includes context, problem, forces, and solution. Whether this makes every piece of technical writing a pattern is another matter for discussion.

One principle of pattern form that I do agree with unreservedly is that they should be named. One advantage of patterns work is how it can enrich the vocabulary of development. By just saying "use a protection proxy here" or "we used observations to record product metrics," we can communicate our design ideas very effectively. Again, there is nothing unique about patterns here; it is a common technique of technical writing to coin new terms for concepts, but looking for patterns encourages this process.

1.2.3   The Author's Level of Abstraction

To many patterns people, one of the key elements of patterns is that they are discovered by looking at what happens in day-to-day development, rather than by academic invention. This is an element that I find particularly important. All the patterns in this book are the result of one or more actual projects and describe useful highlights in that work.

I chose patterns to include in this book that I believe are useful to other developers. These patterns are not only useful to developers within the same domain as the pattern, but frequently a pattern is useful in other domains as well. A good example of this is the portfolio pattern (see Section 9.2). This pattern was originally created as a way of grouping financial contracts together. This pattern can be used to group any kind of object by defining an implicit query and is sufficiently abstract to be used in any domain. I've seen evidence of this: After the early drafts of this book were written, we used this pattern in several places in another project, completely independent of trading.

The question before me is how much should I make of this wide abstraction. If I come across a pattern that I think could be useful in more domains than the one I found it in, how abstract should I make that pattern? The problem with abstracting it beyond its original domain is that I cannot be as certain of its validity. The project that the pattern appeared in tested the pattern through long debate, implementation, and (above all) the knowledge of the domain experts. As soon as I abstract further, I leave those safe harbors behind and guess how my discovery might fare on the open sea. There are many unknowns out there. Thus my view (which many patterns people seem to share) is that you must judge whether the pattern is useful to your domain, which you know infinitely better than I do, or you have access to the appropriate domain experts. In this book I use examples to suggest the wider applicability of a pattern. Any example that lies out of the original domain of the pattern is tentative, but they are there to spark your imagination, to make you ask yourself, "Is this useful for me?"

1.3 The Patterns in this Book

The definition I use for *pattern* is *an idea that has been useful in one practical context and will probably be useful in others.* I use the term *idea* to bring out the fact that a pattern can be anything. It can be a group of collaborating objects, as in the "Gang of Four's" patterns, or Coplien's principles for project organization [5]. The phrase *practical context* reflects the fact that patterns are developed out of the practical experience of a real project. It is often said that patterns are discovered rather than invented. This is true in the sense that models turn into patterns only when it is realized that they may have a common usefulness. A particular project comes first, and not all ideas of a particular project are patterns; patterns are those things that developers think may be *useful in other contexts.* Ideally this comes from actually using them elsewhere, but it may just reflect the opinion of the original developers.

The patterns in this book fall into two categories:

- Analysis patterns are groups of concepts that represent a common construction in business modeling. It may be relevant to only one domain, or it may span many domains. Analysis patterns form the heart of this book.

- Supporting patterns are patterns in themselves and are valuable on their own. They have a special role in this book, however: They describe how to take the analysis patterns and apply them, to make them real.

1.3.1 Examples for Modeling

The average book on analysis and design is an introductory book that typically explains the author's methodology. Such introductory books do not cover many important problems in modeling—problems that can only surface in the context of a large project. Such problems are difficult to understand outside that context and require the reader to have some modeling experience to fully appreciate them.

Patterns provide a good way of looking at these problems. Many patterns in this book deal with general modeling issues by looking at a particular problem in one domain, where it is easier to understand. Examples are the handling of methods that can be linked to individual object instances (see Section 6.6), subtyping of state diagrams (see Section 10.4), separating models into knowledge and operational levels (see Section 2.5) and using portfolios to group objects by a query (see Section 9.2).

1.3.2 Origins of the Patterns

As mentioned above, the patterns in this book are based on my personal experiences applying object modeling to large corporate information systems. This explains their somewhat random selection. I can only write about patterns I know about, that is, patterns that come from projects in which I have participated.

Although these models are based on intensive projects that sometimes took several months to complete, I have made no attempt to discuss full models. I could write a whole book describing one domain. While such a book would be interesting to someone working in that field (and I hope such books will appear one day), I wanted this book to span fields and cross-pollinate between them. A second reason for describing highlights rather than complete models is client confidentiality.

I have not attempted to be entirely faithful to the models. I have made changes for several reasons. I have simplified some of the abstractions, preserving the spirit of the original while making it easier to explain and to follow. I have also abstracted some models a *little* above the specific domain. The abstractions are limited to those that were considered reasonable in the project but fell outside the scope of the project. In some cases I have altered the models so that they reflect my ideas rather than those chosen by the project team. As a consultant, I can only advise, and sometimes my view does not win. In these cases I have presented both points of view in the text but tend to build on my own opinions.

When it comes to the naming of object types, I have followed the principle of using the naming of the source project. There are many points where I have been tempted to change names, but as any modeler knows, naming can be one of the most difficult parts of modeling. Some of the names may seem a little odd, but no name is perfect.

1.3.3   Patterns Across Domains

Whatever domain you work in, I hope that you will study patterns outside your domain. Much of the book includes general modeling issues and lessons applicable outside the domain being modeled. Knowledge of other domains is a valuable tool for abstraction. Specific cases are usually necessary to trigger powerful abstractions. Many professionals do not share my luck in working in many different domains. Looking at models in different domains can often spring new ideas in an unrelated domain.

But the biggest reason for looking at other domains is that it is not always obvious when domains are the same or different. The best example of that in this book comes from the health care field, which is modeled in several chapters. After working on a health care model, I was involved in a project supporting financial analysis of a large manufacturing company. The problem revolved around understanding the causes of high-level financial indicators. The health care model, essentially a model about diagnosis and treatment, proved remarkably appropriate (see Chapters 3 and 4).

I suspect that there are a small number of highly generic processes that cut across traditional boundaries of systems development and business engineering. The diagnosis and treatment model is one; another is the accounting and inventory model (see Chapter 6). Many diverse businesses can use a set of very similar abstract process models. This raises some significant questions about the promised development of vertical class libraries for industry sectors. I believe that true business frameworks will not be organized along traditional business lines but instead along abstract conceptual processes.

1.4   Conceptual Models and Business Process Reengineering

Most readers will analyze the conceptual models in this book to help develop computer systems, but conceptual models have other purposes. Good systems analysts have always known that taking an existing process and simply computerizing it is not a good use of resources. Computers allow people to do things in a different way. Systems analysts have found it difficult to push these ideas far enough, however: Their techniques still seem too dependent on software thinking. IT people have a hard time getting business leaders to take their ideas seriously.

Working with Jim Odell [9] has always immersed me in business modeling rather than software modeling. John Edwards (an early colleague and inspiration) always called his approach process engineering, long before BPR (business process reengineering) became a hot acronym. Using OO techniques for conceptual modeling can really make systems analysis and BPR the same activity. All the domain experts that I have taught have quickly seized on its potential to think about their own field in a new way. Only the domain experts can really use and apply these ideas.

The models in this book thus have as much to say about business engineering as they do about software engineering. Although much of the attention in business engineering is about process, most of these patterns are static type models. The basic reason for this is the experience from the domains I have worked with. In health care we found that although we could make generic type models, which applied to all parts of health care, we could not make many meaningful generic dynamic models.

The type models are important. I like to think of type models as defining the *language* of the business. These models thus provide a way of coming up with useful concepts that underlie a great deal of the process modeling. The concept of accountability has proven very useful in modeling confidentiality policies in health care. In working with payroll I have seen how modeling has changed the language and perception of the process.

1.5   Patterns and Frameworks

If the average professional is asked what the principal benefit of object technology is, the answer is almost always reuse. The vision is that of developers being able to assemble systems from tried and tested off-the-shelf components. Many of these visions have been very slow to appear. In some cases reuse is beginning to show, most notably in GUI development and database interaction. Where they are not appearing is at the business level.

There are no components for health care, banking, manufacturing, or the like because there is no standard framework for these areas. The most successful example of software components is that for Visual Basic. A vital part of this is because all the components are based on a common framework—the Visual Basic environment. Component developers can develop their wares knowing what kind of world they will live in.

To accomplish component reuse for information systems, a common framework must be established. An effective framework must not be too complex or too bulky. It should be widely applicable across a large domain and be based on an effective conceptual model of that domain. Developing such frameworks is difficult, both technically and politically.

This book does not attempt to define frameworks for various industries.[1] This book is about describing alternative ways of modeling a situation; frameworks are about choosing a particular model. I hope this book will encourage people to think about such frameworks and will influence their development.

1.6   Using the Patterns

Patterns are a new development in software. We are still developing ways to help people learn about patterns and use them in their work. Faced with a large body of patterns in this book, it is easy to be overwhelmed.

The first thing to do is to get a general orientation. After reading this introductory chapter, I suggest reading the introduction to each chapter in the book. The chapter introduction gives you an idea of the topics covered in the chapter. Obviously you can then go ahead and read every chapter, but I have tried to write the book so that you don't have to read every chapter to get something out of it. If you are working in a particular area, you can read a couple of chapters that you think may be appropriate. Another approach people have suggested is to look at the diagrams. If something catches your eye as interesting, then read the examples. The examples are often a good

---

[1] It should be mentioned that many chapters are based on a conceptual framework designed for health care— the Cosmos Clinical Process Model [2].

way of giving you an idea of whether the pattern will be useful to you. The Table of Patterns also acts as a summary, so you can start there or use it later to jog your memory.

Once you have identified a potentially useful pattern, then try it out. I've found that the only way I really understand how a pattern works is to try it out on a problem of my own. You can do this mentally by sketching a particular model on paper or by trying out some code. Try to make the pattern fit, but don't try too hard. You may find the pattern just wasn't the right one. You have not wasted your time—you have learned something about the pattern, and probably something about the problem, too. If a pattern does not fit your needs exactly, then don't hesitate to modify it. Patterns are suggestions, not prescriptions. I treat them as recipes in recipe books: They give me a starting point, a basic plan of putting the dish together, and I don't hesitate to adapt them to my particular circumstances. However well it fits, make sure you read the full text of the pattern so you get a sense of its limitations and important features. Do this both before you try to use it and after you have applied it. If you learn something about the pattern that isn't in the text, don't just curse me—send me an e-mail to let me know (100031.3311@compuserve .com). I am very interested to see how people use these patterns.

When I use patterns on a project, I have to be aware of the client's perspective. Some clients don't like to think of themselves as similar to any other client. They see themselves as very different and are suspicious of foreign ideas. With these clients I don't reveal the patterns. If I see where a pattern may apply, I use it to help me frame questions. These questions may well lead the client to something that fits the pattern, but I do it indirectly, using questions to prod them.

Other clients are happy to see me openly using patterns and are reassured to see that I am reusing my past work. With these clients I try the pattern out in front of them and question them closely to see if they are happy with it. It is important to be clear to them that I am not holding them up as gospel, and if are not comfortable, I will try something else. The danger with these clients is that they might take the patterns without questioning them enough.

Patterns are also important for reviews of both your own and others' work. For your own work, look to see if there are any patterns that are similar. If you find any, then try them out. Even if you believe your solution is better, use the patterns and work out why your solution is more appropriate. I find this a useful technique to understand problems better. A similar process works for reviewing the work of others. If you find a similar pattern, use it as a platform to ask questions of the work you are reviewing: What are its strengths compared to the pattern? Does the pattern give you anything the reviewed model does not have, and if so, is it important? I compare models I review with the patterns I know and usually find the process teaches me a great deal about both the problem and the patterns as I ask "Why do it this way?" It is amazing how much you learn by simply asking why.

Writing a book always implies a certain authority. It is easy for a reader to treat a book as a statement of certainty. Although some writers may have a sense of the certain correctness of what they say, I do not. These patterns are based on real experiences, and as such I am sure they will be of value to you. However, I am, more than anyone, painfully aware of their limitations. To be truly authoritative, patterns such as these must be tested by many applications—more than my experience allows.

This does not mean that these patterns will not be helpful. They represent a lot of careful thought. Just as they give me a head start in my modeling work, I hope they will help you, too. The important thing is to be conscious that they are a starting point, not a destination. Spend time understanding how these patterns work, but look for how they were developed and the limitations they have. Don't be afraid to press on further and develop new and better ideas. When I work with a client, I do not take the patterns as gospel, even those I feel I invented. The demands of each project make me adapt, refine, and improve the patterns.

Modeling Principle   *Patterns are a starting point, not a destination.*

Modeling Principle   *Models are not right or wrong, they are more or less useful.*

References

1. Alexander, C., S. Ishikawa, M. Silverstein, M. Jacobson, I. Fiksdahl-King, and S. Angel. *A Pattern Language*. New York: Oxford University Press, 1977.

2. Cairns, T., A. Casey, M. Fowler, M. Thursz, and H. Timimi. *The Cosmos Clinical Process Model*. National Health Service, Information Management Centre, 15 Frederick Rd, Birmingham, B15 1JD, England. Report ECBS20A & ECBS20B <http:// www.sm.ic.ac.uk/medicine/cpm>, 1992.

3. Coplien, J.O. *Advanced C++ Programming Styles and Idioms*. Reading, MA: Addison-Wesley, 1992.

4. Coplien, J.O. and D.C. Schmidt. *Pattern Languages of Program Design*. Reading, MA: Addison-Wesley, 1995.

5. Coplien, J.O. "A Generative Development-Process Pattern Language," In *Pattern Languages of Program Design*. J.O. Coplien and D.C. Schmidt, ed. Reading, MA: Addison-Wesley, 1995, pp. 183–237.

6. Gamma, E., R. Helm, R. Johnson, and J. Vlissides. *Design Patterns: Elements of Reusable Object-Oriented Software*. Reading, MA: Addison-Wesley, 1995.

7. Hay, D. *Data Model Patterns: Conventions of Thought*. New York: Dorset House, 1996.

8. Jacobson, I., M. Christerson, P. Jonsson, and G. Övergaard. *Object-Oriented Software Engineering: A Use Case Driven Approach*. Wokingham, England: Addison-Wesley, 1992.

9. Martin, J., and J. Odell. *Object-Oriented Methods: A Foundation*. Englewood Cliffs, NJ: Prentice-Hall, 1995.

Analysis Patterns

This portion of the book presents patterns from a number of business domains. We start in Chapter 2 by looking at patterns for describing relationships that define responsibilities between parties. These include formal organizational and contractual relationships, as well as more informal relationships. Chapters 3 and 4 consider observation and measurement, presenting patterns for recording facts about the world. The origins for Chapter 3 are in health care. Chapter 4 provides a number of patterns from the realm of corporate financial analysis.

Chapter 5 looks at how we refer to objects, not the addressing and memory management of languages, but the indexing we need when referring exactly to objects in our working life. Chapters 6 and 7 examine basic patterns for accounting, describing how a network of accounts and posting rules can form an active accounting system. Planning is the subject of Chapter 8, where we examine the relationship between standard plans and one-off plans, and how to plan and record the use of resources.

Chapter 9 examines trading in situations where prices are fluid and we need to understand how these price changes affect the profits of our trades. Chapter 10 then looks at the more specialized area of derivative trading, but with an eye at the problems of situations which lead us to build inheritance hierarchies of business objects. Derivatives are one example of more common problems. Finally in Chapter 11 we look beyond objects, to packages of objects, and visit some of the problems of organizing them in a way that improves their maintainability and flexibility.

Accountability

The concept of accountability applies when a person or organization is responsible to another. It is an abstract notion that can represent many specific issues, including organization structures, contracts, and employment.

This chapter begins by introducing the important pattern of *party (2.1)*—the supertype of person and organization. The organization structure problem is then used to show the development of the accountability model. Simple organization structures can be modeled with *organization hierarchies (2.2)*. When many hierarchies develop the model becomes too complex, and the *organization structure (2.3)* pattern is required. The combination of the party and organization structure patterns produces *accountability (2.4)*. Accountabilities can handle many relationships between parties: organization structures, patient consent, contracts for services, employment, and registration with professional bodies.

When accountabilities are used it is valuable to describe what kinds of accountabilities can be formed and the rules that constrain these accountabilities. These rules can be described by instances of types at the *accountability knowledge level (2.5)*. This level includes the party type, which allows parties to be classified and subtyped with *party type generalizations (2.6)* without changing the model. *Hierarchic accountability (2.7)* represents those interparty relationships that do require a strict hierarchy. In this way accountabilities can be used for both hierarchic and more complex networks of relationships.

Accountabilities define responsibilities for parties. These responsibilities can be defined through *operating scopes (2.8)*. Operating scopes are the clauses of the accountability's contract, rather like line items on an ongoing order. As these responsibilities accumulate it can be useful to attach them to a *post (2.9)* rather than to the person who occupies it.

This chapter is based on many projects: Accountabilities are a common theme. Original ideas developed with a customer service project for a utility and an accounting project for a telephone company. The accountability model was developed in the Cosmos project for the UK National Health Service [2].

Key Concepts   Party, Accountability

2.1   Party

Take a look through your address book, and what do you see? If it's anything like mine, you will see a lot of addresses, telephone numbers, the odd e-mail address... all linked to something. Often that something is a person, but once in awhile a company shows up. I call Town Taxi frequently, but there's no particular person I want to speak to there—I just want to get a cab. A first attempt at modeling the address book might be Figure 2.1, but it has a duplication that is painful to my eye. Instinctively I look for a generalization of person and company. This type is a classic case of an unnamed concept—one that everybody knows and uses but nobody has a name for. I have seen it on countless data models on various names: person/organization, player, legal entity, and so on.

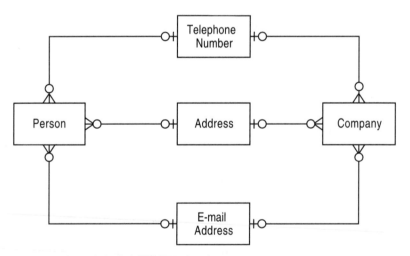

Figure 2.1   Initial model of an address book.

This model shows the similar responsibilities of person and organization.

The term I prefer is *party.* In Figure 2.2 I define a party as the supertype of a person or organization. This allows me to have addresses and phone numbers for departments within companies, or even informal teams.

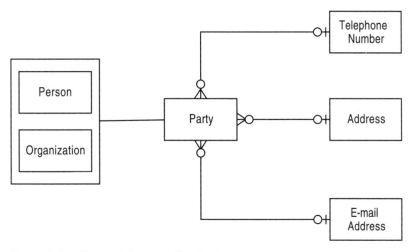

Figure 2.2   Figure 2.1 generalized using party.
Party should be used in many situations where person or organization is used.

It is surprising how many things relate to party rather than to person or organization. You receive and send letters to both people and organizational units; I make payments to people and organizations; both organizations and people carry out actions, have bank accounts, file taxes. These examples are enough, I think, to make the abstraction worthwhile.

Example   In the UK National Health Service, the following would be parties: Dr. Tom Cairns, the renal unit team at St. Mary's Hospital, St. Mary's Hospital, Parkside District Health Authority, and the Royal College of Physicians.

2.2   Organization Hierarchies

Let us consider a generic multinational: Aroma Coffee Makers, Inc. (ACM). It has operating units, which are divided into regions, which are divided into divisions which are divided into sales offices. We can model this simple structure using Figure 2.3. This is not a model that I would feel content with, however. If the organization changes, say regions are taken out to provide a flatter structure, then we must alter the model. Figure 2.4 provides a simpler model—one that is easier to change. The danger with the recursive relationship shown in Figure 2.4 is that it allows a division to be part of a sales office. We can deal with this by defining subtypes to correspond with the levels and by putting constraints on these subtypes. Should the organizational hierarchy change, we would alter these subtypes and rules. Usually it is easier to change a rule than to change the model structure, so I prefer Figure 2.4 over Figure 2.3.

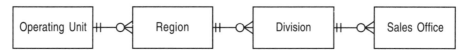

Figure 2.3   Organization structure with explicit levels.
Such a structure is inflexible and not reusable.

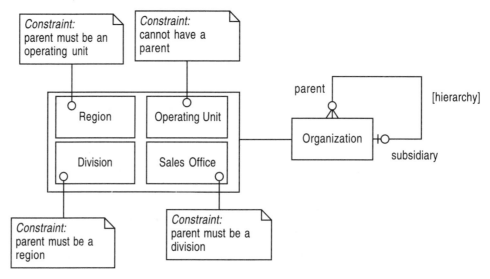

Figure 2.4   Organization supertype with hierarchic relationship.
The hierarchic association provides the most flexibility. Constraints due to levels have to be added as rules on the subtypes.

The hierarchic structure provides a certain amount of generality but has some limitations, including the fact that it only supports a single organizational hierarchy. Assume that ACM attaches service teams for its major lines of coffee makers to its sales offices. These teams have a dual reporting structure: They report to the sales team as well as the service departments for each product family, which in turn report to product type support units. Thus the service team for the 2176 high-volume cappuccino maker in Boston (50 cappuccinos a minute) reports to the Boston sales office but also to the 2170 family service center, which reports to the high-volume Italian coffee division, which reports to the high-volume coffee products service division, which reports to coffee products service division. (I'm not making this up entirely!) Faced with this situation we can add a second hierarchy, as shown in Figure 2.5. (More rules would be required, similar to those in Figure 2.4, but I will leave the addition of those as an exercise for the reader.) As it stands this approach works well, but as more hierarchies appear the structure will become unwieldy.

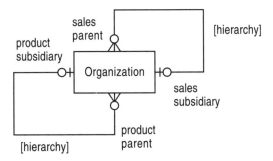

Figure 2.5   Two organizational hierarchies.

Subtypes of the organization are not shown. If there are many hierarchies, this will soon get out of hand.

2.3   Organization Structure

If it looks like the model will have several hierarchies, we can use a typed relationship, as shown in Figure 2.6. We turn the hierarchic associations into a type and differentiate the hierarchies by using varied instances of the organization structure type. This would handle the above scenario with two instances of the organization structure type: sales organization and service organization. Additional hierarchies could be added merely by adding more organization structure types. Again, this abstraction gives us more flexibility for a modest increase in complexity. For just two hierarchies it would not be worth the effort, but for several it would be. Note also that the organization structure has a time period; this allows us to record changes in the organization structure over time. Note further that I have not modeled the organization structure type as an attribute—a very important factor with type attributes, as we will see later.

Example   The service team for the 2176 high-volume cappuccino maker in Boston reports to the Boston sales office. We would model this as an organization structure whose parent is the Boston sales office, subsidiary is the Boston 2176 service team, and organization structure type is line management.

Example   The service team for the 2176 high-volume cappuccino maker in Boston also reports to the 2170 family service center in the product support structure. We would model this as a separate organization structure whose parent is the 2170 family service center, subsidiary is the Boston 2176 service team, and organization structure type is product support.

Simplifying the object structure puts more emphasis on the rules. The rules are of the form, "If we have an organization structure whose type is sales organization and whose child is a division, then the parent must be a region." Note that the rules are expressed by referring to properties of the organization

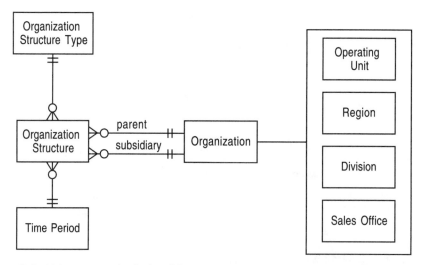

Figure 2.6 Using a typed relationship.

Each relationship between organizations is defined by an organization structure type. It is better than explicit associations if there are many relationships.

structure, which implies that the rules should be on the organization structure. However, this means that extending the system by adding a new organization structure type would require changing the rules in the organization structure. Furthermore, the rules would get very unwieldy as the number of organization structure types increases.

The rules can be placed instead on the organization structure type, as shown in Figure 2.7. All the rules for a particular organization structure type are held in one place, and it is easy to add new organization structure types.

Figure 2.7 does not work well, however, if we change the organization structure types rarely but add new subtypes of organization frequently. In that case each addition of a subtype of organization would cause rule changes. It is better to place the rules on the subtypes of the organization. The general point here is to minimize the model changes that occur. Thus we should place the rules in the most volatile area in such a way that need not touch other parts of the model.

Modeling Principle   *Design a model so that the most frequent modification of the model causes changes to the least number of types.*

2.4   Accountability

Essentially Figure 2.7 shows one organization having a relationship with another for a period of time according to a defined rule. Whenever any statement is made about organizations, it is always worth considering whether the

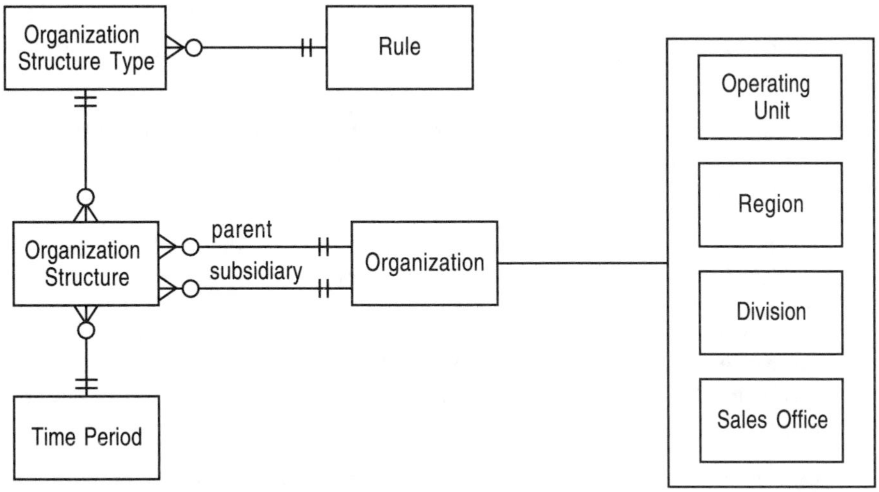

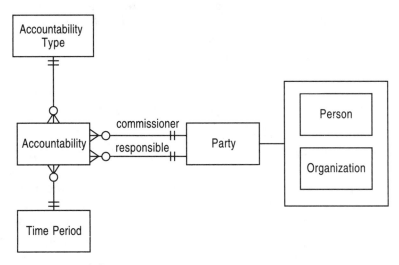

Figure 2.7 Adding a rule to Figure 2.6.

The rule enforces constraints such as sales offices reporting to divisions.

same statement can also apply to people. In this case I ask, "Can people have relationships to organizations or other people for a period of time according to a defined rule?" This is certainly true, and thus I can, and should, abstract Figure 2.7 to apply to a party. As I do this I name the new abstraction an accountability, as shown in Figure 2.8.

Figure 2.8 Accountability.

Using a party allows accountability to cover a wide range of interparty responsibilities, including management, employment, and contracts.

Example John Smith works for ACM. This can be modeled by an accountability whose commissioner is ACM, responsible party is John Smith, and accountability type is employment.

Example John Smith is the manager of the Boston 2176 service team. This can be modeled as an accountability whose type is manager, with John Smith responsible to the Boston 2176 service team.

Example Mark Thursz is a member of the Royal College of Physicians. This can be modeled as an accountability whose type is professional registration, with Mark Thursz responsible to the Royal College of Physicians.

Example John Smith gives his consent to Mark Thursz to perform an endoscopy. This can be modeled as an accountability whose type is patient consent, with Mark Thursz responsible to John Smith.

Example St. Mary's Hospital has a contract with Parkside District Health Authority to perform endoscopies in 1996/97. This can be modeled as an accountability whose type is endoscopy services, with St. Mary's Hospital responsible to Parkside. The time period on the accountability would be January 1, 1996, to December 31, 1997. A subtype of accountability could provide additional information, such as which operations were covered and how many should be performed during the contract's duration.

Modeling Principle *Whenever defining features for a type that has a supertype, consider whether placing the features on the supertype makes sense.*

As the examples indicate, abstracting from organization structure to accountability introduces a wide range of additional situations that can be captured by the model. The complexity of the model has not increased, however. The basic model has the same structure as Figure 2.7; the only change is that of using party instead of organization.

2.5 Accountability Knowledge Level

Complexity has been introduced, however, in that there are many more accountability types than there would be organization structure types. The rules for defining accountability types would thus become more complex.

This complexity can be managed by introducing a knowledge level. Using a knowledge level splits the model into two sections: the operational and knowledge levels. The operational level consists of accountability, party, and their interrelationships. The knowledge level consists of accountability type, party type, and their interrelationships, as shown in Figure 2.9.

At the operational level the model records the day to day events of the domain. At the knowledge level the model records the general rules that govern this structure. Instances in the knowledge level govern the configuration of instances in the operational level. In this example instances of

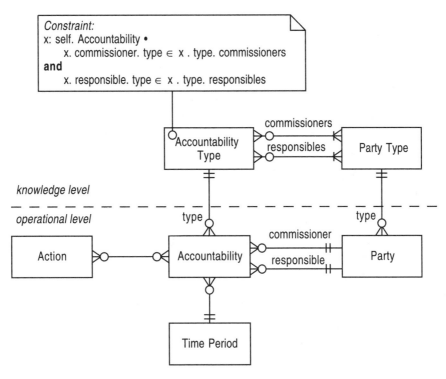

Constraint:
x: self. Accountability •
    x. commissioner. type ∈ x . type. commissioners
and
    x. responsible. type ∈ x . type. responsibles

commissioners
responsibles
Accountability Type
Party Type

knowledge level

operational level

type

type

commissioner
responsible

Action
Accountability
Party

Time Period

Figure 2.9   Knowledge and operational levels of accountability.

The knowledge level objects define the legal configurations of operational level objects. Accountabilities can only be created between parties according to corresponding accountability types and party types.

accountability (links between actual parties) are constrained by the links between accountability type and party type.

Example   Regions are subdivided into divisions. This is handled by an accountability type of regional structure whose commissioners are regions and responsibles are divisions.

Example   Patient consent is defined as an accountability type whose commissioners are patients and responsibles are doctors.

Note how mapping to the party type replaces subtyping of the party. This is an example of what Odell [3] refers to as a *power type*, which occurs when a mapping defines subtypes. The party type is closely linked to the subtypes of party in that the subtype region must have its type as the party type region. Conceptually you can consider the instance of the party type to be the same object as the subtype of party, although this cannot be directly implemented in mainstream programming languages. The party type is then a power type of party. Often we need only one of either the mapping or the subtyping.

However, if the subtypes have specific behavior and the power type has its own features, then both subtypes and mapping to the power type are needed. (Odell has a special notation for this case [3].)

This reflection between the knowledge and operational levels is similar but not identical, in that the parent and subsidiary mappings are multivalued at the knowledge level but single-valued at the operational level. This is because the operational level records the actual party for the accountability, while the knowledge level records the permissible party types for the accountability type. This use of a multivalued knowledge mapping to show permissible types for a single-valued operational mapping is a common pattern.

Knowledge and operational levels are a common feature of models, although the difference between the levels is often not made explicitly. I make the divisions explicit because I find this helps to clarify my thinking when modeling. There are lots of examples of operational and knowledge levels in this book, particularly in Chapter 3.

Modeling Principle   *Explicitly divide a model into operational and knowledge levels.*

A lot of data modelers use the term *meta-model* to describe the knowledge level. I am not entirely comfortable with this terminology. *Meta-model* can also define the modeling technique. Thus a meta-model includes concepts such as type, association, subtyping, and operation (such as the meta-models of Rational Software's Unified Method [1]). The knowledge level does not really fall into that category because it does not describe the notation for the operational level. I thus only use the term *meta-model* to describe a model that describes the language (semantics of notation) for a model.[1]

Accountability represents some pretty heady abstraction and as in any climb we should stop and take stock before altitude sickness sets in. Although we have a very simple structure in the object model, a lot of knowledge is buried in the instances of the knowledge level. Thus to make this work it is not enough to implement the object model; the knowledge level must also be instantiated. Instantiating the knowledge level is effectively configuring the system, which is a constrained, and thus simpler, form of programming. It is still programming, however, so you should consider how you are going to test it.

Rich knowledge levels also affect communication between systems. If two systems are to communicate, they must not only share the object model but also have identical knowledge objects (or at least some equivalence between knowledge levels, as discussed in Section 5.4). In the end it comes

---

[1] Of course, if I defined a diagram that showed instances of accountability type and party type, then the knowledge level would act as the meta-model for that diagram. This kind of diagram can be useful if there is a complicated web of accountability types.

down to the question, If the number of accountability types is large, is it easier to use the structure of Figure 2.9 or to extend Figure 2.5 with one association for each accountability type? The complexity of the problem cannot be avoided; we can only ask ourselves which is the simpler model, taking both type structure and knowledge objects into account.

We need to be careful, as with any typed relationship, that this does not become a catch-all for every relationship between two parties. For example, biological parent would not fit as an instance of an accountability type because neither party is responsible to the other, nor is there an inherent time period; legal guardian would fit, however.

2.6   Party Type Generalizations

The model as it stands is quite powerful, but some useful variations will add even more flexibility. These variations are useful with any model that uses a knowledge/operational split.

Consider a general practitioner (GP), Dr. Edwards. Using the model shown in Figure 2.9, we can consider him to be a GP or a doctor but not both. Any accountability types that are defined on doctor that would apply also to GP would have to be copied over. We can use various techniques to alleviate this problem. One approach is to allow party types to have sub- and super-types relationships, as shown in Figure 2.10. This essentially introduces

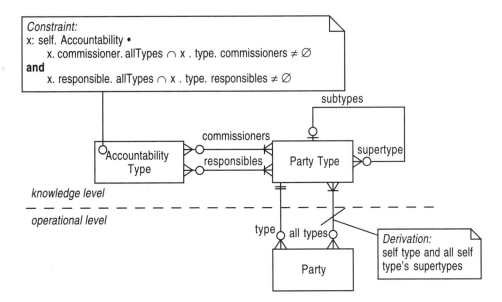

Figure 2.10   Allowing party types to have sub- and supertypes.

Adding generalization to party types makes it easier to define the knowledge level.

generalization to party types in a similar way that generalization works on types. Generalizations cause a change in the constraint on accountability type, so that both the party's type (from the type mapping) and the supertypes (from the all types mapping) are taken into account.

Figure 2.10 provides a single inheritance hierarchy on party type. Multiple inheritance can be supported by allowing the supertype mapping to be multivalued. In addition, Figure 2.10 only supports single classification. This means that if Dr. Edwards is both a GP and a pediatrician, we can record that only by creating a special GP/pediatrician party type, with both GP and pediatrician as supertypes. Multiple classification allows party to be given multiple party types outside of the generalization structure of party type. This can be done by allowing the type mapping on party to be multivalued.

Much of the discussion about the interrelationships between the knowledge level and operational level is similar to the relationships between object and type in a modeling meta-model.

2.7   Hierarchic Accountability

The flexible structure that accountabilities provide requires more effort to enforce the constraints of some accountability types. For example, the organization structure shown in Figure 2.3 defines a strict series of levels: operating units are divided into regions, that are divided into divisions that are divided into sales offices. It is possible to define an accountability type of regional structure, but how can we enforce the strict rules of Figure 2.3?

The first issue is that Figure 2.3 describes a hierarchic structure. The accountability models do not have a rule to enforce such a hierarchy. This can be addressed by providing a subtype of accountability type with an additional constraint, as shown in Figure 2.11. This constraint acts with the usual constraint on accountability types to enforce the hierarchic nature of the operational level structure. A similar accountability type subtype can be used to enforce a directed acyclic graph structure.

Using Figure 2.11, we can support the case shown in Figure 2.3 by a series of accountability types. An accountability type regional structure level 1 would have regions responsible to operating units, regional structure level 2 would have divisions responsible to regions, and so on. This approach works but would be somewhat clumsy. An alternative is to use a leveled accountability type, as shown in Figure 2.12. In this case there would only be a single regional structure accountability type. The levels mapping would map to the list of party types—operating unit, region, division, and sales office. This model makes it easier to add new leveled accountability types and to modify the levels in those structures that need it. The hierarchic accountability type captures the responsibility of the parties forming a hierarchy, the

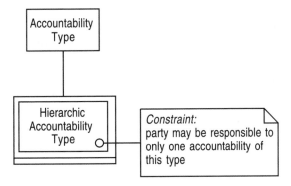

Figure 2.11   Hierarchic accountability type.

The added constraint means that the parties linked by accountabilities of this type must form a hierarchy.

leveled accountability type captures the responsibility of a fixed sequence of party types. The regional structure accountability type would be both leveled and hierarchic.

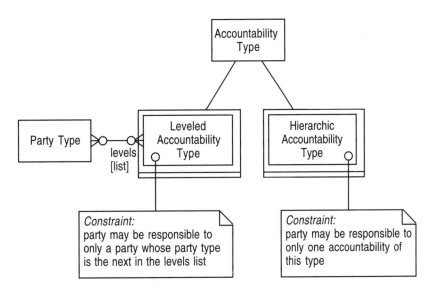

Figure 2.12   Leveled accountability type.

Leveled accountabilities supports fixed levels such as sales office, division, region.

The constraints applied on the subtypes act with the constraint defined on accountability type, following the principles of design by contract [4]. In the case of the leveled accountability type, the constraint subsumes that of the supertype, and indeed makes the commissioners and responsibles mappings superfluous. This thinking leads to a model along the lines of Figure 2.13. It is important to note that Figure 2.12 is not incorrect. Leveled accountability type is a perfectly good subtype of accountability type because the constraint on accountability type will still hold for leveled accountability type. The commissioners and responsibles mappings will also continue to hold, although they would be derived from the levels mapping. I would be inclined to stick with Figure 2.12. The leveled accountability type is not always needed, and can easily be added without violating the model. Figure 2.12 also has the advantage of making the knowledge/operational relationship more explicit.

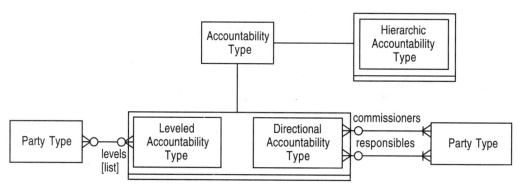

Figure 2.13   Rebalancing the subtypes of accountability type.
A better way of organizing the accountability type hierarchy.

2.8   Operating Scopes

Accountability, as it stands, provides a valuable way of describing how parties relate to each other. The type of accountability describes what kind of relationship they have. There are usually other details, however, that describe more of the meaning of accountability. Consider a doctor who might be employed as a liver surgeon to carry out 20 liver transplants for southeast London in 1997. A diabetic care team at a hospital might be asked to care for insulin-dependent diabetes patients in western Massachusetts for the Red Shield HMO (Health Management Organization).

Such details are the operating scopes of accountability, as shown in Figure 2.14. Each operating scope defines some part of consequences of accountability on the responsible party. It is difficult to enumerate the attributes of an operating scope in the abstract. Thus we see that accountability has a number of operating scopes, each of which is some subtype that describes the actual characteristics.

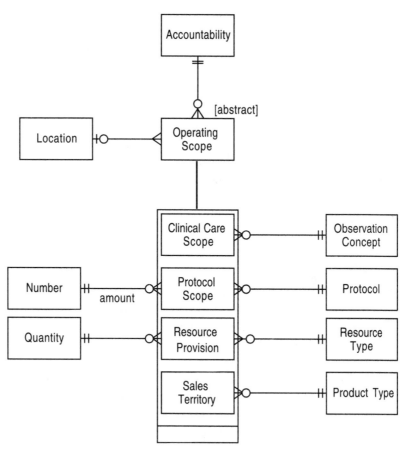

Figure 2.14   Operating scope.

Operating scopes define the responsibilities that are taken on when an accountability is created. They can be used for job descriptions.

Example   A liver surgeon who is responsible for 20 liver transplants a year in southeast London has a protocol scope on employment accountability with amount of 20, protocol of liver transplant, and location of southeast London.

Example   A diabetic care team has accountability with Red Shield. This accountability would have a clinical care scope whose observation concept is insulin-dependent diabetes and location is western Massachusetts.

Example   ACM has a contract with Indonesian Coffee Exporters (ICE) for 3000 tons of Java and 2000 tons of Sumatra over the course of a year. This is described by accountability between ACM and ICE with a year's time period and two resource provisions: 3000 tons/ year of Java and 2000 tons/year of Sumatra.

Example   John Smith sells the 1100 and 2170 families of high-volume coffee maker for ACM. He sells both the 1100 and 2170 in New England and sells the 2170 in New York. He has employment accountability to ACM with sales territories for 1100 in New England, 2170 in New England, and 2170 in New York.

When using operating scopes for a particular organization, you need to identify the kinds of operating scopes that exist and the properties for them. It is very difficult to generalize about operating scopes in the abstract, but location is a common factor. The subtypes of operating scope may form an inheritance hierarchy of their own if there are many of them. In particularly complex cases you might see an operating scope type[2] placed on the knowledge level to show which accountability types can have which operating scope types.

2.9   Post

Often the operating scopes of a person—their responsibilities, including many of their accountabilities—are defined in advance as that person's job description. When a person leaves a job, the replacement may inherit a full set of responsibilities. These responsibilities are tied to the job rather than the person.

We can deal with this situation by introducing the post as a third subtype of party, as shown in Figure 2.15. Any responsibilities that are constant to the job, whoever occupies it, are attached to the post. A person fills a post by having an accountability to the post. The notion is that a person is responsible for the responsibilities of the post for the period of time that they are appointed to the post.

Example   Paul Smith is the head of the high-volume product development team. We can describe this by having a post for the head of the high-volume product development team. This has a management accountability with the high-volume product development team (a party). Paul Smith has a separate accountability (of type appointment) to this post.

Example   The transplant surgeon post at a hospital has in its job description the requirement to do 50 renal and 20 liver transplants in a year. This post has an accountability with the hospital and protocol scopes for 50 renal transplants and 20 liver transplants.

Posts should not be used all the time. They add significant complexity to the operational level with their extra level of indirection. Only use posts

---

[2] In this case the instances of operating scope type must match the subtypes of operating scope. Operating scope type is thus a *power type* [3] of operating scope.

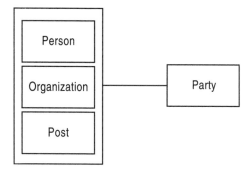

Figure 2.15   Post.

Posts are used when accountabilities and scopes are defined by the post and do not change when the holder of the post changes. Appointments to posts are accountabilities.

when there are significant responsibilities that are static in a post and people change between posts reasonably often. Posts are not necessary in models in which all responsibilities can be attached to a person.

References

1. Booch, G., and J. Rumbaugh. *Unified Method for Object-Oriented Development.* Rational Software Corporation, Version 0.8, 1995.
2. Cairns, T., A. Casey, M. Fowler, M. Thursz, and H. Timimi. *The Cosmos Clinical Process Model.* National Health Service, Information Management Centre, 15 Frederick Rd, Birmingham, B15 1JD, England. Report ECBS20A & ECBS20B, http://www.sm.ic.ac.uk/medicine/cpm, 1992.
3. Martin, J., and J. Odell. *Object-Oriented Methods: A Foundation.* Englewood Cliffs, NJ: Prentice-Hall, 1995.
4. Meyer, B. "Applying 'Design by Contract,'" *IEEE Computer*, 25, 10 (1992), pp. 40–51.

3

Observations and Measurements

Many computer systems record information about objects in the real world. This information finds its way into computer systems as records, attributes, objects, and various other representations. The typical route is to record a piece of information as an attribute to an object. For example, the fact that I weigh 185 pounds would be recorded in an attribute of a person type. This chapter examines how this approach fails and suggests more sophisticated approaches.

We begin by discussing *quantity (3.1)*—a type that combines a number with the unit that is associated with it. By combining numbers and units, we are able to model the world more exactly. With quantities and their units modeled as objects, we can also describe how to convert quantities with a *conversion ratio (3.2)*. The quantity pattern can be extended by using *compound units (3.3)*, which represent complex units explicitly in terms of their components. Quantities are required for almost all computer systems; monetary values should always be represented using this pattern.

Quantities can be used as attributes of objects to record information about them. This approach begins to break down, however, when there is a very large number of attributes that can bloat the type with attributes and operations. In these situations *measurement (3.4)* can be used to treat measurements as objects in their own right. This pattern is also useful when you need to keep information about individual measurements. Here we begin to see the use of operational and knowledge levels (see Section 2.5) in this chapter.

Measurements allow us to record quantitative information. *Observation (3.5)* extends this pattern to deal with qualitative information and thus allows *subtyping observation concepts (3.6)* in the knowledge level. It is also often essential to record the *protocol (3.7)* for an observation so that clinicians can

35

better interpret the observation as well as determine the accuracy and sensitivity of the observation.

A number of small patterns extend observation. The difference between the time an observation occurred and when it is recorded can be captured with a *dual time record (3.8)*. Often it is important to keep a record of observations that have been found to be incorrect; this requires a *rejected observation (3.9)*. The biggest headache with observation is dealing with certainty, for it is often important to record hypotheses about objects. The subtyping of *active observation, hypothesis, and projection (3.10)* is one way of dealing with this problem.

Many statements about observations are made using a process of diagnosis. We infer observations based on other observations. *Associated observation (3.11)* can be used to record the evidence observations, plus the knowledge that was used for the diagnosis.

The preceding patterns are structural and are used to make records of our observations. To understand how they work, it is useful to consider the *process of observation (3.12)*, which can be modeled with an event-based technique.

Few professions have such complex demands on measurements and observations as medicine. The models in this chapter come from an intense effort in modeling health care from a clinical perspective—the Cosmos project [3] of the UK National Health Service. In this project a joint team of doctors, nurses, and analysts worked together on a notoriously difficult domain. We do not include a pure description of the Cosmos model here. Those interested should refer to the complete model [1]. The ideas here can be transplanted to other areas: Chapter 4 discusses how this was done for corporate finance.

Key Concepts   Quantity, Unit, Measurement, Observation, Observation Concept, Phenomenon Type, Associative Function, Rejected Observation, Hypothesis.

3.1   Quantity

The simplest and most common way of recording measurements in current computer systems is to record a number in a field designed for a particular measurement, such as the arrangement shown in Figure 3.1. One problem with this method is that using a number to represent a person's height is not very appropriate. What does it mean to say that my height is 6, or that my weight is 185? To make sense of the number, we need units. One way of doing this is to introduce a unit into the name of the association (for example, weight in pounds). The unit clarifies the meaning of the number, but the representation remains awkward. Another problem with this technique is that the recorder must use the correct units for the information. If someone tells me their weight is 80 kilograms, what am I to record? Ideally a good record, especially in medicine, records exactly what was measured—no more, no less. A conversion, however deterministic, does not follow that faithfully.

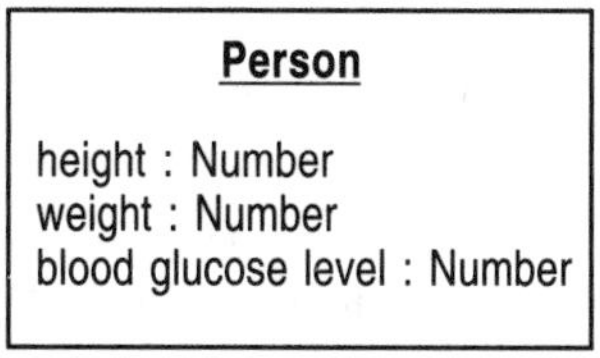

```
                   Person
     ────────────────────────────────
     height : Number
     weight : Number
     blood glucose level : Number
```

Figure 3.1   Number attribute.

This approach does not specify the units.

In this context a very useful concept is that of quantity. Figure 3.2 shows an object type that combines number and units, for example, 6 feet or 180 pounds. Quantity includes appropriate arithmetical and comparative operations. For example, an addition operation allows quantities to be added together as easily as numbers but checks the units so that 34 inches are not added to 68 kilograms. Quantity is a "whole value" [2] that the user interface can interpret and display (a simple print operation can show the number and the unit). In this way quantity soon becomes as useful and as widely used an attribute as integer or date.

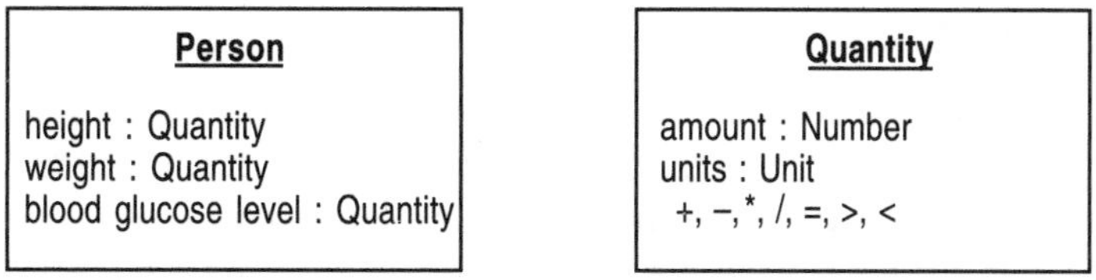

```
              Person                                   Quantity
   ──────────────────────────────       ────────────────────────────────
   height : Quantity                     amount : Number
   weight : Quantity                     units : Unit
   blood glucose level : Quantity        +, −, *, /, =, >, <
```

Figure 3.2   Measurements as attributes using quantity.

Quantity should always be used where units are required.

Example   We can represent a weight of 185 pounds as a quantity with amount of 185 and unit of pounds.

Monetary values should also be represented as quantities (I use the term *money* in this book), using a currency as the unit. With quantities you can easily deal with multiple currencies, rather than being tied to a single currency (if only my personal finance program did that!). Money objects can also control the representation of the amount. Often rounding problems occur in financial systems if floating point numbers are used to represent monetary values; monetary quantities can enforce the use of fixed point numbers for the amount attribute.

Example $80 would be represented as a quantity with amount of 80 and units of US dollars.

The use of quantity is an important feature of object-oriented analysis. Many modeling approaches make a distinction between attributes and associations. Associations link types in the model, and attributes contain some value according to some attribute type. The question is, what makes something an attribute rather than an association? Usually attributes are the typical built-in types of most software environments (integer, real, string, date, and so on). Types such as quantity do not fit into this way of choosing between attribute and association. Some modelers say quantity should be modeled with an association (because it is not a typical built-in type), while other modelers recommend an attribute (because it is a self-contained, widely used type). In conceptual modeling it doesn't really matter which way you do it, the important thing is that you look for and use types such as quantity. Since I don't distinguish between attributes and mappings, I don't get into this argument. (I'm laboring this point because I find types such as quantity conspicuously absent from most of the models I see.)

Modeling Principle *When multiple attributes interact with behavior that might be used in several types, combine the attributes into a new fundamental type.*

3.2 Conversion Ratio

We can make good use of units represented explicitly in the model. The first service that units can perform is to allow us to convert quantities from one unit to another. As shown in Figure 3.3 we can use conversion ratio objects between units and then give quantity an operation, convertTo (Unit), which can return a new quantity in the given unit. This operation looks at the conversion ratios to see if a path can be traced from the receiving object's quantity to the desired quantity.

Example We can convert between inches and feet by defining a conversion ratio from feet to inches with the number 12.

Figure 3.3 Adding conversion ratios to units.

Example   We can convert between inches and millimeters by defining a conversion ratio from inches to millimeters with the number 25.4. We can then combine this ratio with the conversion ratio from feet to inches to convert from feet to millimeters.

Conversion ratios can handle most but not all kinds of conversion. A conversion from Celsius to Fahrenheit requires a little more than simple multiplication. In this case an individual instance method (see Section 6.6) is required.

If we have a lot of different units to convert, we can consider holding the dimensions of a unit. For example, force has dimensions of $[MLT^{-2}]$, and we also need a scalar for units that are not S.I. units. With the dimensions and the scalar, we can compute conversion ratios automatically, although it is a bit of work to set it up.

Be aware that time does not convert properly between days and months because the number of days in a month is not constant.

If we have several alternative paths in conversion, we can make use of them in our test cases. The tests should check that the conversions work in both directions.

For monetary values, whose units are currencies, the conversion ratios are not constant over time. We can deal with this problem by giving the conversion ratios attributes to indicate their time of applicability.

When converting between units, we can use either conversion ratios, as described here, or scenarios, as described in Section 9.4. I use scenarios if the conversions change frequently and I need to know about many sets of consistent conversions. Otherwise, the simpler conversion ratio is the better model.

3.3   Compound Units

Units can be atomic or compound. A compound unit is a combination of atomic units, such as feet^2 or meters per second. A sophisticated conversion operation can use conversion ratios on atomic units to convert compound units. The compound units need to remember which atomic units are used and their powers. Figure 3.4 is an example of a straightforward model that can convert compound units. Remember that the power can be positive or negative.

Example   We can represent an area of 150 square yards by a quantity whose number is 150 and whose unit is a compound unit with one unit reference to feet with power 2.

A variation on this model takes advantage of representing mappings with bags. Unlike the usual sets, bags allow us to use an object more than once in a mapping, as shown in Figure 3.5. Bags are particularly useful when we have a relationship that has a single numeric attribute.

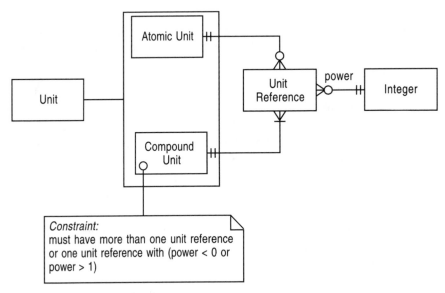

Figure 3.4 Compound units.

This model can be used for acceleration and similar phenomena.

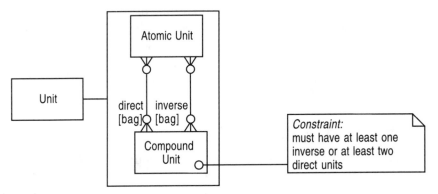

Figure 3.5 Compound units using bags.

This model is more compact than Figure 3.4.

Example The acceleration due to gravity can be expressed as a quantity with number 9.81 and a compound unit with direct units of meter and inverse units of seconds and seconds.

The difference between Figures 3.4 and 3.5 is not great. I have a mild preference for Figure 3.5 because it avoids unit reference—a type that does not do much. The choice between these models does not matter to most clients of a compound unit. Only clients that need to break the compound unit down into atomic units are involved, and most of the type's clients would only need some printing representation. Obviously we must use Figure 3.4 if our method does not allow bags in mappings.

3.4   Measurement

Modeling quantities as attributes may be useful for a single hospital department that collects a couple of dozen measurements for each in-patient visit. However, when we look across all areas of medicine, we find thousands of potential measurements that could be made on one person. Defining an attribute for each measurement would mean that one person could have thousands of operations—an untenably complex interface. One solution is to consider all the various things that can be measured (height, weight, blood glucose level, and so on) as objects and to introduce the object type phenomenon type, as shown in Figure 3.6. A person would then have many measurements, each assigning a quantity to a specific phenomenon type. The person would now have only one attribute for all measurements, and the complexity of dealing with the measurements would be shifted to querying thousands of instances of measurement and phenomenon type. We could now add further attributes to the measurement to record such things as who did it, when it was done, where it was done, and so on.

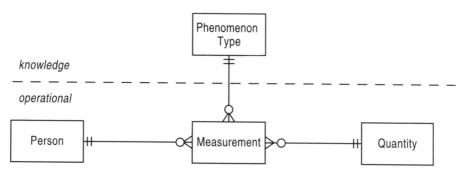

Figure 3.6   Introducing measurement and phenomenon type.

This model is useful if a large number of possible measurements would make person too complex. The phenomenon types are things we know we can measure. Such knowledge is at the knowledge level of the model.

Example   John Smith is 6 feet tall, which can be represented by a measurement whose person is John Smith, phenomenon type is height, and quantity is 6 feet.

Example   John Smith has a peak expiratory flow rate (how much air can be blown out of the lungs, how fast) of 180 liters per minute. This can be represented as a measurement whose person is John Smith, phenomenon type is peak expiratory flow rate, and quantity is 180 liters per minute.

Example   A sample of concrete has a strength indicated by a force of 4000 pounds per square inch. Here the person is replaced by a concrete sample with a measurement whose phenomenon type is strength and quantity is 4000 pounds per square inch.

This model has a simple division that was found to be very useful in later analysis. Measurements are created as part of the day-to-day operation of a system based on this model. Phenomenon types, however, are created on a much more infrequent basis because they represent the knowledge of what things to measure. The two-level model was thus conceived: the *operational level* consists of the measurement, and the *knowledge level* consists of the phenomenon type (see also Section 2.5). Although it does not seem important in this simple example, we will see that thinking about these two levels is useful as we explore modeling more deeply. (Although Figure 3.6 shows the dividing line, we have left it out of most of the following figures; however, we have a convention of drawing knowledge concepts toward the top of the figure.)

Modeling Principle   *The operational level has those concepts that change on a day-to-day basis. Their configuration is constrained by a knowledge level that changes much less frequently.*

Modeling Principle   *If a type has many, many similar associations, make all of these associations objects of a new type. Create a knowledge level type to differentiate between them.*

We could choose to add the unit of measurement to the phenomenon type and use numbers instead of quantities for the measurement. I prefer to keep quantities on the measurement so that I can easily support multiple units for a phenomenon type. A set of units on a phenomenon type can be used to check the unit of an entered measurement and to provide a list for users to choose from.

3.5   **Observation**

Just as there are many quantitative statements we can make about a patient, there are also many important qualitative statements, such as gender, blood group, and whether or not they have diabetes. We cannot use attributes for these statements because there is such a large range of possibilities, so a construct similar to that for measurement is useful.

Consider the problem of recording a person's gender, which has two possible values: male and female. We can think of gender as being what we are measuring, and male and female are two values for it, just as any positive number is a meaningful value for the height of a person. We can then devise a new type, category observation, which is similar to measurement but has a category instead of quantity, as shown in Figure 3.7. We can also devise another new type of observation that acts as a supertype to a measurement and a qualitative observation.

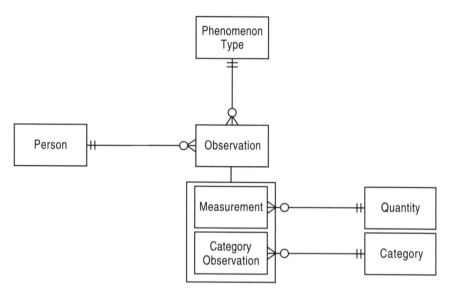

Figure 3.7   Observations and category observations.

This model supports qualitative measurements, such as blood group A.

Using Figure 3.7, we can say that gender is the instance of phenomenon type, and male and female are instances of category. To record that a person is male, we create an observation with a category of male and a phenomenon type of gender.

We now have to consider how we can record that certain categories can be used only for certain phenomenon types. Tall, Average, and Short might be categories for the phenomenon type height, while A, B, A/B, and O might be categories for the phenomenon type blood group. This could be done by providing a relationship between category and phenomenon type. The interesting question then is the cardinality of the mapping from category to phenomenon type. We might ask, does the object A used in blood group potentially link to more than one phenomenon type? One answer is, of course it does: We grade liver function on the Childs-Pugh scale, which has values A (reasonable), B (moderate), and C (poor). This raises the question of what we mean by A. If we mean merely the string consisting of the character 'A,' then the mapping is multivalued and the category is independent of the phenomenon type. The category's meaning is only clear when a phenomenon type is brought in through a qualitative observation. The alternative is to make the mapping single-valued, where the category is only defined within the context of the phenomenon type; that is, it is not A but blood group A.

What difference is this to us? The single-valued case allows us to record useful information about the categories, such as A is better than B with respect to liver function, while no such ordering exists for blood groups.

My initial investigations of the clinical process revealed a common sequence: The patient comes to the facility, evidence is collected about the patient's condition, and a clinician makes an assessment. For example, a patient might come in complaining of excessive thirst, weight loss, and frequent urination (polyuria). This would lead a clinician to diagnose diabetes. A couple of things are important about recording this diagnosis. First, it is not sufficient simply to note that the patient has diabetes; the clinician must also explicitly record the evidence used to come up with this diagnosis. Second, the clinician does not make this kind of deduction out of thin air. Random evidence is not assembled into random deductions. The clinician must rely on clinical knowledge.

Consider placing this process in the model we have so far. The patient is suffering from weight loss. We can capture this by saying that there is a phenomenon type of change in weight, with linked categories of gain, loss, and steady. Similarly there is a phenomenon type of diabetes with categories of present and absent. Clearly we can record the link between the observations by placing a suitable recursive relationship on observation, as shown in Figure 3.8. We can thus record the link between the observation of diabetes and its evidence. We also need to record the clinical knowledge of the link between weight loss and diabetes. Using the model shown in Figure 3.7, we would have difficulty recording this link. The phenomenon type of change in weight and the category of loss are only linked when an observation is made. We need a way to say that weight loss, which can exist without any observations, is at the knowledge level. Making the mapping from category to phenomenon type single-valued provides the way. (Section 3.11 discusses this further.)

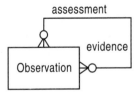

Figure 3.8   Recursive relationship to record evidence and assessment.

This was the compelling evidence for making the mapping from category to phenomenon type single-valued. It moved category to the knowledge level and renamed it phenomenon, as shown in Figure 3.9. Phenomena define the possible values for some phenomenon type.

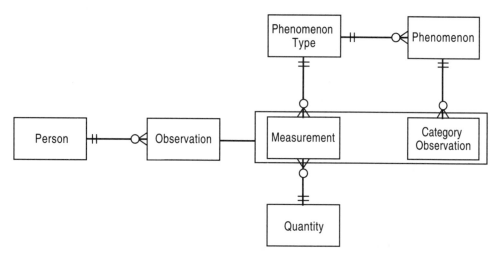

Figure 3.9   Phenomenon (formerly category) in the knowledge level.

Placing qualitative statements (such as blood group A) in the knowledge level allows them to be used in rules.

Example   The fact that a person is blood group A is indicated by a category observation of a person whose phenomenon is blood group A. The blood group A phenomenon is linked to the phenomenon type of blood group.

Example   We can model a low oil level in a car as a category observation of the car. The phenomenon type is oil level with possible phenomena of over-full, OK, and low. The observation links the car to the low phenomenon.

The model in Figure 3.9 works well for category observations with several values for a phenomenon type. But many observations involve merely a statement of absence or presence rather than a range of values. Diseases are good examples of these: Diabetes is either present or absent. We could use Figure 3.9 with the phenomena diabetes absent and diabetes present. This ability to explicitly record the absence of diabetes is important, but it may also be sensible to record absence of weight loss. (If a patient comes in with symptoms of diabetes but has not been losing weight, then that would contra-indicate diabetes. This does not imply that the weight is increasing or steady, merely that it is not decreasing.) Indeed we can record the absence of any phenomenon, particularly to eliminate hypothetical diagnoses. Thus the model shown in Figure 3.10 allows any category observation to have presence and absence. Observation concept is added as a supertype of phenomenon. This is done to allow diabetes to be an observation concept without attaching it to some phenomenon type.

Example   We record the fact that John Smith has diabetes by a presence observation of John Smith linked to the observation concept diabetes.

Example   We represent spalling (deteriorating) concrete in a tunnel by an observation with the tunnel instead of the person, and an observation concept of spalling concrete. We also need a feature on the observation to indicate where in the tunnel the spalling occurs. (Medical observations may also need an anatomical location for some observation concepts.)

3.6   Subtyping Observation Concepts

Figure 3.10 introduces a supertype relationship that allows generalization of observation concepts. This is quite common in medicine and is valuable because observations can be made at any level of generality. If an observation is made of the presence of the subtype, then all supertypes are also considered to be present. However, if an observation is made of the absence of a subtype, then that implies neither presence nor absence of supertypes. Observation of absence does imply all subtypes are also absent. Thus presence is propagated up the supertype hierarchy, while absence is propagated downward.

Example   Diabetes is an observation concept with two subtypes: type I diabetes and type II diabetes. An observation that type I diabetes is present for John Smith implies that diabetes is also present for John Smith.

Example   Blood group A is called polymorphic because it can be subtyped to A1 and A2. The other blood groups are not polymorphic.

3.7   Protocol

An important knowledge concept for recording observations is the protocol—the method by which the observations were made. We can measure a person's body temperature by placing a thermometer in the mouth, armpit, or rectum. Usually the temperature readings these techniques yield can be considered the same; nonetheless, it is vital to record which approach we used. A strange observation can often be explained by understanding the technique that was used to reach it. Thus in health care it is accepted practice to always record what tests are used to record observations.

One of the values of a protocol is that it can be used to determine the accuracy and sensitivity of a measurement. This information could be recorded

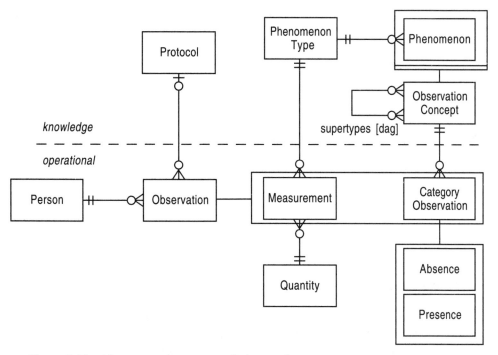

Figure 3.10   Absence and presence of observation concepts.

The absence of a phenomenon can be as valuable as finding a presence.

on the measurement itself, but usually it is based on the protocol that is used for the observation. Holding it at the protocol makes it easier to capture this information.

3.8   Dual Time Record

Observations often have a limited time period during which they can be applied. The end of the time period indicates when the observation is no longer applicable. This time period is different than the time at which the observation is made. Thus there are two time records (which may be periods or single time points) for each observation: one to record when the observation is applicable and the second when it is recorded, as shown in Figure 3.11.

Example   At a consultation on May 1, 1997, John Smith tells his doctor that he had chest pain six months ago that lasted for a week. The doctor records this as an observation of the presence of the observation concept chest pain. The applicability time record is a time period starting at November 1, 1996 and ending at November 8, 1996. The recording time is the timepoint May 1, 1997. (Note that some way of recording approximate timepoints would be valuable here.)

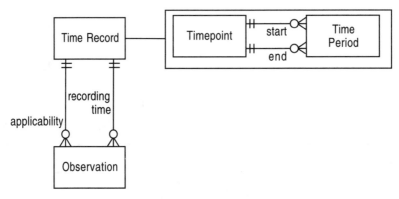

Figure 3.11 Dual time record for observation.

A time record allows both periods and single points to be recorded. Most events have a separate occurring and recording time.

3.9 Rejected Observation

Inevitably we make mistakes when making observations. In the case of medical records, however, we cannot just erase them. Treatments may have been based on these mistakes, and there are usually legal restrictions. To handle this consideration, we can classify observations as rejected observations when it is found that they were and are untrue, as shown in Figure 3.12. (Note the difference between this and an observation that was true but is no longer true, such as a healed broken arm. A healed broken arm is never rejected, but its applicability time record is given an end date.) Rejected observations must be linked to the observation that rejects them.

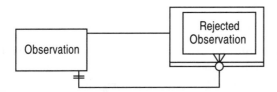

Figure 3.12 Rejected observations.

Observations cannot be deleted if a full audit trail is needed.

Example John Smith has a blood test that indicates a large mean corpuscular volume. This can be due to either pernicious anemia or alcohol abuse. John Smith informs the doctor that he drinks very little alcohol. This indicates the presence of pernicious anemia, which leads to further tests and treatment. Six months later it is discovered that John Smith drinks heavily. This information indicates that the observation of pernicious anemia should be rejected by an observation of alcohol abuse. The rejected observation of pernicious anemia must be retained to explain the treatment that ensued.

3.10   Active Observation, Hypothesis, and Projection

As observations are recorded, many levels of assurance are given. A clinician might be faced with a patient showing all the classic symptoms of diabetes. The clinician records that she thinks the patient probably has diabetes, but she cannot be certain until a test is done, and in many diseases even a test does not provide 100 percent certainty. One approach to recording this kind of information is to assign probabilities to observations, but this method is unclear and does not seem natural. The alternative is to use two classifications: active observation and hypothesis, as shown in Figure 3.13. The distinction is subtle: An active observation is one that the clinician "runs with," probably using it as a basis for treatment. A hypothesis more likely leads to further tests.

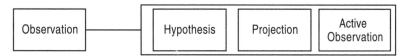

Figure 3.13   Active observation, hypothesis, and projection.

Example   A patient with observations of the presence of thirst, weight loss, and polyuria indicates diabetes. With just these symptoms, however, a clinician makes a hypothesis of diabetes and orders a measurement of the fasting blood glucose. The result of this test indicates whether to confirm the hypothesis or reject it.

Both subtypes, active observation and hypothesis, represent observations of the current state of the patient. Projections are observations that the clinician thinks might occur in the future. Often clinicians decide on treatments by considering future conditions that may occur. If the prediction is true, it is recorded with an additional active observation.

Example   If a patient has rheumatic fever, or consequent rheumatic valve disease, there is a risk of endocarditis. This risk is recorded as a projection of endocarditis. Treatments will then be based on this projection.

The certainty of observations was one area of much discussion in the Cosmos project. More changes were made in this area and more time was spent by both the team and quality assurance panel than any other part of the model. The final model reflects the clinicians' views of what was the most natural. The classic approach of assigning probabilities might make sense to science fiction aficionados, but it clearly did not to clinicians (who could predict asking questions such as "What am I to make of the difference between 0.8 and 0.7?"). With active observation and hypothesis, the final concept is more clear, although the choice of which classification to use is more problematic. In the end only the group of experienced clinicians connected with the project could make a useful decision on this area in an almost instinctive way. The professional analyst in the team could only point out some formal consequences.

3.11 Associated Observation

At this point we can look at ways to record the chain of evidence behind a diagnosis. The basic idea is to allow observations to be linked to each other (the patient's thirst indicated the patient's diabetes) and observation concepts to be so linked (thirst indicates diabetes). Thus we see that the knowledge and operational levels are reflections of each other, as shown in Figure 3.14. These reflections are linked by associations that show how knowledge concepts are applied to the operational level. In this case the links occur not only between the observation and the observation concept but also between the evidence conclusion links. Thus when we say the patient's thirst indicates that the patient has diabetes, we are making use of, and should explicitly record that we are making use of, the general connection between thirst and diabetes. Figure 3.14 shows how we make types to hold not just observations and observation concepts but also types for the links at the operational (associated observation) and the knowledge (associative function) level.

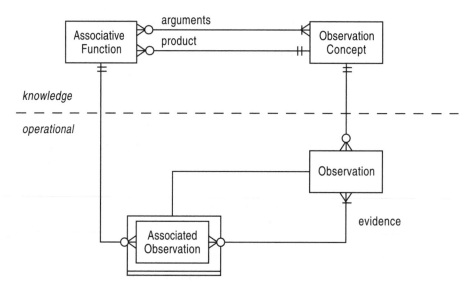

Figure 3.14   Links between observations.

Actual evidence chains for a patient are recorded at the operational level. The knowledge level describes what chains are possible.

Example A clinician observes weight loss, thirst, and polyuria in a patient and makes an associated observation (and hypothesis) of diabetes based on the evidence observations. The associated observation is linked to an associative function whose arguments are the observation concepts—weight loss, thirst, and polyuria—and whose product is diabetes.

Example If my car does not start and the lights do not work, then both of these observations are evidence for the associated observation of a dead battery. Car not starting, lights not working, and dead battery are all observation concepts linked by an associative function.

Note that the knowledge and operational levels are not complete mirror images of each other. Associated observation is a subtype of observation, but associative function is not a subtype of observation concept. It seemed natural to make associated observation a subtype of observation since, at the operational level, one particular observation is made with supporting evidence. At the knowledge level, the rule with arguments and conclusion is recorded. One observation concept may have several associative functions for which it is the result, but a particular observation has only one set of observations as evidence.

3.12   Process of Observation

This chapter has concentrated on the static elements of observation: what an observation or measurement is and how we can record it in a generic way to support the analysis that clinicians need to perform on it. It is significant that in modeling we found that we could conceive of a general static model, but the behavioral part was much more dependent on individual departments. Of course, a static model implies a great deal of behavior. Behaviors exist to create observations and to provide various ways of navigating associations to understand how those observations fit with other observations. The behavior we cannot imply, however, is the sequence of observations that a typical department makes. Often a clinician has some path of observations that can be taken. Departmental policy may be to record this path in terms of higher-level protocols (see Chapter 8). It is difficult, and almost certainly impossible, to design a general process that all clinicians could use.

It is possible, however, to sketch an outline of the process involved in making observations. I begin by looking at how making a new observation can trigger further observations, as shown in Figure 3.15. Whenever clinicians make observations, they consider the possibility of other associated observations. They use the associative functions they know to come up with a list of possible observation concepts that might be associated with the triggering observations. They can then propose further observations as needed.

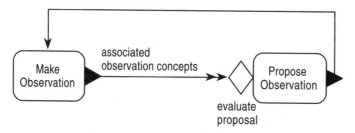

Figure 3.15 Making an observation triggers further observations.
Further observations are suggested by the knowledge level.

In Figure 3.15 the concurrent trigger rule is labeled "associated observation concepts." In event diagrams, trigger rules have two purposes. First, they show cause and effect. When we are considering business processes, this is usually enough, but as we delve deeper we see a second purpose. Any operation has input and output. The trigger that connects two operations must describe how to get from the output of the triggering operation to the input of the triggered operation. In many cases this is trivial, as they are the same object (as in the trigger from propose observation to make observation shown in Figure 3.15). However they can get quite complex, as in finding associated observation concepts.

When we have a more complex trigger rule, we can represent the trigger rule with another event diagram. Figures 3.16 and 3.17 do this for the associated observation concepts trigger. We begin by finding all the associative functions whose input includes the initial observation's observation concept. We then evaluate each of these associative functions. For each one that evaluates to true, we find the product and add it to the answer. Since these event diagrams describe a trigger rule query, all the operations must be accessors and hence must not change the observable state of any object.

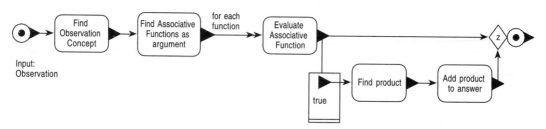

Figure 3.16 Event diagram to describe the query for finding associated observations.
This lies on the concurrent trigger of Figure 3.15 or in the operation of Figure 3.18.

When the trigger rule query is complex, you can also represent the query as an operation in its own right, as shown in Figure 3.18. Either method is correct.

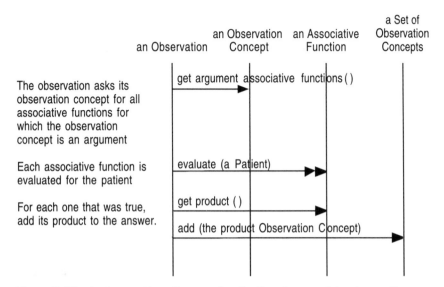

Figure 3.17   An interaction diagram for finding the possible observation concepts implied by an observation.

This interaction diagram supports Figure 3.16.

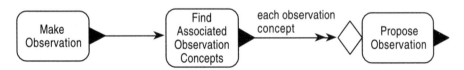

Figure 3.18   Notating the query explicitly as an operation.

This is equivalent to Figure 3.15. You can either show queries as operations or consider them part of the trigger, trading simplicity for compactness.

Even after the query, there is a control condition (evaluate proposal) before an observation is proposed. The query suggests possible observation concepts to look for based on the associative functions. This step could easily be done by software in a decision support system. The control condition represents the extra step of deciding whether the suggested observation concept is worth testing for. We did not feel we could formally model this process, implying that this step is beyond software and can only be done in the clinician's head.

Figure 3.19 includes additional triggers that arise from projections and active observations. The triggers to propose intervention work in a similar way to the previous case. We suggest interventions that are evaluated by the clinician before they are proposed. This reinforces the fact that although any observation can lead to further observations being made, only active observations or projections (not hypotheses) lead to interventions. (An intervention is an action which either intends or risks a change in state of the patient.) The trigger queries work in a similar way with the knowledge level but involve start functions, which are discussed briefly in Section 8.7.

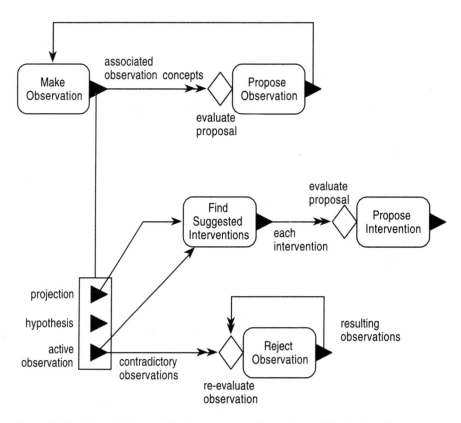

Figure 3.19 Event diagram for the process of working with observations.

This extends Figure 3.15 with similar triggers for interventions and rejections.

The final trigger on Figure 3.19 shows how the appearance of an active observation can contradict other observations and thus lead to those observations being rejected. Again this can involve associative functions, but this time we are looking for a contradiction. Once an observation (which may be a hypothesis) is rejected, further observations which were supported by this observation must be reconsidered.

One of the interesting things about the work that produced these patterns is the way the abstractions were found. Although the final results discussed here are usually structural, behavioral modeling played a central role in understanding how the concepts worked. The fact that clinicians did the modeling themselves was also crucial. The abstraction of observation is central to these patterns; it ties together signs, symptoms, and diagnoses, which clinicians have long considered to be very different. It was only by going through the modeling process that clinicians could pull out the abstraction. If software engineers had come up with such an abstraction, I doubt if they could ever convince clinicians that it was valid. And there would be good reason to be doubtful, since software engineers can never have that deep knowledge of medicine. The best conceptual models are built by domain experts, and they are often the best conceptual modelers.

References

1. Cairns, T., A. Casey, M. Fowler, M. Thursz, and H. Timimi. *The Cosmos Clinical Process Model*. National Health Service, Information Management Centre, 15 Frederick Rd, Birmingham, B15 1JD, England. Report ECBS20A & ECBS20B <http://www.sm.ic.ac.uk/medicine/cpm>, 1992.

2. Cunningham, W. "The CHECKS Pattern Language of Information Integrity," In *Pattern Languages of Program Design*. J.O. Coplien, and D.C. Schmidt, ed. Reading, MA: Addison-Wesley, 1995, pp. 145–155.

3. Thursz, M., M. Fowler, T. Cairns, M. Thick, and G. Gold. "Clinical Systems Design," In *Proceedings of IEEE 6th International Symposium on Computer Based Medical Systems*, 1993.

4

Observations for Corporate Finance

To fully understand this chapter, you will need to read Chapter 3 first.

In large corporations it is easy to identify high-level problems, but finding out the root causes of these problems is more tricky. Such corporations generate a deluge of information that can quickly drown anyone trying to analyze it.

For example, one of the principal measures of a company's performance is its final revenue. If the revenue shows a notable dip, then some analysis needs to be done to find out why. Such an analysis for Aroma Coffee Makers (ACM) showed that their equipment sales income was reduced, although their costs were still reasonable. This was most noticeable in their Northeast region. Looking further showed that their 1100 high-volume coffee maker family was well below its planned income, particularly in the government sector. Much of this is analysis of numbers, but further analysis may be more qualitative than quantitative. Perhaps this poor performance is due to a weak sales compensation plan, or government budget cuts, or a very hot summer, or strong competitor presence in the area.

All of this is much the same diagnostic process that is done by clinicians when investigating a patient's symptoms. From the obvious symptom we track back through likely causes, guided by our knowledge of the field. We hope to identify the root causes and then treat them. From this broad view of similar processes, we might hypothesize that we can apply the clinical models to corporate finance.

Chapter 3 gives a description of how qualitative and quantitative statements can be made about patients in a health care context. At the end of that chapter, I briefly mentioned that that model can be applied to other contexts, such as analyzing corporate finances. This chapter looks at how this can be done. The model works very well, but some modifications are required. Fortunately the patterns that describe these modifications are all extensions of the existing model rather than changes to it.

The first pattern replaces the person with some way of describing the segment of the enterprise under analysis. This *enterprise segment (4.1)* describes a part of the enterprise defined along a series of dimensions. Each dimension represents some way of hierarchically breaking down the enterprise, such as location, product range, or market. The enterprise segment is a combination of these dimensions, a technique widely used by multidimensional databases.

The *measurement protocol (4.2)* pattern describes how measurements can be calculated from other measurements using formulas that are instances of model types. Chapter 3 discusses how each measurement measures a phenomenon type; here we discuss how the measurement protocol defines ways of creating measurements for a particular phenomenon type. We cover three varieties of measurement protocols: *Causal measurement protocols (4.2.2)* describe how different phenomenon types are combined to calculate another (sales revenue is the product of units sold and average price). *Comparative measurement protocols (4.2.2)* describe how a single phenomenon type can vary between *status types (4.2.3)* (actual versus plan deviation of sales revenue). *Dimension combinations (4.2.5)* use the dimensions defined in the enterprise segment pattern to calculate summary values (calculate northeast sales revenue by totaling the values for individual states). Each of these subtypes of measurement protocol uses polymorphism to determine its value.

Often we use qualitative phenomena to describe quantitative phenomenon types. In this case we can define the phenomena by linking them to a range of values for the phenomenon type. First we need a *range (4.3)*, which allows us to describe a range between two quantities and various operations we want to do with the range. We can then define a *phenomenon with range (4.4)* either by adding a range to the phenomenon using a *phenomenon with range attribute (4.4.1)* or by using a *range function (4.4.2)*.

We can combine the patterns examined in this chapter with those of Chapter 3 to analyze a business' financial data. Section 4.5 shows how we can use these patterns to identify the causes of problems in large corporations.

The models in this chapter are based on work done by a team from a large manufacturing company. This team explored using a health care model for corporate finance and found it to be a very useful foundation. The models in this chapter were prototyped using C++.

Key Concepts   Enterprise Segment, Dimension, Measurement Protocol, Status Type

4.1   Enterprise Segment

The most noticeable difference between the problem we examine in this chapter and the one discussed in Chapter 3 is that here not a single patient is being observed. In some cases we look at the whole company, but in other cases we observe only part of the company, such as 10–11 espresso sales to the government in the Northeast region. This could be handled by treating each part of the company, and the whole, as separate parties. However, it is important to ensure that the relationships between these corporate parts is understood.

Thus we have to alter the mapping from procedure to patient to point to some other type. This is an issue that I skimmed over in the discussion of mapping in Chapter 3, so actually it is not such a problem as it may first appear. The original Cosmos model [1], on which Chapter 3 is based, does not actually link from observation to person. In reality the link is to a type called object of care. Object of care is itself a generalization of patient and population. A population is a group of people and is used to allow observations to be made of groups of people, which is particularly important for public health.

For corporate finance we need a new subtype of object of care, which we call enterprise segment, as shown in Figure 4.1. An enterprise segment is a part of a company, a part defined in a very particular way.

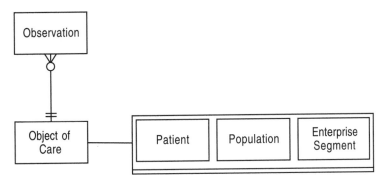

Figure 4.1   Object of care and its subtypes.

The patient of Chapter 3 is one kind of object of care that can be observed.

When we look at an enterprise, we can see that we can divide it into parts according to several criteria. It may be divided due to organizational unit, to geographical location, by product, by the industry sector that the product is being sold into, and so on. Each of these methods of division can be carried out more or less independently. Each can also be expressed as a hierarchy. For example, a multinational company can be divided first by market (USA), then by region (Northeast), then by area (New Hampshire). Each of these independent hierarchies is a dimension of the enterprise. New Hampshire and Northeast are elements at different levels in the geographical dimension. An enterprise segment is a combination of dimension elements, one for each dimension of the enterprise. Thus the part of ACM that is northeast, 11-10, government can be defined as the enterprise segment with dimension elements of northeast on the geographical dimension, 11-10 on the product dimension, and government on the industry dimension, as shown in Figure 4.2. This approach to analysis, often referred to as a star schema [4], is commonly used in multidimensional databases [2].

With this enterprise segment defined, we can form a model of the relationships between the various types, as shown in Figure 4.3. We can link dimension elements together into hierarchies. Many hierarchies of dimension elements can be defined. Note how the hierarchies constraint on the parent association is necessary because the cardinalities alone do not enforce a hierarchy (although they might allow cycles). The enterprise segment must have one element from each of these hierarchies, as indicated by the three associations from the enterprise segment. The constraint on the dimension element ensures that the hierarchies are all within the same dimension. The model will handle the situation quite well, but it has a couple of disadvantages. First, the concepts of dimension and dimension level are not properly defined, although they can be derived. Second, adding a new dimension will cause a model change.

The model shown in Figure 4.4 uses an explicit dimension type. Each dimension holds a hierarchy of dimension elements. The enterprise segment then needs to have one link to a dimension element in each dimension. We can do this by using the keyed mapping (see Section 15.2). When combined with cardinality this mapping states that for each instance of the key (dimension) there is one and only one dimension element.

Example   We can define the 11-10, Northeast government enterprise segment, linking it to the dimension elements 11-10, Northeast, and government. 11-10 is in the product dimension, Northeast is in the location dimension, and government is in the industry dimension.

Note that each hierarchy needs a top, and this does not necessarily show a named thing. A common convention is to label the top "all," showing that any segment that references it does not have any breakdowns along that dimension. Another convention would be to let the mapping to the dimension element be optional; then "nil" would indicate the top of the tree. The former approach is more consistent, despite this slightly artificial top element.

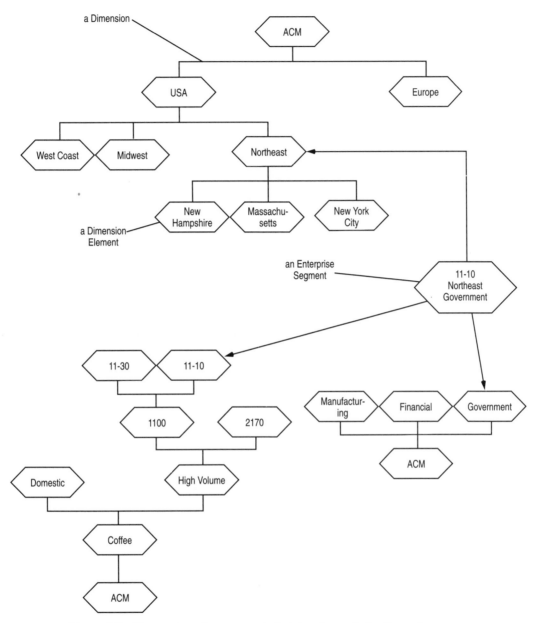

Figure 4.2   How enterprise segments link to elements in dimensions.

One enterprise segment is a combination of elements from each dimension.

Example   If we add a channel dimension, then the enterprise segment 11-10 Northeast government has a link to the top dimension element of the channel hierarchy. We call this dimension element all.

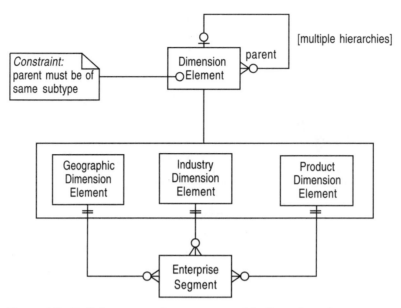

Figure 4.3   Defining enterprise segments with dimension elements.

Using this model requires adding a new subtype whenever a dimension is added.

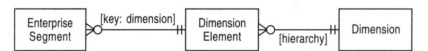

Figure 4.4   Defining enterprise segments by using dimensions and dimension elements.

This model allows us to add new dimensions without changing the model. It is also more compact.

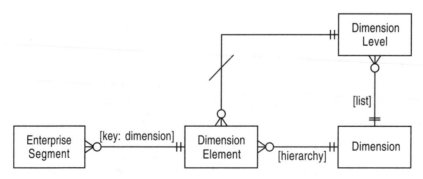

Figure 4.5   Adding dimension levels to Figure 4.4.

Dimension levels allow us to name each level of a dimension.

Adding a type for dimension level is not entirely obvious. Naturally every dimension element has a dimension level. However, the level is determined by its position in the dimension's hierarchy. The model shown in Figure 4.5 deals with this by assigning each dimension a list to define its dimension elements. The dimension element uses its level in the hierarchy and the list of dimension levels to determine its dimension level.

Example   In the ACM example the location dimension has a list of dimension levels: market, region, and area. New Hampshire is defined in the hierarchy with parent Northeast, whose parent is USA, whose parent is all. Since it is three levels down, New Hampshire's dimension level is the third in the list: area.

4.1.1   Defining the Dimensions

How can we define dimensions? The simplest definition is that they are the ways in which a large organization can be broken down via some organizational structure. However, that is not generally the most satisfactory definition. An organization can be broken down in many ways, depending on the situation. In addition, some dimensions are not necessarily appropriate to an organization system. The model in Figure 4.2 includes a breakdown by industry to which ACM sells, but this need not represent an organization structure within ACM.

We can find a better way to define dimensions by looking at the bottom of the hierarchy and asking what is being classified by the dimensions there. In the example we can see that ACM is focusing on the sale or rental of a coffee machine. We can classify this dimension according to which machine was sold, which sales area sold it, and which industry it was sold into. The dimensions come from the classification of this *focal event,* which is the fact table of a star schema [4].

In determining the dimensions to use in this kind of analysis, first we need to understand what the focal event is. We can then look at the ways in which this focal event can be classified. From Figure 4.2 we see the focal event involves a product that has a product family, which has a product group, which has a beverage. On the sales dimension we see area, region, and market.

These dimensions and levels should be defined by business analysts; Figure 4.6 shows a good way to do this. As Figure 4.6 indicates this structure can become quite complex. The dimensions are not necessarily completely independent. For example, note how the price range dimension intersects the product dimension. This indicates that any product will have one particular parent along the product and price range dimensions. The model of Figure 4.5 would need to be modified to take this into account properly, although it is questionable whether it is worth undertaking this since it does complicate the model somewhat. This issue could be handled by the dimension creation process.

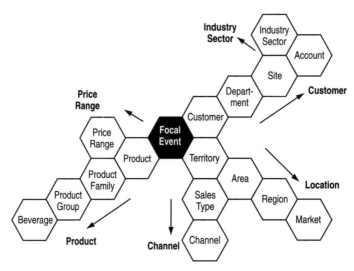

Figure 4.6   A Tilak chart showing a typical set of dimensions and levels.

This is a useful diagram providing we do not have more than six branches from any level. In practice we rarely do.

The dimensions need not be measurable to the lowest level. In this case it might not be worthwhile, or even possible, to analyze down to an individual salesperson's territory or to an individual customer. In this case the dimensions are elaborated part of the way down to the underlying event. It is still useful to understand what the lower levels are, both for future development and to see the foundations of the higher levels.

A full analysis of the customer's domain would involve producing a business model for the customer's area. This would include a structural model, which would be used to rigorously define the dimensions. Each dimension should represent a hierarchical path along the structural model. The details of this process are beyond the scope of this chapter. For the sake of discussion we will assume the dimensions have been determined.

The dimensions can be defined explicitly by the user of the analysis system. Otherwise, they can be determined from corporate databases. For the latter, each dimension needs a builder operation to tell it how to query corporate databases. This allows the system to add nodes to the dimension over time.

4.1.2   Properties of Dimensions and Enterprise Segments

An important rule about dimensions is that the measurements for dimensions at lower levels can be properly combined into the higher level. Thus if we want to look at sales revenue for the Northeast, we can do this by adding together the values for sales for all subregions of the Northeast region.

Any dimensions that are defined must support this property. Usually dimensions are combined through addition, but there are some exceptions (see Section 4.2.5).

Along with dimensions defined through business structures, another common dimension is time. Time is treated as a dimension by classifying the underlying event into a time period. If these periods are months then we can talk about such figures as revenue for (11-10, Northeast, March 1994). This implies a dimension element for March 1994 that would be a child of the dimension element for 1994. The time dimension satisfies the combinability property discussed above, providing the figures are only for that month (and not year-to-date figures). We can easily calculate year-to-dates from month-only figures but typically not by combining along a dimension.

Enterprise segments share an interesting property with more fundamental types: All enterprise segments conceptually exist. There is no notion of conceptually creating the number 5, the quantity $5, or the date 1/1/2314. These things all exist in our minds but may need to be created as objects in the computer. Enterprise segments share this property. Once all dimensions have been specified with their dimension elements, then all enterprise segments conceptually exist, although they may not be created as software objects.

This shared property raises the question of whether an enterprise segment should be treated as a fundamental type (see Section A.1.5). If so, it should not have any mappings to nonfundamental objects. A dimension element and an observation (inherited from an object of care) are both non-fundamental. Although the latter could be excluded, the former is part of the definition of enterprise segment and thus cannot be excluded. There is also a lot of sense in holding the mapping from an enterprise segment to an observation since a very common request is to find all observations for a given enterprise segment. In balance it seems that enterprise segments are not fundamental, despite this property of universal conceptual existence.

Treating enterprise segments as nonfundamental does have an effect on the interface. The create operation is really a find-or-create. It first looks to see if the required instance of the enterprise segment exists; if so it returns it, if not it creates it. (Or you can think of it as not having a create operation but only a find operation, which creates silently when it needs to.)

4.2   Measurement Protocol

The corporate analysis we have been discussing uses a lot of measurements. These measurements are not entered by hand; usually they are either loaded from one of many databases or calculated from other measurements. We need to remember how we can make these measurements, that is, the protocol we use to create the measurement. Figure 4.7 shows a general outline of measurement and protocols, much of it similar to that of Chapter 3.

Two kinds of measurement protocol are shown in Figure 4.7. Source measurement protocols refer to queries against some corporate database. Typically an object knows logically which database it is accessing, although the actual commands are in another layer. The user should decide which database is accessed. A calculated measurement protocol represents a calculation done on measurements already present in this domain.

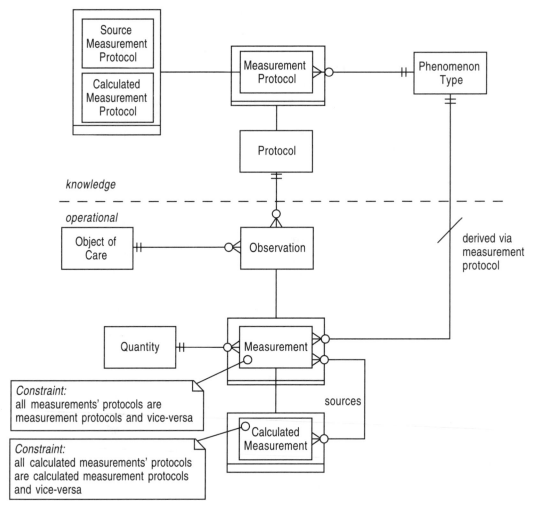

Figure 4.7   Measurement and measurement protocols.

Source measurements are from a database, and calculated measurements use formulas.

An important point about this model—a reflection of its clinical background—is that any phenomenon type can have several measurement protocols to determine its value. This point may strike some readers as odd. What is the point of a measurement that we can calculate in more than one way? If there is more than one formula, surely it is a different phenomenon type. The first and most obvious point is that the phenomenon type can have both calculations and source protocols. We can use different protocols at different times. There can also be multiple source protocols; which one we use depends on system availability. Some databases are more reliable than others, but availability can never be perfect.

Similarly the user could consider using different calculations to produce the same phenomenon type. Which calculation the user chooses can depend on which sources are available or on the user's opinion about subtle points within the calculation. A good example of this is the value of inventory. Usually inventory is physically counted only at the end of the year, but its value needs to be estimated at other times. In either case the value is used in the same way for further financial information.

Some users of this model may choose to specify which measurement protocol to use to come up with a value. Others, however, may just want a phenomenon type and leave it to the system to come up with how it gets it. In the latter case some way is needed to prioritize the measurement protocols for a phenomenon type. This can be done by making the mapping from phenomenon type to measurement protocol a list. The front of the list defines the preferred protocol and so on.

Note the presence of calculated measurement, with its link back to its source measurements. This follows the general rule that the result of a computation, when treated as an object, should know what computation caused it (the protocol) and what the inputs to this protocol were (the sources).

4.2.1   Holding the Calculations

The calculated measurement protocols include the formulas by which they are calculated, as shown in Figure 4.8. This is an example of an individual instance method (see Section 6.6). The formulas for calculated measurement protocols are often very simple, so we can use a simple interpreter [3] and hold the formulas as spreadsheet-style formulas.

An important feature of the model is the way the arguments are presented. Each calculated measurement protocol has a list of arguments. This list represents those phenomenon types that are combined in the formula. Note that the mapping is a list. For the formula to make sense, the elements in the mapping must be identifiable. A list is a good way to do this. Alternatively they can be keyed by a string.

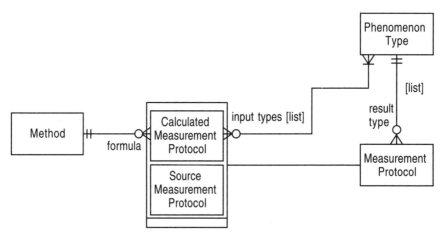

Figure 4.8   Methods for calculated measurement protocols.

Example   Sales revenue is a phenomenon type with a causal calculation as its measurement protocol. The arguments to the causal calculation are a list of two phenomenon types—number of sales and average price. The method is the formula arg[1]*arg[2].

Example   Body mass index is a phenomenon type in medicine. It has a causal calculation with arguments of weight and height. The method is the formula weight/height^2.

4.2.2   Comparative and Causal Measurements Protocols

In a corporate finance application the measurements are not absolute values. The users are usually not too interested in a figure that says revenues are x, rather they are interested in the difference between the actual and a planned figure or this year's revenues compared to last year's.

To consider these comparative measurements, we need to describe the various kinds of measurements that can appear. Typical comparisons are between an actual value and either a prior or a planned value. Prior values can be considered by either looking at the applicability time reference (see Section 3.8) or by looking for a measurement for the enterprise segment that has a prior time dimension. Planned measurements require us to make a distinction between actual or planned values, which correspond to the active and projected observations discussed in Section 3.10. In addition, the projected observation must record what plan was the source for the projection, so that we can distinguish between annual plans, quarterly forecasts, and the like, as shown in Figure 4.9.

At this point a fundamental distinction between two types of calculation should be apparent. One kind is determining a value for a phenomenon type based on values of other phenomenon types. For example, we can calculate sales revenue by multiplying the number of sales by the average price. This type of calculation is called a causal calculation because it follows the cause

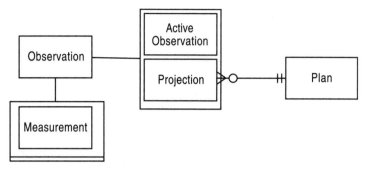

Figure 4.9   Kinds of observations to support planned and actual values.

and effect analysis. Causal calculations can have any number and any relationship of input phenomenon types, and the formulas by which they are computed can be any expression.

Comparative calculations, on the other hand, are more structured. They always have two input measurements, which must be of the same phenomenon type. The output measurement's phenomenon type is always derived from the form of the calculation and the input phenomenon type. Thus if we are looking at the deviation of number of sales, then the inputs will be the phenomenon type number of sales and the output phenomenon type will be deviation for number of sales. The formulas for these calculations will generally be of a fairly limited set: such things as absolute deviation $(x-y)$ or percentage deviation $((x-y)/y)$.

The differences between these two types of calculations can be formalized by subtyping the calculated measurement protocol, as shown in Figure 4.10. The calculated measurement protocol carries the key elements of the structure. Each calculated measurement protocol has a single result type and a number of input types. For comparative calculations they are limited to two arguments, which must be the same phenomenon type. All calculated measurement protocols have a method that contains the formula by which a new value is calculated from the inputs. Two protocols can share a single method, for example the method `arg1-arg2` is shared between all the protocols that determine absolute deviation for all the phenomenon types. Indeed, this case is so common it is worth making a special subtype for it that fixes the method to the type.

4.2.3   Status Type: Defining Planned and Actual Status

Measurements determined by source or calculated measurement protocols are always calculated through their measurement protocol. The measurement protocol provides a factory method for the measurement [3].[1] A client asks the

---

[1] Note that the reason for this is that the method of creation varies, rather than the type of the final result. This is another reason to use the factory method in addition to those indicated by Gamma et al [3].

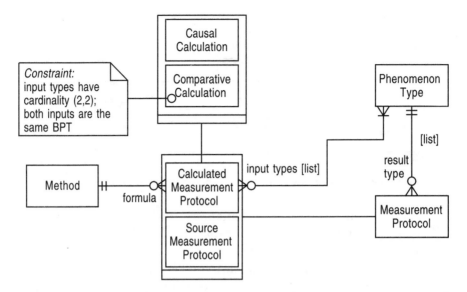

Figure 4.10   Types of calculation as shown by calculated measurement protocols.

Causal calculations link different phenomenon types, and comparative calculations show the difference in one phenomenon type between status types.

measurement protocol to create a measurement. The client needs to tell the measurement protocol what object of care it needs to reference. The client also needs to tell the protocol whether it is an actual or planned value: which plan for the planned value or which date for the actual value.

At this point the model shown in Figure 4.9 shows a weakness. There is no simple way we can provide the information needed for the protocol. Figure 4.9 does provide a good way to determine this information from an existing measurement, but it does not provide a convenient single way to ask for the information. This can be overcome by the model shown in Figure 4.11, which puts these properties together into a single status type. Two subtypes exist of the abstract status type. Actual status types may have a time offset. For current values there will be no offset (or it can be zero). Six months or one year ago will have the appropriate offset. Planned status types have the appropriate plan, just like projections.

Example   A corporation assesses four kinds of financials: actual value, prior year, the annual plan, and the latest quarterly forecast. The actual would be an actual status type with time offset of zero. The prior year is an actual with time offset of one year. The annual plan is a planned status type linked to the annual plan. The quarterly forecast is also a planned status type linked to the latest quarterly forecast. All the quarterly forecasts are instances of the plan.

Effectively we have moved the knowledge of what kind of observation we have from the observation itself to a separate type. This type can enumerate

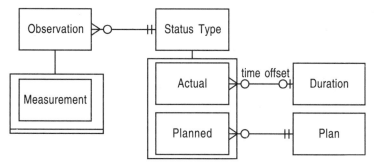

Figure 4.11   Status types as an alternative to Figure 4.9.

This alternative makes it easier to specify the kind of comparative measurement required (see Figure 4.12).

all possible variations independently of existing observations. The type resides at the knowledge level so we can calculate new measurements, but it need not be at the knowledge level. We should note that this is not inconsistent with the model in Figure 4.9. Both expressions say the same thing, in slightly different ways, and both could be supported at the same time.

Now the client needs only to specify the status type for the measurement protocol to have enough information to create the measurement, assuming the protocol is a causal protocol. Comparative calculations need two status types, one for each input. One way of dealing with this is to vary the create measurement operation so that it requires one status type for causals and two for comparative measurements. Another method is to allow comparative status types, as shown in Figure 4.12. I prefer the latter method because the comparison is now an object in its own right, and the interface for creating all measurements is the same.

Example ACM management wants to see the actual vs. planned deviation for sales revenue. To satisfy this request, the model must include a phenomenon type for sales revenue and a phenomenon type for sales revenue deviation. The sales revenue deviation is a comparative calculation with a method of arg[1] – arg[2]. The request creates an observation of sales revenue deviation with a comparative status type. The status type will have datum of planned and comparator of actual.

4.2.4   Creating a Measurement

Now that we know how to ask for a new measurement, we can look at the process for creating a measurement, which is illustrated in Figures 4.13 and 4.14. The process has three steps: finding the arguments, executing a formula, and creating a new measurement object with the resulting value.

The argument-finding operation is polymorphic depending on whether we have a causal or comparative measurement protocol. The causal protocol, shown in Figure 4.15, needs to find all measurements of the same status type

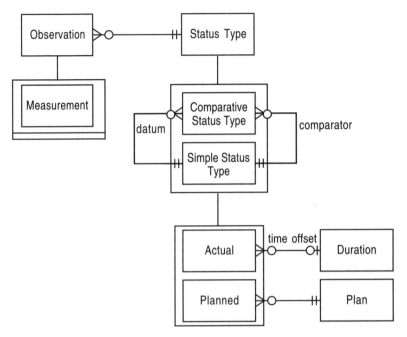

Figure 4.12   Using comparative status types to ease the specification of comparative measurements.

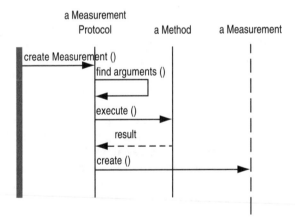

Figure 4.13   Interaction diagram for creating a measurement.

and object of care whose phenomenon types match the input types of the protocol. The comparative formula, shown in Figure 4.16, looks for two measurements whose phenomenon type is that of the input type, who have the same object of care, and whose status types are the datum and comparator for the protocol.

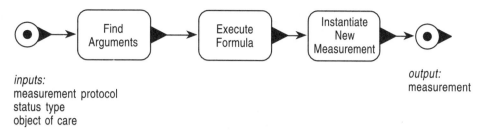

inputs:
measurement protocol
status type
object of care

output:
measurement

Figure 4.14   Event diagram that describes the process for creating a measurement.

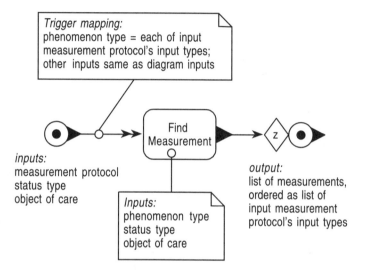

inputs:
measurement protocol
status type
object of care

output:
list of measurements,
ordered as list of
input measurement
protocol's input types

Figure 4.15   The find arguments operation for a causal calculation.

This operation finds a measurement for each argument type with all other factors the same.

When we have found the arguments, we can pass them on to the formula and then create a measurement with the resulting value.

4.2.5   Dimension Combinations

A third kind of calculation is the combination of values along a dimension. The example mentioned above was that of calculating sales revenue for the Northeast by adding together the values for sales for all child regions of the Northeast region. More precisely, the measurement of a phenomenon type for an enterprise segment that refers to Northeast is calculated by finding all measurements of that phenomenon type attached to enterprise segments that refer to child regions of the Northeast dimension element but have the same dimension elements along the other dimensions. These values are added together for the new value.

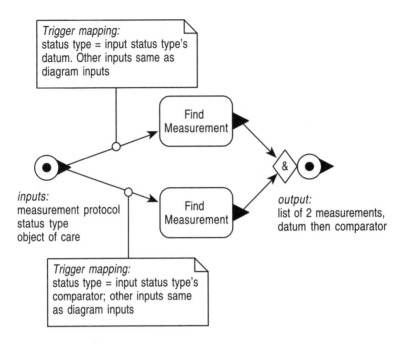

Figure 4.16 The find arguments operation for comparative calculations.

This operation finds one argument for each leg of the comparative status type.

We can thus add a dimension combination protocol as shown in Figure 4.17. We must specify the dimension that is being combined. The calculation does not need any input types (since it is always the same phenomenon type as the output type). We could consider reducing the input type mapping's cardinality to zero, but I think we can preserve the sense better by keeping the mapping mandatory and adding a constraint. Creating the measurement follows the usual steps shown in Figure 4.14, with the find arguments operation again being altered as in Figure 4.18.

The role of the calculation method is very simple: It takes all the arguments and adds them together. Usually addition is used for combining, but not always. For example, the phenomenon type average price is not added in dimension combination; instead a mean is found. These variations depend on the phenomenon type, so each phenomenon type needs to have a combination method. The calculation method applies the combination method to the arguments to determine the result.

Note that the comparative and dimension combination protocols can be automatically generated. For dimension combination, one protocol can be defined for each combination of phenomenon type and dimension. For comparative calculations, one protocol can be defined for each combination of phenomenon type and kind of comparative calculation.

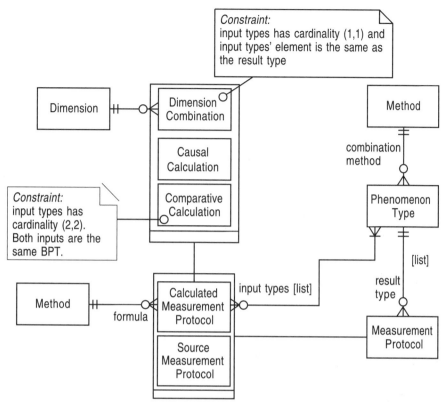

Figure 4.17 Adding dimension combination to the calculated measurement protocols.

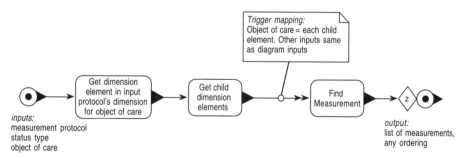

Figure 4.18 The find arguments operation for dimension combination calculations.

This operation finds a measurement for each child enterprise segment along the indicated dimension.

Calculated measurements are just as useful in health care. We discuss calculated measurements in this chapter, rather than in Chapter 3, primarily because they were used extensively in our work on corporate finance. Thus they are an illustration of how taking a model to a different domain causes more thought that may well feed back into the original domain.

4.3 Range

So far we have looked at how we can use measurements, both calculated and sourced, to investigate a company's financial performance. The measurement protocol pattern gives us a way of looking at this information quantitatively. To make sense of a forest of numbers, however, it is often useful to group measurements into categories. We might want to divide the absolute revenues into a number of bands, or we could highlight as problems all comparative measurements that are 10 percent below the datum.

Our first step is to describe ranges of measurements, which is the subject of this pattern. The second step is to link these ranges into the broader system of observations, as we will discuss in Section 4.4.

We often come across the need to hold a range of some values. The range can consist of numbers (such as 1..10), dates (such as 1/1/95..5/5/95), quantities (such as 10..20kg) or even strings (such as AAA..AGZ). Usually a range is placed on the type that is using it by giving that type separate mapping for an upper and lower value, as shown in Figure 4.19.

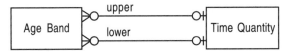

Figure 4.19   Representing a range with upper and lower bounds on the type that uses it.

I do not recommend this approach to ranges; use a range type instead.

The problem with this approach is that there is rather more to ranges than just an upper and lower value. We might want to know whether a particular value is within a range, whether two ranges overlap, whether two ranges abut, or whether a set of ranges form a continuous range. Such behavior would have to be copied for every type that has upper and lower values. The solution is to make the range an object in its own right, as shown in Figure 4.20. In this situation all responsibilities which are essentially about ranges are contained within the range, and do not need to be duplicated in those types that use ranges.

In general a range can be formed between any two magnitudes. A magnitude, in essence, is a type that defines the comparative operators ($>$, $<$, $=$, $\geq$, $\leq$).

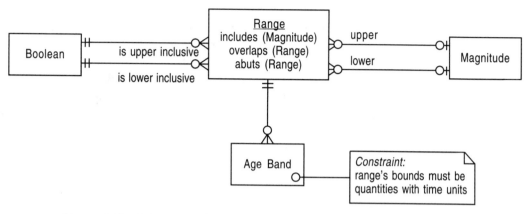

Figure 4.20   Using an explicit range object.

This should always be done when an upper and lower value are needed. Upper and lower mappings are optional, thus allowing open-ended ranges, such as less than 6 months. The Booleans are needed to differentiate less than 6 months from less than or equal to 6 months.

The range needs only these operations to define its own key operations: includes, overlaps, and abuts. When a range is used, the using type usually indicates what kind of magnitudes it wants in its range. There are several ways of modeling which kind of magnitude is required. One way is to declare a subtype, such as I do with time period (a range whose magnitudes are time-points). Another way is to use a constraint, as in Figure 4.20. A third way is to use something along the lines of parameterized classes, where a range of integers is defined by a type called range<Integer>. Conceptually all of these modeling techniques are equivalent, so we can use whatever we find the easiest. In implementation we need to choose more carefully, and the trade-offs vary depending on the implementation environment. The choice of conceptual model does not imply anything about the implementation.

4.4   Phenomenon with Range

Ranges give us a way to define categories of measurements. We now need to link them into the broader model of observation and measurement. To do this, we can form phenomena of certain phenomenon types. If our phenomenon type is revenue percentage deviation, we can form a phenomenon of revenue problem, which exists when our revenue percentage deviation is less than −10 percent. This implies that a measurement of −12 percent of revenue percentage deviation also implies a category observation (see Section 3.5) of revenue problem.

The first question we need to answer is whether there are one or two observations. According to the model shown in Figure 3.9, observations are either measurements or category observations, they cannot be both. We can allow a single observation to be both by using the model shown in Figure 4.21. The choice between the models depends on whether we consider the conceptual process as being first a measurement and then a separate step of observing the revenue problem (which implies using Figure 3.9), or whether we see the measurement and observation as one process. For simple cases such as these, the domain experts I have worked with preferred the latter.

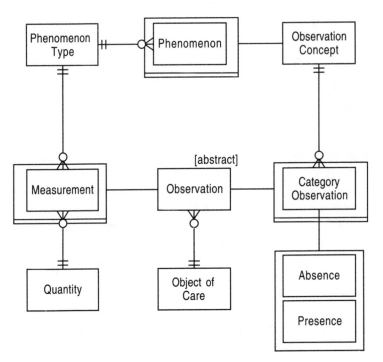

Figure 4.21 Allowing an observation to be both a measurement and a category observation.

The [abstract] statement implies that an observation must be at least one of its subtypes.

Since we have a well-defined range, it seems natural to let the computer automatically link any such measurement to the relevant phenomenon. To do this we need a way of defining the range within the knowledge level.

4.4.1 Phenomenon with Range Attribute

The simplest approach is to add a range to a phenomenon, as shown in Figures 4.22 and 4.23. Then when we create a measurement we can look to see if it falls in the range for any phenomenon of that measurement's phenomenon types. We do have to consider whether we want the range for a phenomenon type not to overlap or to be complete. Either of these conditions indicate the need for a constraint.

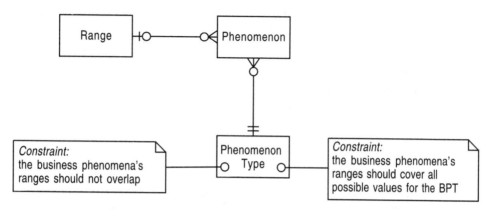

Figure 4.22   Adding a range to a phenomenon.

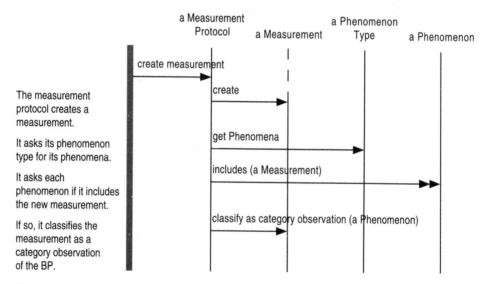

Figure 4.23   Interaction diagram for creating a measurement and checking the phenomena.

The responsibility for checking the phenomena could be done equally well by the measurement object. I prefer the protocol, as I think that is a more likely place for overriding.

Example   Revenue percentage deviation is divided into four categories: greater than 5% is good, 5% to –5% is OK, –5% to –10% is warning, and less than –10% is a problem. This can be represented as four phenomena for the phenomenon type revenue percentage deviation (RPD). The phenomenon good RPD has a range with no upper bound and 5 lower bound, the phenomenon OK RPD has a range with upper bound 5 and lower bound –5, the phenomenon warning RPD has a range with upper bound –5 and lower bound –10, the phenomenon problem RPD has a range with upper bound –10 and no lower bound. It is important to check exactly what the boundaries are and include this information in the ranges; so we ask if exactly 5% is good RPD or OK RPD?

Example   Body mass index is used to define four groups: normal 20–25 kg/m^2, overweight 25–30 kg/m^2, obese 30–40 kg/m^2, morbid obese >40 kg/m^2. This would be represented as four phenomena for the phenomenon type body mass index. The overweight phenomenon would have a range with lower bound 25 kg/m^2 and upper bound 30 kg/m^2. Each of the other phenomena would have similar ranges.

4.4.2   Range Function

An alternative approach is to create a separate range function as a subtype of associative function, as shown in Figures 4.24 and 4.25. This is useful when different ranges apply, depending on the context described by an observation concept. This model allows several series of ranges to be present, depending on which observation concepts apply. The range function evaluates some expression of the arguments, as in an associative function, but also checks whether the measurement falls in the range over a phenomenon type. If both are true,

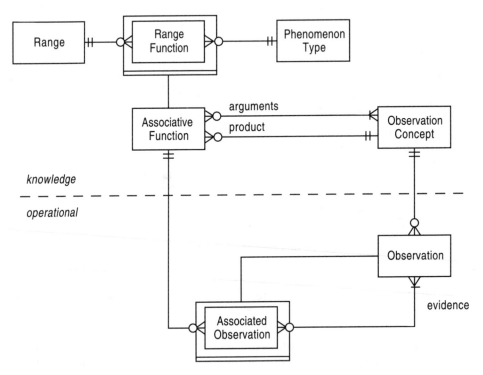

Figure 4.24   Range function.

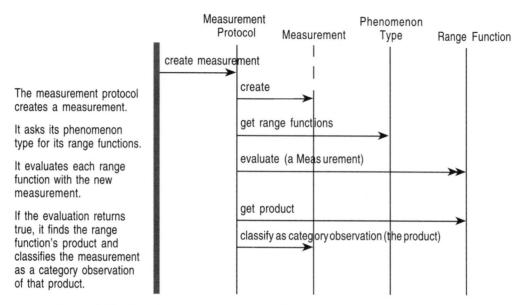

The measurement protocol creates a measurement.

It asks its phenomenon type for its range functions.

It evaluates each range function with the new measurement.

If the evaluation returns true, it finds the range function's product and classifies the measurement as a category observation of that product.

Figure 4.25   Creating a measurement and checking range functions.

then the product observation concept applies. Developing constraints to ensure that only one range function will be true for any given measurement is considerably more difficult than when ranges are applied directly to phenomena.

Example   Certain enterprise segments are defined as key. For these segments the problem revenue percentage deviation (RPD) is defined at –5% instead of –10%. To handle this we would define an observation concept of key segment. Those segments that were key segments would have an appropriate observation applied to them. (This would also give us the ability to change key status over time.) We would define a range function with arguments of {key segment}, product of problem RPD, a range of <5% and a phenomenon type of RPD.

Example   The normal range of a person's beta HCG increases with pregnancy. To represent this, we would have two range functions with the product normal beta HCG. One would have arguments of pregnancy and the other arguments of nonpregnancy. The phenomenon type on the range functions would be beta HCG.

Both of these approaches have their merits, and it can be plausible to use them both together. Linking directly to the phenomenon is certainly the easiest way of doing it, and that is the one to use if it correctly describes the situation. Range functions are more complex but can represent more complicated situations. So you should use the direct link to phenomenon when you can and range functions when you must. If the situation gets more complex than the models described here can handle, you should add features to range function, either directly or by way of a subtype.

4.5   **Using the Resulting Framework**

So far this chapter has described patterns that represented expansions of those introduced in Chapter 3. Now we can look at how we can use these models.

We begin by looking for the total revenue for ACM. This would be a measurement whose enterprise segment is the whole company; that is, the enterprise segment's dimension elements are all at the top of the dimension hierarchies. The measurement normally would not be an absolute value; rather it would be a comparative value with some plan or prior time period. Furthermore, the fact that it is a problem might be indicated by highlighting it according to a ranged phenomenon. The analyst would then begin by looking for problem observations defined by phenomena.

To identify that the problem is with equipment sales income, we need to roll back the causal calculation of total revenue as sales income minus sales cost. Note that the causal calculation indicates a possible path of analysis, whether or not the measurement was determined that way. It may be that this final figure was actually sourced from a database. (Due to dirty data, it may be that it doesn't exactly fit the result of the formula.)

The next step is to use dimension combination protocols. Looking along the location dimension shows that the Northeast segment had a noticeably higher deviation. We can now focus on the enterprise segment that points to the Northeast dimension element on the location dimension, and at the top for all other dimensions. Repeating this process two more times would lead us to the enterprise segment with location of Northeast, product of 1100 family, and industry sector of government.

There is a certain amount of indirection here. When comparative calculations are involved, the route may not be direct. It may not be that the deviation in total revenue is calculated by subtracting the deviation in sales cost from the deviation in sales income. A more likely scenario is that the separate actual and planned sales revenues are calculated, and then these are used in the causal. With absolute deviation, either route will work, but this is not true for percentage deviation. The presence or absence of protocols will indicate what will and will not be appropriate calculations.

We can use alternative routes. Instead of first doing the causal, and then dimension combinations, we could break down on the location dimension, then use a causal, and then other dimension breakdowns. There are many possible paths for analysis, and these need not be the same as those used for calculating the figures.

We can describe qualitative statements, such as "a strong competitor may cause a decrease in sales," using the associative functions described in Section 3.11. Qualitative and quantitative observations are linked by assigning ranged phenomena.

Applications can use several techniques to explore this structure. Current multidimensional databases lean toward ad-hoc exploration by the user, which provides the maximum flexibility. Another alternative is to fix a decomposition path, defined by a hierarchy of protocols. This technique has been found to be effective in getting to the root of problems quickly. These hierarchical analyzers can easily be built on top of this framework. Other approaches would use agents to burrow in the structure to highlight interesting measurements.

This chapter reflects an actual attempt to take a model from health care and apply it to corporate finance. The extensions made to the health care model can be fed back into that model. Measurement protocols are certainly applicable; the enterprise segment pattern may be useful in epidemiology, although that is yet to be analyzed. By allowing patterns to migrate like this, I hope that more and more useful patterns will emerge, patterns that would never have appeared had we been more inclined to keep patterns shut up inside their home.

References

1. Cairns, T., A. Casey, , M. Fowler, M. Thursz, and H. Timimi. *The Cosmos Clinical Process Model*. National Health Service, Information Management Centre, 15 Frederick Rd, Birmingham, B15 1JD, England. Report ECBS20A & ECBS20B <http://www.sm.ic.ac.uk/medicine/cpm>, 1992.

2. Dejesus, E.X. "Dimensions of Data," in *Byte*, April 1995, pp. 139–148.

3. Gamma, E., R. Helm, R. Johnson, and J. Vlissides. *Design Patterns: Elements of Reusable Object-Oriented Software*. Reading, MA: Addison-Wesley, 1995.

4. Peterson, S. "Stars: a pattern language for query-optimized schemas," In *Pattern Languages of Program Design*. J.O. Coplien and D.C. Schmidt, ed. Reading, MA: Addison-Wesley, 1995, pp. 163–177.

5

Referring to Objects

Much of object orientation focuses on the idea of object identity. Within an OO computer system, each object has a unique ID, which is used as a guarantee that any object can be directly accessed. This notion affects our conceptual thinking, too. Few object methods use primary and secondary keys, which play a major role in traditional data modeling. We still need some way to refer to a particular object: For example, I might need to find a particular person to whom I need to send a bill, and a doctor may need to mark a patient as suffering from diabetes. Object systems provide us with powerful browsing capabilities that exploit the natural relationships between conceptual objects, but sometimes a more explicit identifier is required.

The simplest identifier for an object is a *name (5.1),* a sequence of characters that usually identifies an object. The problem is that names are not guaranteed to refer to a specific object in all circumstances. A more artificial creation may be required: an identifier within the context of an *identification scheme (5.2).*

Matters are further complicated when we realize that objects are not always as well defined and static as we think they are. In the world outside computers, it is easy to find situations where what we thought was two objects is actually one. For such situations we need to do an *object merge (5.3).* We may also need to split them again later, since we can merge in error, too. We can do the merge by copy and replace, superseding, or essence/appearance. Sometimes we have separate objects that perhaps ought to be the same, but we cannot be entirely sure, or we cannot reach an agreement with other people involved. At this point we can only say that there is an *object equivalence (5.4).*

Remember that this chapter is about *conceptual* references to objects—references that humans use. These references appear in a model in addition to any object identity schemes used by software. I don't discuss any software identity techniques in this chapter, but I would assume they exist in any OO implementation. I would also assume they would be hidden from the users.

Key Concepts   Identifier, Identification Scheme, Superseded Object, Object Essence, Equivalence.

5.1   Name

An exercise I use in an OO design class I teach involves recording details of a person's birth. Part of this problem requires us to record the hospital and city of someone's birth. As guidance I point out that if the we know the hospital someone is born in, we should automatically know the city, since every hospital lies in only one city. Inevitably someone points out that this is not the case because many cities of the world have a St. Mary's Hospital.

The error here is one of the oldest in logic and philosophy—the confusion between the name of a thing and the thing itself. A hospital is much more than a sequence of letters: It is buildings, an organization, people, a legal entity, many things that make St. Mary's Hospital on the Isle of Wight different from St. Mary's Hospital in London. Clearly nobody would actually mistake one for the other if they actually ran into the object. The point is that there may be many hospital objects that share the same name, but the name is merely a sequence of letters associated with the hospital, not the hospital itself. We model objects, not names, thus it is perfectly reasonable to say that every hospital lies in only one city.

What is a name? It is an informal way of identifying an object. I stress the word informal, for names rely more on convenience of use than any other feature. The string "Martin" is a useful identifier that in many contexts is enough to identify me. But I once shared a house with someone else named Martin. Both occupants shared that character string, so its value as an identifier was reduced. Among our circle of friends, "Martin" was still the most commonly used identifier for both of us, but occasional confusions did occur. In many applications we consider it reasonable to give a person a single name, as shown in Figure 5.1, although that name might be structured. More sophisticated examples might give a person many names to allow for aliases, as shown in Figure 5.2. For example, I could be referred to by the string "Martin F" to distinguish me from the other Martin.

Names are often a valuable way to identify objects, but no one serious about building a system that records people would ever use a name as a

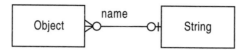

Figure 5.1 Object with one name.

The model implies that not all objects have to have a name. You could argue that not having a name implies a link to an empty string, hence the mapping is mandatory. In either case this model indicates that a string can be used as a name for many objects. Conceptually all equal strings are the same string; that is, you don't have identical copies.

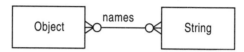

Figure 5.2 Object with many names.

This models an object with aliases. A variation may be to have one (usual) name and several aliases.

person's sole identifier. People have many names, the same name is used by different people, and people change names. All of these factors make names unreliable identifiers, although still by far the most common one.

There is another aspect to names and identifiers that is important to remember: A name is a compact way of telling someone about an object. It can describe some of the properties of an object. Naming a car model 16GL tells someone about the engine size and the level of comfort. Although this name is a compact report on the model, it is not an identifier because many models could be called 16GL.

A true identifier has several properties: It must reliably lead the user to one and only one object and it must always lead to the same object whenever it is used. Figure 5.3 shows a common model of an identifier. Unlike the usual case with fundamental objects, the mapping back to the object is single-valued.

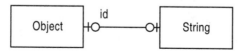

Figure 5.3 An identifier for an object.

This model implies that not all objects have an identifier, which can be true conceptually even if it is not true in software systems. Since the id is a string, not all strings identify an object, but to be a true identifier, it should identify only one. If an identifier type were used, and that would usually be preferable, then that would have a mandatory mapping to an object.

5.2   **Identification Scheme**

In simple systems a single identifier for each object is typical, but more complex systems have many identifiers for one object. The health care industry has many schemes for identifying patients: Each hospital assigns a case number, and departments have individual numbers. Banking uses several schemes to identify banks: SWIFT, sort codes, CHAPS, and so on. This more general approach can be supported by a model along the lines of Figure 5.4.

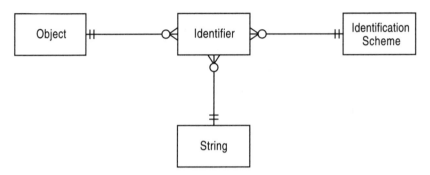

Figure 5.4   Identification schemes.

Example   The World Health Organization's International Classification of Diseases uses the code E10 for type I diabetes. This can be represented as an identifier with string 'E10,' identification scheme ICD-10, and object the disease diabetes mellitus type I.

Example   Suppose I have a passport number of 123456. This is represented as an identifier with string '123456,' identification scheme UK passport, and object myself. Depending on the situation, however, the object could be my passport.

Identification schemes represent the context used to identify an object. A single account will have separate SWIFT and CHAPS numbers. The same character sequence can indicate two different banks in SWIFT and CHAPS, but this is not a problem if these strings are in different schemes.

The model in Figure 5.4, although a start, is not the whole story. Its crude form includes nothing to stop one string from being used to represent more than one object within the same scheme. A useful concept here is the uniqueness constraint [1], which is used to indicate that a particular combination of mappings must have unique values for an object type.

Consider a uniqueness constraint on the mappings identification scheme and string. Such a constraint would say that no two identifiers can have the same identification scheme and the same string. Since the mapping from identifier to object is single-valued, the combination of identification scheme and string identifies a single object—exactly what we need. The other possibilities are also worth considering. How about a uniqueness constraint on object and string? This constraint would say that a particular object and a particular string uniquely reference an identification scheme; in other words, an object cannot have the same string in two different identification schemes. This type of uniqueness constraint is not only unenforceable but also inconvenient. People often like to use the same string for different schemes so they don't have to remember too many identifiers. Bank card PINs and social security numbers are two examples.

A uniqueness constraint on identification scheme and object would mean that within one scheme only one string can identify an object. This would disallow aliases within an identification scheme. Aliases can be useful but are not essential; they can be inconvenient, especially if people confuse the identifier with the object, but are not necessarily disastrous. A constraint for all three mappings would stop useless duplication of identifiers but would not materially alter the picture.

The second part of a uniqueness constraint states that an objects's identifier cannot be changed. This implies that, within a scheme, the same string cannot be switched from one object to another. This can be enforced by ensuring that identifiers cannot be deleted and that the mappings from the identifier are immutable—that is, they are assigned at creation and cannot change. Once an identifier is assigned, it is assigned for good. In reality some schemes do recycle identifiers, but only identifiers that have never been used can be recycled.

How are uniqueness constraints implemented in a typical object-oriented language? The immutability of the identifiers is a considerable help. Immutability allows no update of the mapping within software, so there is no public modifier operation. The mappings must be set in the creation operation by passing the values as arguments. During the creation operation a check needs to be made that no other identifier exists with the same combination of mappings that make up the uniqueness constraint.

Usually the identification scheme would be responsible for checking the format of the strings used by its identifiers. This check would be made when the identifiers are created. If the string embeds any meaningful information about the referenced object, then this information should also be checked. I might have an identifier U123, where the U indicates I live in United States. This identifier would cause a problem should I return to England. In general it is bad practice to embed information about features of an object into an identification string, because such practice implies that the string should change when the features change. It is better to generate a separate string that provides this kind of compact information.

5.3   Object Merge

We like to think of objects as somehow complete: Once identified, an object is so identified forever. Alas, the vagaries of real life are not so simple. Imagine a patient arriving and being treated at a hospital. After several days they realize that this patient is also an out-patient at another department. However, they have created a separate record for the patient on the hospital computer system. This situation is not uncommon, and it may be weeks or months before the duplication is spotted.

This duplication affects not only the computer system but also the perception of the people who work in the hospital. Realizing that a patient you are currently treating for left ventricular failure is the same patient who was in for thyrotoxicosis (overactive thyroid) a year ago is important for the whole clinical process, not just the computer system. We need a conceptual mechanism to tie the two objects together.

I will outline three strategies for this: copy and replace, superseding, and essence/appearance.

5.3.1   Copy and Replace

Usually the first strategy we think of is to copy all the properties of one object over to the other and delete the copied object (copy and replace). The identifier to the old deleted object would be altered so that it mapped to the object that remained, thus breaking the immutability rule. This strategy works when alias identifiers are allowed, but a problem remains in dealing with any references within the software to the deleted object. Unless you can catch all such references, there is the risk of a dangling reference, which often has painful consequences.

Example   John Smith enters the emergency room for some treatment and is given the hospital number JS777. Later the hospital discovers that he was previously registered in the hospital under the number JS123. The information from the JS777 object must be added to the record of the JS123 object, all references to the JS777 object switched to the JS123 object, and the JS777 object deleted.

5.3.2   Superseding

The second strategy is to supersede the object, as shown in Figure 5.5. One object is classified as superseded and linked to the other active object. In the future all work will be done to the active object, and the superseded object is held for historical reasons. There is no need to replace the references to the superseded object. Either the data currently in the superseded object is copied to the active object, or any messages to the active object must check data on all objects that the receiver supersedes. All messages to the superseded object are

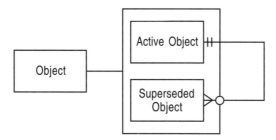

Figure 5.5   Object superseded by another.

delegated to the active object. If all data is copied, then the active object can safely ignore the presence of superseded objects.

Example   With the superseding strategy the JS777 object is marked as superseded and the JS123 as the active object. Any messages sent to JS777 are delegated to JS123.

Example   Researchers discovered two varieties of hepatitis: post-transfusion hepatitis and non-A non-B hepatitis. In time these were considered the same and called hepatitis C. This can be represented by superseding both the post-transfusion and non-A non-B hepatitis, linking them to the active hepatitis C object.

Conceptually the copy and replace strategy and the superseding strategies are much the same. The only difference is that you can look to see what was originally attached to the superseded object. This can be important: If a hospital performed treatment on Mr. Smith without realizing the two patients were the same, only the superseding strategy would give an accurate reflection of what happened.

5.3.3   Essence/Appearance

The final strategy to consider is the essence/appearance model, shown in Figure 5.6. The object remains much the same, but sitting behind it is another object—the object essence. The object essence exists only to link together objects; it has no other properties. In this strategy merging is done by connecting the objects to a single object essence. This implies some message passing modification, in that objects must know about their other appearances and take them into account when responding.

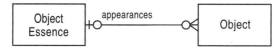

Figure 5.6   Object essence and appearance.

Example   With the essence/appearance strategy, a new object essence is created with JS123 and JS777 as its appearances.

Example   This model does not apply well to the preceding hepatitis example because the concepts of post-transfusion and non-A non-B hepatitis fell out of use, and hepatitis C became the one that was generally accepted.

The discussion above has focused on merging objects; however, merging may need to be undone later. Having merged two patients, the hospital may find out a few months later that there really were two different patients after all. Splitting the objects again is easiest if the essence/appearance strategy was used, because it preserves the original objects. Thus the essence/appearance strategy is the best one to use should the merging not be certain in the long term.

Example   Should the two John Smiths be found to be different after all, the object essence linking them together must be removed.

5.4   Object Equivalence

The previous sections have focused on how one object can be identified by different people in different ways. A related, though subtly different, point is that different objects can be considered similar. For example, medical terminology includes various more-or-less standard words to define various clinical conditions. The emphasis, however, is on "more-or-less." The definitions are fairly precise, certainly in comparison to most software terms, but are not completely so. To handle this imprecision, various coding schemes for medical terms have been set up, which means we have several such coding schemes we must choose from.

We could use a coding scheme as an identification scheme for our own terms. Thus if a particular clinician uses a particular set of biological phenomena, that clinician can map the various coding schemes to the biological phenomena by treating the coding scheme as an identification scheme. Other clinicians can do the same. This allows information to be transferred, at least to the level of granularity of the coding scheme. An important issue that can get lost here is when the equivalence is not universally agreed on. Some parties may think that two objects are the same while other parties do not. The model in Figure 5.7 deals with this by defining an equivalence that is held by certain parties. A party can make use of the equivalence only if it approves of it.

Example   Many doctors consider the diseases hepatitis G and hepatitis GBC to be the same disease, but this is not universal. This can be represented by an equivalence be-

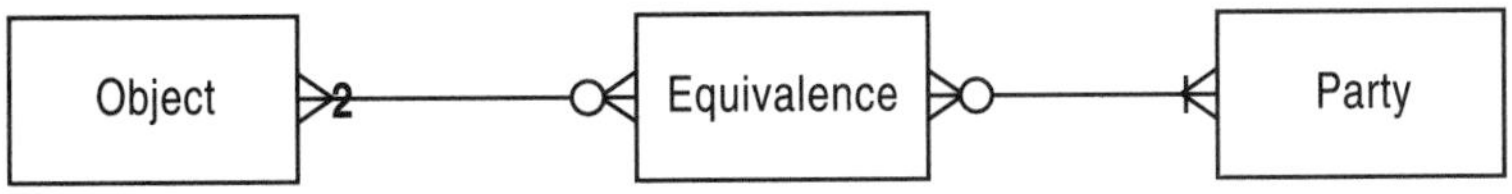

Figure 5.7   Equivalences between objects.

tween these two diseases. If a doctor wants a list of patients suffering from hepatitis G and that doctor is a party on the equivalence, then those patients suffering from hepatitis GBC are also returned.

References

1.   Martin, J. and J. Odell. *Object-Oriented Methods: A Foundation.* Englewood Cliffs, NJ: Prentice-Hall, 1995.

6

Inventory and Accounting

A large proportion of commercial computing systems are designed to track the money moving through an enterprise, recording how it is earned and spent. The fundamental idea behind accounting and inventory tracking is that there are various pots of money and goods, and we must record how money and goods move among these pots.

The inventory and accounting patterns in this chapter are born from this fundamental idea. They present a core set of concepts that we can use as the basis for financial accounting, inventory, or resource management. The patterns do not describe these processes directly, rather they describe the underlying ideas from which processes can be built. Chapter 7 describes a simple example that uses these ideas for billing telephone calls.

In this chapter I use a simple personal financial example to explain the basic ideas of accounting and inventory. Although similar, the terms I use are not the terms traditionally used in financial accounting. In my search for a more abstract model, I found that I needed new terms and concepts. A particular feature of the patterns in this chapter is how the rules for processing are embedded into the accounts system. This approach allows the accounts to update and manage themselves. This turns a traditionally passive recording system into an active system that can be configured by wiring up the accounts in the appropriate manner.

The first pattern is that of an *account (6.1)*. An account holds things of value—goods or money—which can only be added or removed by entries. The entries provide a history of all changes to the account. When we use an account to record the history of changes to a value, it is important to check that items do not get lost. *Transactions (6.2)* add a further degree of auditability by linking entries together. In a transaction, the items withdrawn from one account must be deposited in another; items cannot be created or destroyed.

There are two kinds of transactions: A two-legged transaction moves an amount from one account to another. A multilegged transaction can have entries in several accounts as long as the transaction as a whole balances.

Accounts can be grouped together using a *summary account (6.3)*, which applies most of account's reporting behavior to groups of accounts. Sometimes we need to make account entries that are not designed to be kept in balance; a *memo account (6.4)* deals with this task.

An account can include fixed rules that govern how amounts are transferred between accounts. *Posting rules (6.5)* allow us to build active networks of accounts that update each other and reflect business rules. To achieve this, instances of a posting rule require their own executable methods, a requirement that introduces the important modeling concept of an *individual instance method (6.6)*. Individual instance methods can be implemented with some combination of a single subtype, the strategy pattern, an internal case statement, an interpreter, and a parameterized method.

The *posting rule execution (6.7)* pattern describes ways in which posting rules can be triggered: while a transaction is created; by asking an account to process its rules; by asking a posting rule to fire; or by asking an account to bring itself up to date, thus firing its predecessors in a backward chaining manner.

To use posting rules with many accounts, we need a way of defining *posting rules for many accounts (6.8)*. One way is to use a knowledge level, in which case posting rules are defined on account types. Another way is to link posting rules to summary accounts.

In an accounting system, various objects will want subsets of the account's entries and their balances, both of which require a pattern for *choosing entries (6.9)*. This pattern is useful whenever we want a selection of objects from a multivalued mapping. Our alternatives are to return the whole set and let the client do the selection, adding extra operations to the account, or using an account filter.

We can divide large networks of posting rules into groups by using the *accounting practice (6.10)* pattern. In long calculations we often need to go back to see why various transactions gave the result they did; then we need to use the *sources of an entry (6.11)* pattern.

Balance sheets and income statements (6.12) distinguish between accounts that record items being held and accounts that record where items come or go. Different people can have similar views of accounts; for example, my view of my bank account is probably similar to my bank's view. One is a *corresponding account (6.13)* of the other.

The resulting patterns are quite abstract; particular cases need a *specialized account model (6.14)* to apply them to everyday practice. Such accounts are developed by subtyping the general accounting patterns.

The final pattern in this chapter describes *booking entries to multiple accounts (6.15)*. This pattern is useful when there is more than one way of reporting the trail of entries. The two alternative techniques are using memo entries or using derived accounts. We can use derived accounts instead of accounting patterns when we want the reporting behavior of accounts but not the balancing and audit capabilities.

These models are the results of ideas generated during several projects. They originated from working on a customer service system for a US utility company, and were further developed while examining accounting structures for an international telecommunications company. The models also draw deeply from the recent development of a payroll system for a major US manufacturing company.

Key Concepts   Account, Transaction, Entry, Posting Rule

6.1   Account

In many fields it is important to keep a record of not only the current value of something but also details of each change that effects that value. A bank account needs to record every withdrawal and deposit; an inventory record needs to record each time items are added or removed.

An account is similar to a quantity attribute, with an added entry for every change to its value, as shown in Figure 6.1. The balance, which represents the current value of the account, is the net effect of all entries linked to the account. This does not mean that the balance needs to be recalculated each time it is asked for. Derived values can be cached, although the cache would be invisible to the account user. By using the entries, a client can also determine the changes over a period of time and the total amount of deposits or withdrawals (see Section 6.9). The sign on the amount indicates whether the entry is a deposit or a withdrawal. A statement is a list of all the entries that have been carried out against an account over a period of time.

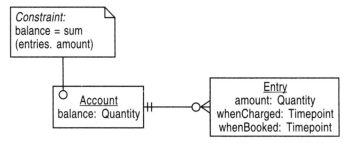

Figure 6.1   Account and entry.
The entries record each change to the account.

Example   I withdraw $100 from my checking account. This is represented as an entry with amount –$100 attached to my checking account.

Example   I buy 4 reams of standard letter paper from a shop. The shop represents this as an entry on their standard letter paper account with amount –4 reams.

Example   In January I use 350 KWH of electricity. This is represented as an entry with amount 350 KWH to my domestic electricity usage account.

Modeling Principle   *To record a history of changes to a value use an account for that value.*

One way an implementation can compute a balance is to take a collection of entries and form a collection of quantities. Smalltalk has a specific operation, collect, to do this. The danger is that the collect operation collects the objects into the same kind of collection as the original. Thus running collect on a set of entries yields a set of quantities. Sets allow no duplicates, so if we have two entries with the same amount, only the first entry's quantity is counted, and the balance value is incorrect. To form collections of fundamental values, it is often better to use a bag, which does allow duplicates. In C++ this problem is less common because collect operations are less common and more difficult to use; instead C++ users use an external iterator [1] which does not have this problem. As a check, however, test cases should always include entries with equal amounts (as well as entries with every attribute equal).

Figure 6.1 indicates two timepoints for the entry: one indicates when the charge is made and the other when the entry is booked to the account. This is particularly important when retroactive charges occur. A price for a charge may have changed between the charge date and the booked date, so both dates are required. We need to know both the history of events and our knowledge of that history (see Section 15.3.1). Timepoints also include both the time of day as well as the date; many applications are happy with just the date.

Example   I have a meal at Jae's Café on April 1. The credit card company receives notice of payment on April 4. The entry has a charged date of April 1 and a booked date of April 4.

6.2   Transactions

Using entries help keep a record of changes to an account. These changes usually involve moving an item from one account to another. When I withdraw money from my bank account, I am adding money to my wallet, or cash account. With many items it is not enough to just record the comings and goings; we must also record where they come from and go to.

The transaction helps by explicitly linking a withdrawal from one account to a deposit in another, as shown in Figure 6.2. The double entry approach reflects a very basic accounting principle that money (or anything else we must account for) is never created or destroyed, it merely moves from one account to another.

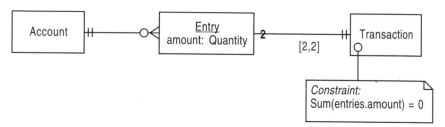

Figure 6.2 A transaction with two entries.

Example I use my credit card to pay Boston Airlines $500 for an airline ticket. This is a transaction from the credit card account to the Boston Airlines account with an amount of $500. Later I will make a transaction from my checking account to the credit card account to bring the credit card account's balance to zero.

Example Aroma Coffee Makers (ACM) moves 5 tons of Arabian Mocha from New York to Boston. This is transaction from the New York account to the Boston account with an amount of 5 tons.

In complex accounting structures we aim to get the accounts to balance—that is, to reach zero—at various points in the business cycle. By building the principle of conservation into the model, we make it easier to find any "leaks" in the system. Although it's not essential to use transactions when you are using accounts, I prefer to.

Modeling Principle *When working with accounts, follow the* principle of conservation: *The item being accounted for cannot be created or destroyed, only moved from place to place. This makes it easier to find and avoid leaks.*

6.2.1 Multilegged Transactions

Figure 6.2 implies that each transaction consists of a single withdrawal and a single corresponding deposit. In fact we can have many withdrawals and deposits in a transaction. Say I receive $3000 from Megabank and $2000 from Total Telecommunications. I decide to deposit both checks into my checking account. My bank statement will show a $5000 credit. Note that although two checks have hit my bank account, a single entry is shown. This transaction is represented by the multilegged transaction model shown in Figure 6.3. The upper bound on the mapping is lifted from transaction to entry. The overriding rule is that the entries must balance with respect to the whole transaction, but no match is required among individual entries. Thus I can model my bank account situation with a transaction that consists of three entries: [account:

checking account, amount: $5000], [account: Megabank, amount: ($3000)], [account: Total Telecommunications, amount: ($2000)]. The transaction is responsible for ensuring that money is not created or destroyed.

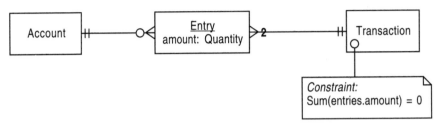

Figure 6.3   Multilegged transactions.

These allow more flexibility in forming transactions than the two-legged model.

Example   Aroma Coffee Makers removes 5 tons of Java from New York and sends 2 tons to Boston and 3 tons to Washington. This is a single transaction with three entries: [account: New York, –5 tons], [account: Boston, 2 tons], [account: Washington, 3 tons].

The two-legged model is a particular case of the multilegged model where the transaction has only two entries. In some applications the two-legged model predominates, and we have a model similar to Figure 6.4. Other applications might have a large number of multilegged transactions. I would recommend the multilegged approach because it provides more flexibility. Two-legged transactions can easily be created by a special creation operation on a multilegged transaction, which is a useful convenience. The rest of this discussion assumes the multilegged model.

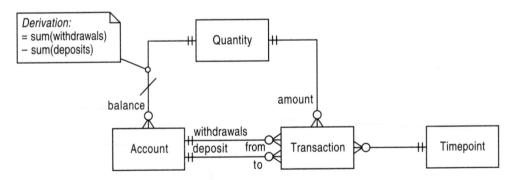

Figure 6.4   A model of a two-legged transaction that does not use entries.

This model may be found where all the transactions are two-legged. It has much the same capabilities as Figure 6.2. However, I would prefer using Figure 6.2 since it is easier to migrate to a multilegged transaction.

The mutual mandatory relationship between transaction and entry introduces a chicken and egg problem. I cannot create an entry without creating a transaction because of a constraint. Similarly I can't create a transaction without an entry because transaction is similarly constrained.

One solution is to provide a creation operation on transaction that takes a list of partially defined entries, or even a list of arrays with appropriate arguments. Entry would have its creation operation made private but accessible to the transaction's creation. The transaction's creation would then be the only place that could create entries. Obviously, during the execution of this creation operation, objects would be in violation of their constraints. The rule with constraints, however, is that *public* operations should end with all constraints satisfied [5]. Providing only the transaction's creation routine is made public, this rule can be enforced.

6.3   Summary Account

In a system of accounts it is often useful to group accounts together. For example, I might want to group my Total Telecommunications and Megabank accounts into a business income account. Similarly I want to put rent and food into personal expenses and my business travel and office expenses into business expenses. This kind of structure can be supported with a simple hierarchy of detail and summary accounts, as shown in Figure 6.5.

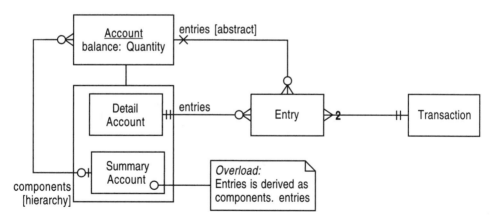

Figure 6.5   Summary and detail accounts.

A summary account can be composed of both summary and detail accounts. This forms a hierarchy, with the detail accounts as leaves (an example of composite [1]). The entries of a summary account are derived from the components' entries in a recursive manner.

In this hierarchy structure we can bring together accounts into summary accounts. We restrict the system to posting entries only to detail accounts and not to summary accounts. Summary accounts can still be treated as accounts because their entries are derived according to their components' entries. A summary account that contains summary accounts will look for entries in its components, its components' components, and so on, recursively. This derivation of the entries mapping allows us to describe the balance attribute, and any other operations and attributes that depend on entries, at the supertype level.

Example I have a summary account for air travel with detail accounts for Mega-bank air travel and Total Telecommunications air travel.

Example Aroma Coffee Makers has a summary account for Java with detail accounts for each warehouse. It can thus find out the total amount of Java that it owns.

Note that the relationship among components needs to be marked to show it is a hierarchy. The cardinalities are not enough to enforce this constraint. We must not have cycles in this structure.

The separation between summary and detail accounts is quite common in accounting, but it is not absolutely necessary. The model in Figure 6.6 shows the distinction removed. In this case an entry can be made to any account, and all accounts can be placed in a hierarchical structure. This can be done by providing two mappings from account to entry: one to show which entries are posted at that level, and another to add together the entries on sub-accounts. The first would be updatable, the latter is derived, not updatable, and used for balance, statements, and other features that were on the supertype in the Figure 6.5 model.

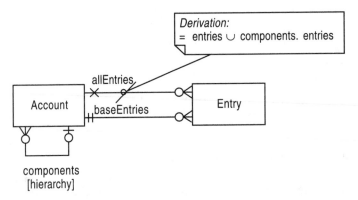

Figure 6.6 Account hierarchies without separating summary and detail accounts.
We can use this model to post entries to summary accounts.

So far we have followed conventions that say that accounts must be arranged in a hierarchy and that entries are booked to only one account. We will continue with these assumptions for a while, but we will consider some alternative possibilities later on in Section 6.15.

6.4   Memo Account

Benjamin Franklin once said, "In this world nothing can be said to be certain, except death and taxes." We can't eliminate the pain of paying taxes, but I find the pain is lessened somewhat by avoiding surprises on my tax return. Each time I earn some money, I allocate a portion to a tax liability account. I then know how much of my money is really mine, and how much I owe in taxes.

Notice that with this plan, no real money has moved. There is no payment from my checking account until I have to pay the tax. Furthermore, my tax category lumps together state and federal taxes. When I actually pay (and when I pay estimates), I will make transactions from my checking account to the accounts federal tax and state tax. When I do this I need to reduce my tax liability account by the same amounts, but again no money moves between the real accounts (checking account, federal tax, state tax) and this tax liability account. This account acts as a memo to me on how much money I owe in taxes, thus it is referred to as a *memo account*.

A memo account contains amounts of money but not real money. It is important that no real money leaks from or to a memo account. So in my tax example, as I take the money from my income account to my checking account I make an entry at the same time into my tax liability memo account. Memo account becomes another subtype of account, and I have to ensure that transactions do not shift money between that and the other accounts. This can be done by ensuring that the balance constraint on transaction excludes memo accounts.

If we are using transactions, we need to ensure that we always move money between accounts and that we do not create or destroy money. This implies that when an entry is made to the tax liability account, a balancing entry is made somewhere. Since it can be difficult to see what account would be a sensible host to this entry, accountants frequently create a contra account. Thus the tax liability account would have a contra tax liability account, which acts as the other end of all entries in the tax liability account, either withdrawals or deposits. This approach can be used with the usual model, but it is not strictly necessary. If the balance checking constraint ignores memo accounts, then single-sided entries against them are allowed. A contra account can always be generated automatically. This approach would imply that the lower bound on the mapping from transaction to entry can be reduced to 1.

Example   Each time I receive a payment from a client, I record it as a transaction from a client income account to my checking account. I also enter a portion of that amount into the tax liability memo account. When the time comes to pay estimated taxes, I make a transaction from my checking account to my federal tax account. I add a third entry to this transaction to reduce the amount on my tax liability memo account by the same amount.

Of course, if we don't use transactions, we don't run into any balance problems and can post the entries without worry, but the danger is that real money can leak into memo accounts (or into thin air) more easily.

6.5   Posting Rules

Using a memo account I can make a posting to a tax liability account, but I still have to remember to do it. Since I always enter 45 percent of each fee income entry into a memo tax liability account, a computer system should be able to do it for me automatically.

What is needed is a rule that looks at a particular account and, when it sees an entry, creates another entry. A simple example of this kind of rule is shown in Figure 6.7. A posting rule is described by specifying an account as a trigger. Any entry in the trigger account causes a new entry to be made, which is the value of the original entry multiplied by the multiplier.

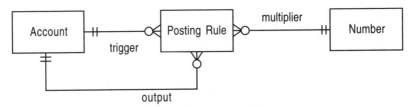

Figure 6.7   A simple structure for posting rules that multiply by a factor.

For each entry in the trigger account, we post an entry to the output account of the value of the triggering entry multiplied by the multiplier.

Example   My tax liability can be handled by a posting rule with the fee income account as the trigger, the tax liability account as the output and the multiplier as 0.45.

Multiplication by a scalar handles a number of useful situations for a posting rule, but the process can easily get complex. Consider a graduated income tax: The first £300 carries no tax, the next £2500 carries a 20 percent tax, the rest is at 40 percent. A simple scalar multiplier is no longer enough. We want posting rules to carry any arbitrary algorithm, which would give us the maximum flexibility.

To give posting rules this flexibility, we have to link a calculation to each instance of a posting rule, since every rule will have a different way of calculating the amount of the new entry. Conceptually this means that each instance of a posting rule needs to have its own method for doing the calculation, as shown in Figure 6.8. The glib notation masks a significant problem. Mainstream object systems allow behavior to vary by polymorphism and inheritance, but this is class based: The behavior varies with the object's class. We want the behavior to vary with each individual instance, which requires the *individual instance methods* pattern, as discussed in Section 6.6. (I discuss a similar problem in Section 9.2.)

Figure 6.8   Posting rules with methods to calculate values for entries.

This notation says that each instance of a posting rule has its own calculation method.

6.5.1   Reversibility

An important property of posting rules is that they must be *reversible*. Usually we cannot delete an incorrect entry because either it has led to an entry that is part of a payment or it appears on a bill. The only way we can remove its effects is by entering a reversal, which is an identical but opposite entry. Thus any posting rule must ensure that two entries that are identical but of opposite signs are both placed in the trigger account and completely cancel each other out in further processing. We can test the reversal by inserting such opposite pairs in routines for a posting rule and ensuring their output amounts are also equal and opposite.

6.5.2   Abandoning Transactions

In some accounts almost all transactions are generated from posting rules. Input accounts are used to record initial entries from the outside world. All further account entries are generated by posting rules. The risk of not using transactions is reduced because all entries are predictable from the initial entries and the posting rules. The responsibility to check that nothing leaks out is transferred from the operational use of the system to the design of the posting rules. If we remove transactions, then it is still valuable to keep a note of the cause and effect trail between entries. On the whole I prefer keeping transactions because they make auditing easier for a small price in overhead. If you don't use transactions, you will still need some audit mechanism.

6.6   Individual Instance Method

A conceptual model should represent a situation as naturally as possible for the convenience of the domain expert. We should minimize dependencies on a particular implementation environment as much as possible. Computer design should reflect human thinking, not the other way round. This philosophy is reflected in the diagram shown in Figure 6.8. After defining this conceptual modeling construct, we need to invent a general way of implementing it. Hence the question is not "How do we put calculations on individual posting rules?" but "How do we attach methods to instances?" This follows the transformational approach discussed in Chapter 14. We want several ways of implementing the model in Figure 6.9 behind a single interface. This follows the overriding principle of template-based design: *The model should define the interface of the classes.* We should be able to exchange the implementations without altering the interface.

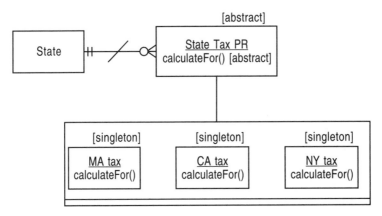

Figure 6.9   Using singleton classes to implement individual instance methods.

6.6.1   Implementation with a Singleton Class

The natural way to vary behavior is to use a polymorphic operation based on subclassing. The simplest way to do this is to subclass the posting rule for each instance of the posting rule, thus creating a number of singleton classes. Here all the standard methods and properties for posting rules are held by the posting rule, and the subtypes merely implement the different `calculateFor` methods.

The main problem with this approach is that the subtypes are rather artificial. They only exist because of the fact we cannot vary `calculateValue` by instance. This artificiality makes the approach less than perfect. Another problem is that this approach leads to many classes, which makes some people feel rather uncomfortable. Classes do not present a particularly large problem because the classes are both small and very constrained. Calculation methods can be shared by manipulating the class hierarchy. However, the process operation on the posting rule can also be the victim of polymorphism, and the two polymorphisms may not match.

6.6.2   Implementation with the Strategy Pattern

On first sight the strategy pattern [1] implementation shown in Figure 6.10 looks very similar to the pattern using singletons. The main difference is that Figure 6.10 performs subtyping on a separate method, or strategy, object. The posting rule is simpler because the whole issue of method choice is eliminated. The posting rule just knows it can ask a method object to do the calculation.

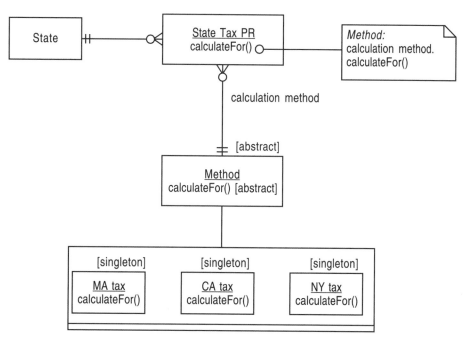

Figure 6.10   Using the strategy pattern [1] implementation for individual instance methods.

Figure 6.11 shows the interactions that occur in an example case. An account asks a process rule to process it. The process rule gets all the entries that have not been processed by this rule (see Section 6.7.2). For each of these entries, it calls its method to calculate the value of the new entry. The method may need to ask questions; for example, tax rates often vary depending on whether a person is married or not. It passes the result back to the posting rule, which then creates the new entry.

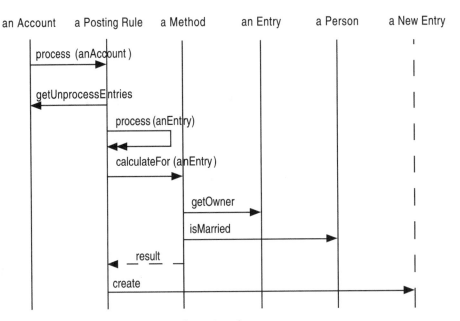

Figure 6.11   Interaction diagram for using the strategy pattern.

The method gets any information it needs by asking the supplied entry.

It should be stressed that this method object is not a "free subroutine," in the manner of functional designs (or some OO approaches). The method is encapsulated within the posting rule, since only the posting rule can reference and use it.

Posting rule methods can be shared between objects. An example of such a method is the flat tax method, which applies a flat rate of tax with some standard deductions. If the method is the same for several kinds of taxes, with only the rate of tax varying, then a method can be designed that asks the posting rule for its flat rate but otherwise allows the processing to be reused. This method can be seen as a cross between the method object and the parameterized method (see Section 6.6.4) implementations.

A variation on this approach in Smalltalk is to use a block as the method. By doing this we eliminate the need for a new method class and eliminate the method class' subclasses. Blocks are elegant to use but can be very tricky to debug: If an error occurs in the block's code, it can be difficult to follow what is going on. If the block is simple, however, this approach can work very well.

6.6.3   Implementation with an Internal Case Statement

Faced with creating subclasses just to handle one polymorphic method, we might wonder why we should bother. Instead we can have a series of private operations for the posting rule: `computeFederalTax`, `computeMassTax`, computeSalesCommision, and so on. Then a single computeFor on the posting rule has a simple case statement that chooses which private method to use depending on which instance is the receiver, as shown in Figure 6.12.

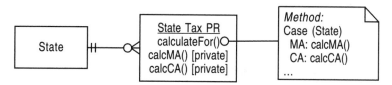

Figure 6.12 Using an internal case statement for an individual instance method.

This is not a violation of object-oriented principles as long as the case statement is encapsulated within the posting rule.

Object designers tend to recoil at the idea of using case statements like this, but in this situation there is a lot to be said for it. Modifying this implementation means adding a new private operation and adding a clause to a case statement. This is not much different from the new subclasses required with the strategy or singleton implementation. If the number of methods is large, then we have a large (but simple) case statement, or a large number of subclasses. Thus it is a trade-off between managing a lot of singleton classes and having to change the case statement with each new posting rule.

6.6.4 Implementation with a Parameterized Method

The parameterized method strategy uses a single method in the posting rule and handles the different behavior by using conditions based on properties of the posting rule, or of related classes. For example, if all the entries are a flat percentage, then the posting rule can hold the percentage, and a single method that deducts that percentage is sufficient, as shown in Figure 6.13. If some posting rules have different percentages for married and single people,

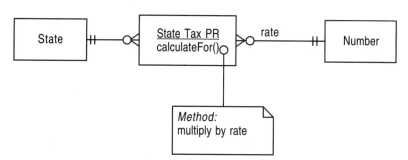

Figure 6.13 Using a parameterized posting rule.

then a married and single rate can be held in the posting rule, and the method asks the employee for marital status and then uses the appropriate rate.

This strategy works if all the variations in the calculation can be captured by varying a few parameters. In such cases, however, we must model it that way. Individual instance methods are only present if the situation is more complicated than that. This is a potential implementation because in some cases we can combine parameterization with another technique.

6.6.5   Implementation with an Interpreter

If the method is simple, then we can hold the method as a string in a simple language and build an interpreter for it. Each instance of the method holds its particular string and the method class can interpret the string (perhaps using the interpreter pattern [1]).

Good candidates for this implementation are methods that use simple formulas that use the arithmetic operators, parentheses, and a couple of simple functions. If the language is simple, it is not too difficult to build the interpreter. The only limitation is what can be expressed in the language.

6.6.6   Choosing an Implementation

All of the implementations work well and can be hidden behind a single operation. I use a parameterized method if I can. My next choice is to use the parameterized method implementation in conjunction with one of the other patterns to see if I can find a blend that uses only a few variant methods to handle the larger variations and many parameters to handle the smaller variations. If only a few variant methods are needed, then either singletons or an internal case statement works well. If there are many variants, then the strategy pattern is the best. On the whole the strategy pattern is never much worse than singletons or internal case statements, but it may be a little bit more difficult to understand at first sight. If the method can be expressed with a simple language, such as an arithmetic formula, then the interpreter is a good idea. As the "Gang of Four" patterns become more widespread, a combination of the strategy pattern and a parameterized method will become the dominant choice.

All four of the above strategies show ways in which the problem of individual instance methods can be handled. We can say that the model shown in Figure 6.8 is the analysis statement of specification, and the designers can choose whichever strategy is the best for the implementation conditions. This works as long as a common interface exists for each strategy. The principle of one analysis model defining a single interface that can be implemented in many ways is the foundation of the approach of using design templates for development.

Many modelers would prefer another way of modeling the problem than that shown in Figure 6.8. They might prefer an expression closer to one of the other strategies. They can still make the separation of analysis from implementation if they substitute another implementation behind the same interface. Other modelers would prefer to model in the same form as the implementation. In this situation they are trading off implementation independence for a greater seamlessness between analysis model and implementation.

This illustrates clearly the difficulty in drawing a line between analysis and design. Just as various combinations of classes may satisfy a particular interface in software, we may use different combinations of types to model the same situation in conceptual models. The choice of types can influence the choice of classes. The overriding influence is that the choice of types defines the interface of classes, but what lies behind that interface need not match the conceptual picture.

6.7   Posting Rule Execution

So far we have looked at how a posting rule is structured and how it responds to being fired, that is, told to execute. This is a good point to step back and look at some of the strategies we can use to fire posting rules. The first point I want to stress is that posting rules should be designed in such a way that they can be fired by different approaches. It is important to separate the strategy of firing the posting rules from the rules themselves as much as possible to reduce the coupling between these mechanisms.

6.7.1   Eager Firing

In this approach posting rules are fired as soon as a suitable entry is made in a trigger account. There are two ways we can do this. One is to put the responsibility in the transaction or entry creation methods, as shown in Figure 6.14. Creating a transaction leads to several entries being posted to accounts. Each posting of an entry prompts a search for posting rules that are using that account as a trigger. Each of these posting rules is then fired.

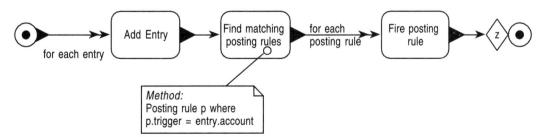

Figure 6.14   Event diagram showing how transaction creation can trigger posting rules.

The finding and firing of posting rules can be done either during transaction creation or in the individual entry creation methods, as shown in Figure 6.15. The latter is a better factoring of the process.

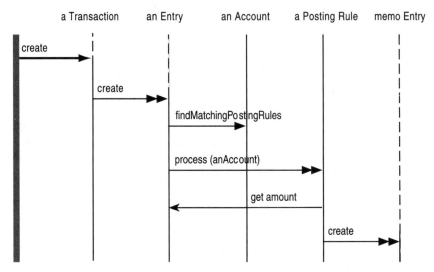

Figure 6.15 Interaction diagram for firing posting rules within entry creation.

A second approach is to make posting rules observers of their trigger account [1]. When a posting rule is set up, it registers itself to the trigger account. When an entry is attached to an account, the account broadcasts to all observers that a noteworthy event has occurred. The posting rule then interrogates the account to find out what has happened and discovers the new entry. It then generates the appropriate new entry to the memo account. The advantage of this scheme is that the transaction no longer needs to activate the posting rule. The observer is a very useful mechanism, but I tend to use it only when there is a need to ensure that visibilities run solely from the observer to the observed, particularly when they lie in different packages. I don't like to use observers when I don't need to, because too many of them make debugging difficult. I don't think I would put the posting rules in a separate package so there is no need to use the observer.

6.7.2 Account-based Firing

Account-based firing moves the responsibility of firing from transactions to the account. Entries can be added to an account without any posting rules being fired. At some point the account is told to process itself and then fires its outbound posting rules for all entries that have arrived since the last time it processed itself, as shown in Figure 6.16.

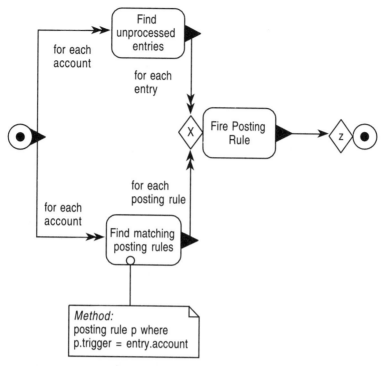

Figure 6.16   Cyclic firing of accounts.

The X notation indicates that the fire posting rule operation is executed for each combination of posting rule and unprocessed entry.

Account-based firing requires the account to keep track of which entries have not been processed yet. It can do this by maintaining a separate collection for unprocessed entries (keeping its entries in a list and keeping track of the last entry to be processed), or by recording the timepoint of the last process and returning entries that were booked after that time (using the when booked property).

Account-based firing can be used in a cyclic accounting system, where accounts are processed once a day. In this case you must be careful that the accounts are processed in the right order. Accounts must be processed before any accounts that may be affected by their outbound process rules. These dependencies can be determined automatically by looking at the process rules.

6.7.3   Posting-rule-based Firing

In posting-rule-based firing the posting rule is explicitly told to execute by some external agent. It looks at its inputs to find what new entries have appeared. As such, posting-rule-based firing is similar to account-based firing, with many of the same advantages and disadvantages. The main difference is that since an account can have many posting rules, the responsibility for deciding which entries have not been processed passes from the account to the posting rule. This usually makes the situation more complicated, so I prefer account-based firing.

6.7.4   Backward-chained Firing

Backward-chained firing is a variant on account-based firing: The accounts do not just process themselves, and they cause all accounts that they are dependent on to process themselves. With this approach we can discover the up-to-date status of any account.

We can start this process by asking an account for its entries, as shown in Figure 6.17. The account first brings itself up to date. The account uses the posting rules to determine which accounts are triggers for a posting rule that has itself as an output. These accounts are asked to bring themselves up to date, which is a recursive process, as shown in Figures 6.18 and 6.19. The whole account graph is brought up to date by simply asking an account at the end to be processed.

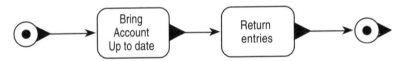

Figure 6.17   Requesting a detail account for its entries with backward-chained firing.

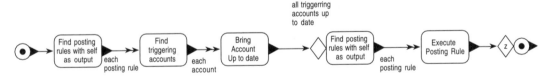

Figure 6.18   Method for bringing an account up to date.

The bring account up to date operation is called recursively on each account that is an input for the processing account.

6.7.5   Comparing the Firing Approaches

The primary considerations in choosing a firing approach is the time taken in executing the posting rule (an implementation decision) and the point at which we want to catch errors. Eager firing allows us to get errors as soon as they are found. This gives us more time to find the cause of the errors. It does force us to do all the calculations when we are making entries. Account-based and backward-chained firing give us more flexibility in the timing of calculations. If we process accounts in a batch method, we can read all the

an Account   a Posting Rule   a Trigger Account

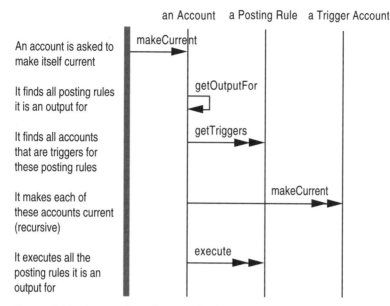

An account is asked to
make itself current

It finds all posting rules
it is an output for

It finds all accounts
that are triggers for
these posting rules

It makes each of
these accounts current
(recursive)

It executes all the
posting rules it is an
output for

Figure 6.19 Interaction diagram for bringing an account up to date for account-based firing.

entries from a file and then fire the posting rules at our leisure, perhaps overnight. The sooner we fire, the sooner we will find any mistakes.

Choosing between account-based and backward-chained firing is really about whether we want to handle the extra complexity of building backward-chained firing. Backward chaining is more awkward to build than account-based, but once built it is easier to use. Thus I would use account-based for simple account structures and backward-chained for complex account structures. On the whole I don't like eager firing because it is not as flexible. I can get all the benefits of eager firing by ensuring that posting rules are fired as soon as I add entries (but not as part of entry creation). Although this is an extra step, it does allow me to choose not to do so if I wish. Eager firing does not give me that choice. If I have so much processing power that the posting rules do not cost anything, then it makes no difference.

There is no reason why you cannot mix the firing approaches. Income accounts might use eager firing into a couple of layers of asset accounts and then use backward chaining for the rest of the way. Using more than one firing scheme will make the system more complex and confusing, however, so I don't mix them unless I have a good reason.

This kind of approach is still new, and we are still learning about the trade-offs inherent in the various firing schemes. Since this is such a fluid area, it is important to retain flexibility so that you can change the firing scheme as you watch the system in action.

6.8   Posting Rules for Many Accounts

So far I have considered the parochial example of myself and my own chart of accounts. We need to extend this to handle many people. We want the posting rules to be consistent, so that a single federal tax posting rule can be used to determine federal tax liability for all the people involved.

With this extension there is no longer a posting rule operating over a single account. Each employee needs a unique account, yet the federal tax liability posting rule should be programmed to work for all employees. We do not want to have to make a separate posting rule for each employee.

There are two ways we can do this. The first is to use the notion of knowledge and operational levels (see Section 2.5). We set up the posting rules at the knowledge level and link them to account types, as shown in Figure 6.20. Thus we would have account types for fee income, pretax earnings, net earnings, and so on. Entries that appear in accounts check the posting rules on their account type, effectively adding a level of indirection to the kinds of expression discussed above.

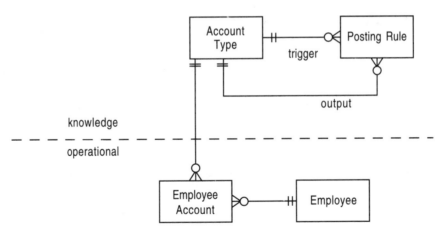

Figure 6.20   Using account types.

This introduces a knowledge level on which the posting rules can be defined.

Example   All employees accrue 1 day of holiday for every 18 days worked. This could be represented as a posting rule with a trigger of the account type days worked and an output of the account type accrued holiday. This method ensures that the accrued holidays account balance was $\frac{1}{18}$ of the days worked balance. Each time the employee account is triggered, it looks for posting rules defined on its account type according to the type of triggering being used.

However a knowledge/operational split, although appealing, is not the only way of handling this situation. A second approach is to use summary accounts. A posting rule defined on a summary account is activated when any entry is placed into any subsidiary of the summary account (or the account itself, if summary account posting is allowed). The output account can similarly be defined on a summary account with the interpretation that this will cause an entry on the appropriate subsidiary account.

Example In this case there are summary accounts for days worked and accrued holiday. The posting rule is the same as the example above. Instead of checking the account type for posting rules, the summary accounts are checked.

The choice between the two methods depends on the degree of difference between account and account type. If all posting rules are defined on account type and entries are made on accounts, then the knowledge/operational split is reasonable. However, sometimes this situation does not occur. Entries can be made at the more general level, perhaps to indicate a general fee to the company (which would require the model shown in Figure 6.6). Similarly, posting rules might vary with each individual payment: This would be required to support deductions for a car loan, for example. When such situations occur, it is better not to make the split.

There is no generally correct approach to take. In any given situation it is necessary to see which model provides the best fit. The key factor is the degree of difference in the behavior of the candidate accounts and account types.

In either case the posting rule needs to determine how to make the correct output entry. In many of the examples above, the posting rule simply looks for the account for the same employee as the triggering entry. More complex situations are possible, however. Consider a situation where a fee entry to a junior consultant causes a percentage of the fee to be posted in a memo account for that consultant's manager. In this case the posting rule needs to be told how to find the lucky manager.

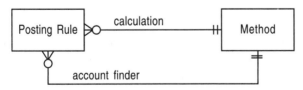

Figure 6.21   Using an account finding method.

Separate methods are used for finding output accounts and calculating the value of the transaction.

One way of handling this is to provide a second method to find the appropriate output account, as shown in Figure 6.21. This second method asks the originating entry for its employee and then that employee for its manager.

This provides the greatest degree of flexibility, at the cost of a second method object, which must be implemented as suggested in Section 6.6.

This hints at another problem. With general posting rules not all employees may be eligible for the posting rule to fire. For example, posting rules can be set up to handle each state tax. A posting rule for Illinois state tax should only fire, however, if the employee is a resident of Illinois. Thus suggests a third method, which is used to express the eligibility condition, as shown in Figures 6.22 and 6.23.

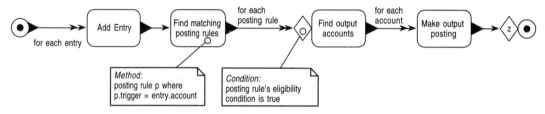

Figure 6.22   Event diagram showing the use of account finder and eligibility condition methods added to Figure 6.14.

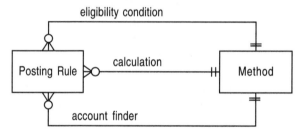

Figure 6.23   Adding an eligibility condition to the above rules.

6.9   Choosing Entries

In many situations a posting rule needs to select some subset of entries from its trigger account. It may want to look at all entries since a certain date booked, the balance of all entries charged in July, or entries of dangerous goods (which would use some subtype of entry). There are three ways of performing selections: getting all entries back and then doing a selection, providing a selection-specific method, and using a filter.

The first technique is the simplest: The account returns all the entries, and the client processes this collection to select the entries it needs. This requires no additional behavior on the account but passes all responsibility to the client. If many clients need to carry out similar selections, a lot of duplication can occur. If there are many entries, there may well be an overhead in passing the set out, especially if the set needs to be copied. Remember that an account should never pass out an unprotected reference to its own way of storing entries (see Section 14.1). Using this approach with entries also means that the client is responsible for summing the entries to get a balance.

If many clients are asking for a similar kind of selection, such as entries in a time period, then an additional behavior can be added to the account to satisfy this (such as `entriesChargedDuring (TimePeriod)`). This has the advantage of saving all the clients from repeatedly going through the same selection process. We can save the clients even more effort by providing a method that gives a balance over a time period (such as `balanceChargedDuring (TimePeriod)`). The problem with this solution is that if there are many such selections, the account interface grows very large.

A filter (see Section 9.2) is an object that encapsulates a query. Using that pattern here would result in an account filter. An account filter includes various operations to set the terms of the query. Once the filter is set up, it is applied to the account to get the answer, as shown in Figure 6.24. The account uses the filter to select the subset of entries by conceptually taking each of its entries and testing it with the filter's `isIncluded` method. It may apply its private knowledge of how the entries are stored to optimize this process. With this approach the account can support most selections of entries with `entriesUsing (AccountFilter)` and give corresponding balances with `balanceUsing (anAccountFilter)`. Note that if subtypes of entries have additional features that are used as a basis for selection, then subtypes of account filter may be needed for each type of entry.

With a multivalued association I start by returning all the objects and leave it up to the client to select them. If there are a few frequently used selections, I might consider using an additional behavior, but only for a few behaviors. If a selection results in too much duplication to return all the objects, but there are too many behaviors to add, I set up a filter. Setting up and maintaining a filter does require extra work, so I use it only when I really need it. This need often appears with accounts and their entries.

6.10 Accounting Practice

When we run into a large network of accounts with many posting rules, the network becomes too big to deal with. In this situation we need some way to break down the network into pieces. Consider a utility's billing procedures. They bill the various types of customers they have with different billing processes. This can be represented as a network of accounts. Each type of customer has different rules and can be handled with a slightly different network of accounts.

an Account Filter   an Account

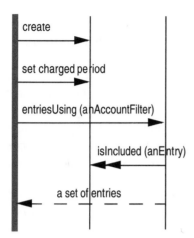

Figure 6.24   Interaction diagram for using an account filter.

A particular network of accounts is an accounting practice. Conceptually an accounting practice is simply a collection of posting rules, as shown in Figure 6.25. The notion is that each type of customer is assigned an accounting practice to handle billing.

Figure 6.25   Accounting practice.

These are used to group posting rules into logical groups.

Example A power utility divides its residential customers into regular and lifeline categories. The lifeline category is for those who the state deems need to be charged minimum rates. The regular customers are divided into three different rate schedules depending on the area in which they live. This is handled by four accounting practices: one for lifeline and one for each of the three areas.

Example ACM has many union workers and each union negotiates a different deal. ACM has a pay practice for each union.

The same posting rule can exist in more than one practice. This is often the case when similar behavior is needed across practices. We need to be aware of the difference between copying a rule from one practice (leading to two identical rules) and having the same rule in more than one practice. Having a rule in more than one accounting practice implies that when the rule is changed it changes for all practices that use it. Copies allow one copy to change without the others changing.

Accounting practices are assigned to some user object so that each user has a single accounting practice. Thus each customer of a power utility or employee of a company uses a particular accounting practice. This assignment can be done manually or a rule can determine it.

Example In ACM the pay practice is assigned to a worker based on his union.

Instead of using an accounting practice, you can use a posting rule that divides up entries depending on an attribute of the employee. Instead of using one practice for each union, you can use only one practice. The first posting rule looks at the union of the employee that the entry is made for and makes an entry for the appropriate union account (see Section 7.6 for an example of this kind of split posting rule).

I prefer to use separate practices if the problem is at all complex, providing that we can assign a practice to a user for a period of time. Any splits that always change on an entry-by-entry basis (such as the evening/day split discussed in Section 7.6) must have a posting rule to handle them. If a user changes its accounting practice, we can use a historic mapping (see Section 15.3) to keep a record of these changes.

When different stages of processing have logically separate clumps of posting rules, we can split the rules up into different practice types and give a user a practice from each type. In Figure 6.26 an accounting practice can have users that can, in general, be any object. In a particular model, of course, users would be customers, employees, or the like. Each user has one accounting practice of each type, a constraint that is enforced by the keyed mapping (see Section 15.2).

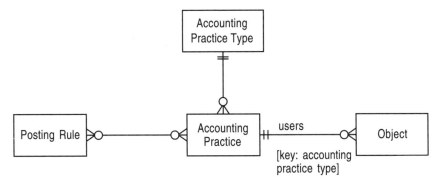

Figure 6.26 Accounting practice type.

In larger account networks we define a configuration of accounting practices that vary for each object that uses them.

Example   A utility has several practices for billing its residential customers, but all residential customers are taxed the same way. We can handle this by having separate charging and taxing practices. All residential customers have the same taxing practice, although they have separate charging practices.

A logical conclusion to this discussion is to treat accounting practices and posting rules as parts of the same composite [1]. This allows composition of practices for many levels. So far I haven't seen a great need for this, so I have not explored it further.

6.11   Sources of an Entry

It is often important to know why a particular entry is in the form it is. For example, if a customer calls to ask about a particular entry, the current model can give us quite a lot of information about how the entry was created. We can determine the state of the account at that time by looking at the dates of other entries. We can also determine which posting rule calculated the entry.

The model shown in Figure 6.27 can handle such customer requests by getting each transaction to remember which posting rule created it and which entries were used as input for the transaction. (If you are not using transactions, the association runs from entry to entry.)

Example   I received $2000 for some work for ACM, which I recorded as a transaction from fee income to checking account. My posting rule created a separate transaction into my tax liability account. The creator of this transaction was the 45 percent posting rule, and the sources for this transaction contained the withdrawal from the fees income account.

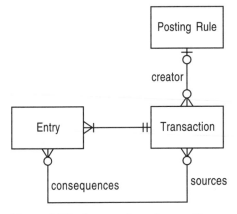

Figure 6.27   Sources for a transaction.

This records a full trail of calculations for each entry in both directions.

Using this pattern, we can form a chain of entries and transactions across the accounting structure. Each entry can determine all the causes and effects by recursive use of the sources and consequences mappings.

Modeling Principle   *To know why a calculation came out the way it did, represent the result of the calculation as an object that remembers the calculation that created it and the input values used.*

6.12   Balance Sheet and Income Statement

When using accounts to describe a system, it can be worth distinguishing between the balance sheet and income statement accounts, as shown in Figure 6.28. My checking account is an asset account, and my credit card account is a liability account. They reflect the money I have (or in the credit card's case, don't have) at any period of time. These appear on my balance sheet. Income and expense accounts reflect where money comes from or goes to. I have an income account for my employer, another income account for interest from my savings, an expense account for traveling, another for food, and so on. The balances of my income and expense accounts do not reflect any money I currently have, merely my classification of where it comes from and goes to.

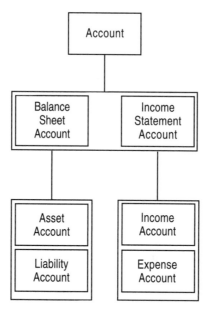

Figure 6.28   Asset, income, and expense accounts.

These are the kinds of accounts usually found in financial accounting. The concepts are useful elsewhere to distinguish between things held and the classification of where they come from and go to.

Accounts are generally used in a pattern where items enter the world via an income account, pass through several asset accounts, and are disposed of via an expense account. Any assets that are saved by the system are kept in particular asset accounts, but many asset accounts are merely staging places intended to be balance regularly. Liability accounts are almost always intended to balanced at some point (which may be far in the future for a long-term debt such as a mortgage).

Example   I buy a ticket from Boston Airlines with my credit card. My credit account is a liability account, and the Boston Airlines account is an expense account. Both accounts are classified by me, and I am the owner of the credit card account (it is my liability).

Example   ACM buys 3 tons of Java from Indonesian Coffee Importers. ACM has an income account for Indonesian Coffee Importers to record the transfer of the 3 tons of Java from Indonesian Coffee Importers to ACM's New York account. The New York account is an asset account, owned by ACM.

At this point I can quickly explain why I have avoided the terms *debit* and *credit*. These are well-known terms that apply to accounts, yet I have ignored them in favor of *from, to, deposit,* and *withdrawal*. The reason is that *debit* and *credit* are not used consistently in the sense of deposit and withdrawal. For income statement accounts, credits increase an account and debits decrease it, which makes sense for the layperson. For balance sheet accounts, however, debits increase assets (that is, they are deposits), and credits decrease assets. This may seem strange to nonaccountants, but it is the usual accounting convention. I have thus avoided *debit* and *credit,* partly because they might confuse any nonaccountant readers, and partly because we are working with a more abstract model than regular financial accounting.

6.13   **Corresponding Account**

Although income and expense accounts are external—the money is not mine—they are my accounts in that I choose the classification. The bank's view of accounts illustrates this. I have a checking account that is an asset within my personal system of accounts. The bank has an account within its system of accounts that looks remarkably similar. The bank is the classifier of the bank's account, but I own the assets within it. We could consider this the same account as the one in my system of accounts, but this would not work. I might post an entry for an ATM withdrawal on March 1, which is the day I made the withdrawal. The bank posts the same withdrawal on March 2 because that is the next working day at the bank. The two accounts both refer to the same asset, but they are not the same because their entries differ. It is better practice to consider the two accounts as corresponding.

Corresponding accounts are expected to match in some way and are usually reconciled at some point. This is what happens when I match my checkbook (my account) against the bank statement (the bank's account). The reconciliation process may be precise, or it may allow some imprecision, such as slight differences in dates.

Figure 6.29 illustrates this situation. Only balance accounts have owners; income statement accounts do not have assets so there is no question of ownership. All accounts have a classifier to indicate who creates and manipulates the accounts; I have used party (see Section 2.1). The correspondents relationship shows a couple of special properties: symmetry and transitivity [3]. First it is *symmetric*: If account *x* is a correspondent of account *y* then account *y* must be a correspondent of account *x*. The usual default for associations is that they are asymmetric. Transitivity indicates that if account *y* is a correspondent of account *x* and account *z* is a correspondent of account *y*, then account *z* is a correspondent of account *x*.

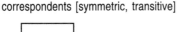

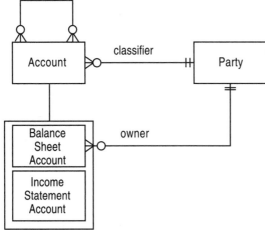

Figure 6.29   Corresponding accounts.

6.14   Specialized Account Model

I have provided several examples to show that this model can be used as a basis for both financial accounting and inventory tracking. With the accounting models it is usual to subtype to provide the information for the particular domain. For example, consider inventory management—a problem suited to the use of accounts. We can form an account for each combination of kind of goods and location (and give it a less accounting name, such as holding).

Thus if we are tracking bottles of Macallans, Talisker, and Laphroig whiskey between London, Paris, and Amsterdam we would have nine holdings (asset accounts, such as London-Macallans, London-Talisker, Paris-Talisker, and so on). Whenever we move goods from one location to another, we create a transfer (transaction) to handle the movement. As with money, transfers have to balance. In addition, the kind of object must be the same throughout the movement. Figure 6.30 shows this kind of extension to the account model.

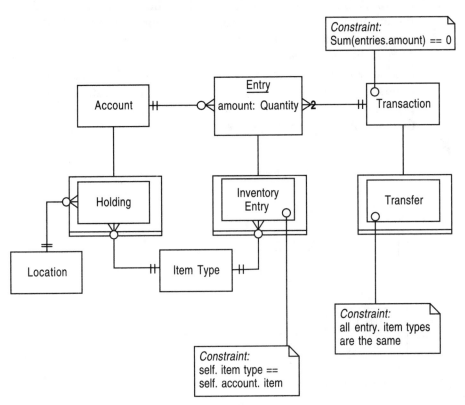

Figure 6.30   Specializing the account model to support inventories.

This kind of specialization should be done to use the accounting model in a particular domain.

This approach could also work to track orders, both incoming and outgoing. Each supplier would have an income account, perhaps more than one if supplier location was important. Similarly each customer would get an expense account. We can track orders in two ways: We could allow subtypes of transfer, either ordered or actual, or we could provide another set of holdings for orders, so we would have, for example, London-Talisker-Ordered and London-Talisker-Actual. When an order is placed, we would make a transfer from a supplier ordered holding to the ordered holding at the location we want it delivered. When the order is delivered, we would make the transfer between the ordered holding and the actual holding at our location. This is exactly the same as using a receivables account in financial books.

We can use summary holdings to get an overall picture. A summary holding of all ordered holdings can give the total ordered position, and a summary holding of Talisker gives the total amount of Talisker in all locations.

6.15   Booking Entries to Multiple Accounts

A common problem in dealing with accounts is when there is more than one place to book an entry. For example, suppose I paid $500 for my airline ticket to attend the OOPSLA conference. Do I book this to an OOPSLA account (so that I can work out how much it cost me to attend OOPSLA) or to an air travel account (so that I can work out how much I spent on air travel)? There are several ways to handle this, which illustrate some useful points about using accounts and also illustrate more complex account structures than the simple account hierarchies mentioned earlier.

A typical consultant's bill illustrates the problem. Let's say that I do three days' consultancy for ACM. I charge them $6000 for the work. In addition, I run up some expenses: $500 for the air fare, $250 for the hotel, $150 for car rental, and $100 for meals. How do I account for this, or more precisely, how do I account for this if I have a decent accounting system? Clearly I need an account for ACM so that I can send them a bill. However, one account is not enough. I am interested in seeing how much I earn from various clients. When I do this analysis, I do not want to see the expenses because they are not earned money. Similarly my tax liability estimates also need to ignore expenses. This indicates that I could use separate accounts for ACM fees and ACM expenses. My ACM bill is then formed by a summary account over these two accounts, as shown in Figure 6.31. The problem with this is that I need a separate account for all earned fees. This fee account would include accounts for ACM fees, Megabank fees, and other clients' fees. This also works as a summary account, but it breaks the hierarchical restriction of Figures 6.5 and 6.6. Thus I need to alter the model to allow a detail account to have multiple summary accounts as parents, as shown in Figure 6.32.

The model in Figure 6.32 allows the accounts to form a directed acyclic graph. Thus an account can have many parents, but we avoid cycles (an account cannot be its own grandparent). This structure allows multiple summary accounts.

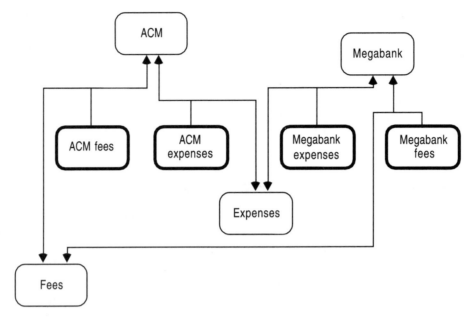

Figure 6.31   A typical fee/expense account structure.

The heavy bordered icons are detail accounts, summarized as shown by the arrows.

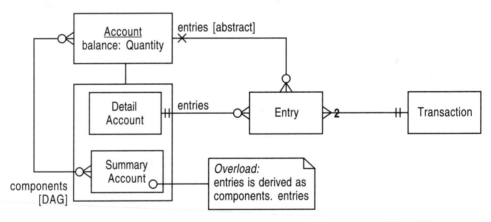

Figure 6.32   Allowing multiple summary accounts.

This diagram replaces the hierarchy of Figure 6.5 with a directed acyclic graph.

However, there is a small wrinkle that we must consider. What would occur if I had the account structure of Figure 6.33? The account X sums over ACM and fees, so the ACM fees account gets counted twice.

According to the model in Figure 6.32, we would still get a correct balance for X. The balance is defined on a derived set of entries. Sets do not

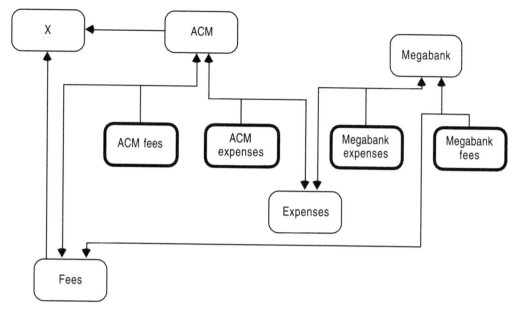

Figure 6.33   Account structure that highlights a problem.

If multiple summary accounts are used, someone could define a summary account that has overlapping detail accounts.

allow duplicates, so all the entries in ACM fees will only appear once in X, thus giving us a correct balance for X. However this balance will not be equal to the sums of the balances for fees and ACM, which might prove confusing. If this confusion is a problem, we need a constraint on the components relationship that would not allow us to select components that had any overlap. This is a reasonable constraint since it is difficult to come up with an example where such an account as X would be useful. Defining this kind of account is more likely to be the product of accident than design.

6.15.1   Using Memo Entries

The model works well at this level, but consider some further details. There may be a need to break down expenses in more detail. Tax regulations may require us to separate expenses for travel, lodging, and meals (for example, ACM-airfare, ACM-lodging, Megabank-airfare, and so on). This could be done by breaking each expense account into detail accounts, but this could become difficult to manage due to all the complex combination accounts. It is worth exploring some other options.

One option is to use entries into memo accounts. Thus $500 for a ticket to visit ACM headquarters would result in depositing into both the ACM expenses account and an airfare account. This method removes the need for an ACM-airfare account but requires additional entries. A posting rule might deal with this to some extent, but we still need some statement about which expense account is needed. This might be done by a special expense transaction creation that takes parameters of from account, to account, and expense type memo account.

Choosing whether the ACM expense account or the airfare account should be a memo account depends on subsequent use of the account. If the ACM expense account is being used to track the payment of invoices, while the airfare account is only being used for tax reporting, then the airfare account would make the better memo account. There's a certain amount of arbitrariness in choosing which accounts hold the main stream of money, compared to those working with memo accounts.

6.15.2 Derived Accounts

A different approach is to use a derived account, as in Figure 6.34. In this case the entries are specified by providing the derived account with a filter (see Section 6.9), which selects matching entries. To work, the derived account needs something on which to base its derivation. A subtype of entry that supports an expense category would do nicely, and then an account where the membership test is expense category = airfare would create the desired information.

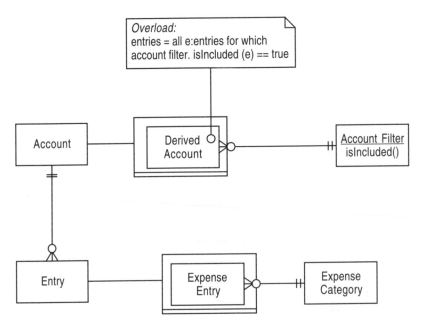

Figure 6.34 Introducing derived accounts.

We might consider taking this approach further. Why not abandon using accounts altogether and just have something like Figure 6.35? We can then work out what is going on just by queries on expense.

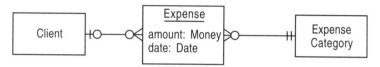

Figure 6.35   Expenses defined to abandon the accounting model.

A derived account can still allow us to use all the reporting behavior, but we lose the tracking behavior.

This question helps define why accounts are useful and why derived accounts are valuable. Accounts work best within relatively static structures where complex movements of assets need to be tracked. If the movements are simple, such as just assigning an expense to airfare, then accounts are not really needed. However, consider the situation where I visit both Megabank and ACM in one trip and charge two-thirds of the airfare to one and one-third to the other. This is the kind of multilegged transaction that accounts handle well. However, the model in Figure 6.35 has a real problem with this. How do I split a simple payment up in this way? Note that the model in Figure 6.35 has another problem: It does not say where the money comes from. I could add a credit card association to it, but then expense looks very similar to a two-legged transaction.

Using attributes for derived accounts is effective when the account structure is not very static. If there are many possible cuts of information, then the derived account allows these to be computed easily using the same reporting facilities that accounts have. However, they only have the reporting facilities. Derived accounts cannot be posted to and thus cannot be used to track the ebb and flow of assets.

So whenever we are trying to represent an aspect of an entry, we have a choice between an attribute of the entry or a new account level. The decision is based on what part of the account behavior you need. If it is simply the reporting side, we can use an attribute and derive an account when it's needed. Otherwise, a new level of accounts is required.

Further Reading

I can recommend a couple of other sources for information on accounts that will give a different perspective to that presented in this chapter. Hay [2] has a chapter dedicated to accounting. His basic concepts of accounts and transactions is very much the same as mine, although he does not present anything on posting rules. He goes into much more depth on the account types that are present in corporations. He also discusses the common transactions that are used in corporations and how they fit into this accounting model. He also presents a knowledge level for these account and transaction types.

There has been a lot of work at the University of Illinois at Urbana-Champaign on developing an accounting framework [4].[1] This takes a very different approach to Hay and myself. It starts with treating the information on an invoice (for example) as a high-level "transaction" against a high-level account. This "transaction" can then be broken down to lower-level "transactions" against lower-level accounts. They use the word *transaction* very differently than I do: They do not follow the principle of conservation. A high-level "transaction" might be an invoice with all its line items. The framework concentrates on breaking this down into lower-level "transactions," such as the line items themselves. Thus the framework is designed to break down a cluster of entries into its component entries, rather than my approach of a network of accounts and transfers between them.

References

1. Gamma, E., R. Helm, R. Johnson, and J. Vlissides. *Design Patterns: Elements of Reusable Object-Oriented Software.* Reading, MA: Addison-Wesley, 1995.
2. Hay, D. *Data Model Patterns: Conventions of Thought.* New York, NY: Dorset House, 1996.
3. Langer, S.K. *An Introduction to Symbolic Logic*, Third Edition. New York, NY: Dover, 1967.
4. Keefer, P.D. *An Object-Oriented Framework for Accounting Systems.* University of Illinois at Urbana-Champaign <ftp://st.cs.uiuc.edu/pub/Smalltalk/st80_vw/accounts/thesis.ps>, 1994.
5. Meyer, B. "Applying 'Design by Contract,'" In *IEEE Computer*, 25, 10 (1992), pp. 40–51.

---

[1] See http://st-www.cs.uiuc.edu/users/johnson/Accounts.html

7

Using the Accounting Models

To fully understand this chapter, you will need to read Chapter 6 first. This is an unusual chapter in this book. Instead of describing a group of patterns, this chapter shows how we can use the patterns presented in Chapter 6. This is a difficult task because the accounting patterns in Chapter 6 are quite abstract. To understand how the patterns really work, we need to look at a fully worked example.

This chapter looks at accounts and posting rules used in a model for a telephone utility, Total Telecommunications (TT). In the best textbook tradition, the examples presented here are somewhat simplistic. They should be sufficient to at least give you a feel for how the models work. The aim is to illustrate the use of the account model, not to model a telephone company.

Since this is an example chapter, I have used some code to illustrate the examples. I chose Digitalk Smalltalk over C++ because Smalltalk makes it easier for me to convey the basic ideas. The concepts should be readily transferable to C++. I have used the patterns from Chapter 14 in transforming the models. I have also used Kent Beck's coding patterns [1], with some variations. I must stress that I have made no attempt to optimize the code. I also have not provided complete code, only highlights.

TT's basic billing plan is very simple. All calls are divided into day and evening calls. Daytime runs from 7:00 a.m. to 7:00 p.m. The classification is based on the time the call begins.[1] Day calls cost 98¢ for the first minute and 30¢ for subsequent minutes. Evening calls cost 70¢ for the first minute, 20¢ for the next 20 minutes, and 12¢ thereafter. The government charges a 6 percent tax on the first $50 of calls in a calendar month and 4 percent on calls thereafter.

---

[1] For the sake of simplicity, I have skipped the case of calls crossing the boundary.

The chapter begins with a discussion of the structural models (7.1), which is naturally based on the patterns presented in Chapter 6. We then look at some interesting features of implementing the structure (7.2). To set up the objects, we begin by setting up new phone services (7.3), followed by setting up calls (7.4). We then take a first look at the posting rules, examining the code for implementing account-based firing (7.5). Three example posting rules are given: separating calls into day and evening (7.6), charging for time (7.7), and calculating the tax (7.8). Each rule illustrates a particular aspect of behavior. The first two rules operate on an entry-by-entry basis, and a common supertype—each entry posting rule—handles the common behavior. Splitting charges into day and evening is handled by a simple singleton subtype of each entry posting rule. A different scale is required for day and evening calls, but since the basic process is the same, we can use a strategy object parameterized by a rate table. This allows us to handle any posting rule that charged according to some scale based on the length of the call. The rate table class used as the strategy object can be used for any calculation based on lengths in this way. Indeed it is used for the next posting rule that calculates tax. Unlike the prior rules, this rule has to work on a month-by-month basis, but we cannot assume it is run once per month.

The three posting rule classes should give a good idea of how we can use the account/inventory patterns to show both monetary and nonmonetary transactions.

In developing code I like to begin with building the skeleton of the structural model. I then prototype, being careful to update the structural model as I go (otherwise, I can forget where I am). As tricky behaviors come up, I may use event diagrams or interaction diagrams at the start or during the programming. If I think it is important to document what I have done with these behaviors (as I do for this book), I produce diagrams once I have the code sorted out. The diagrams are not replacements for the code; they help to illustrate what the code is doing. (With a suitable tool, however, event diagrams could be used as the code.)

7.1 Structural Models

The best place to start is with the structural models because they give an overview of the various pieces of the final model. Figure 7.1 shows the packages within the model. I've split the model into two packages: phone service and account. One virtue of an accounting framework is that it can be used for different industries, so we need to ensure that the accounting model is kept separate from (that is, has no visibility to) any industry-specific concepts.

Figure 7.1 The packages for the TT example.

The account package holds the abstract accounting types, which are extended by the phone service package for this specific domain.

Figure 7.2 shows the accounting model for TT, based on the patterns from Chapter 6. This model has three associations from posting rule to account. Trigger and output are familiar, but the keyed output is new. This allows multiple output accounts for those posting rules that need them. The need will become clear with examples later in the chapter.

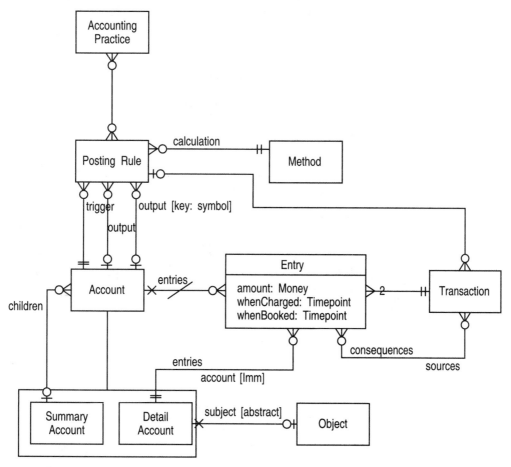

Figure 7.2 Accounts model for TT.

Figure 7.3 shows the model of the phone service. Customers are allowed multiple phone lines. A phone service is really a phone line assigned to a customer. Each phone service is tied to an accounting practice that describes how it will be billed. This diagram illustrates why the subject mapping was added to detail account shown in Figure 7.2. We need a way to find out what detail account is accounting for, but we do not want visibility from the account package into the phone service package because it would compromise reuse. Thus we form a subtype of detail account. With subtyping, visibility only runs from the subtype to the supertype. It is perfectly permissible for the service account to know the phone service because they are both in the phone service package. However, we could have reference to a detail account and not know it is a service account. The abstract mapping on detail account tells us that a detail account could be linked to an object (type unspecified) as a subject. This will all be implemented by subtypes of detail account—a classic case of polymorphism.

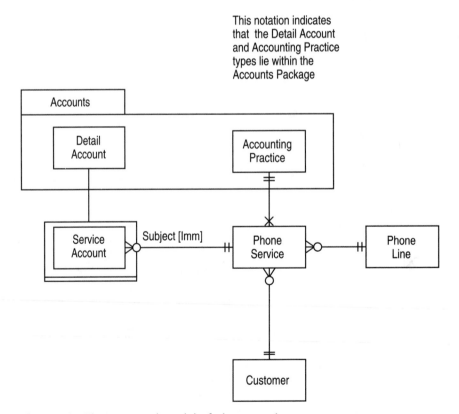

Figure 7.3   The structural model of phone service.

7.2   Implementing the Structure

We can use design templates based on the patterns described in Chapter 14 to implement the models. All associations are represented by access and modify operations. Single-valued mappings follow the usual Smalltalk convention. Thus the mapping named trigger on the posting rule is implemented by the accessor `trigger` and modifier `trigger: anAccount`. Multivalued mappings—for example, posting rules on accounting practice— have accessor `postingRules` and modifiers `addPostingRule: aPostingRule` and `removePostingRule: aPostingRule`.

The entries operation on account is polymorphic—detail account returns an instance variable while summary account sums over its children, (as shown in Listing 7.1).

```
Account>>entries
  ^self subclassResponsibility
SummaryAccount>>entries
  |answer|
  answer := SortedCollection sortBlock:[:a :b| a whenBooked > b whenBooked].
  self detailAccounts
    inject: answer
    into:
        [:total :each |
        total addAll: each entries;
        yourself].
  ^answer
DetailAccount>>entries
  ^entries copy
```

Listing 7.1   Getting the entries of an account.

This model has no account types. The posting rules are defined by summary accounts. For the examples in this chapter, we could use either account types or summary accounts to define posting rules. Using summary accounts is slightly more complicated, making it a better illustration. The high-level summary accounts that are defined are held in a class variable in the account class and are accessible with the class method `findWithName: aString`, following the style of Section 14.5.1.

Various bits of code need to find a service account for a particular phone service under a particular summary account. It's not difficult to think up various ways of doing it: asking a phone service to find the account under a given summary account or asking a summary account to find its descendent attached to a phone service. Both of those ways are reasonable, but it is difficult to choose which one is the best. Furthermore, each implies a certain navigation path, and one may be better than the other. In such cases we can use an entirely different technique, building a class method following Section 14.5.1. Then we can implement the method with either path and change the method without changing the declarative interface. It also makes it easier to remember where these find methods are, as shown in Listing 7.2.

```
ServiceAccount class>>findWithPhoneService: aPhoneService topParent: aTopSummaryAccount
  ^aPhoneService serviceAccounts detect: [:i| i parentTop = aTopSummaryAccount]
PhoneService>>accountNamed: aString
  ^ServiceAccount
     findWithPhoneService: self
     topParent: (Account findWithName: aString)
```

Listing 7.2   Finding a particular account.

In practice a method on phone service, such as `accountNamed: aString`, is often more convenient to use. That method calls `findWithPhoneService: topParent` and provides the advantages of both approaches.

All the examples here use two-legged transactions, although the model supports multilegged transactions. We can create a two-legged transaction with the special creation methods for transaction shown in Listing 7.3. One method carries all the information, including the source entries and the creation posting rule. The other method is used for the initial attributes read in at the beginning.

The listing shows a number of coding techniques. A constructor parameter method [1] (prefixed with `set`) initializes the new object with parameters. Within the creation parameter method, precondition checking is done with the `require:` message. To improve performance, the checking can be removed by redefining the `require:` method. Another element from design by contract [3] is the use of an invariant check.

7.3   Setting Up New Phone Services

Creating a new phone service is not simply a question of instantiating a phone service object. Service accounts must also be created to get the accounting system going. Although this example does not contain more than one accounting practice, it should be flexible enough to set up the accounts for whichever accounting practice is being used, as shown in Figures 7.4 and 7.5, and Listing 7.4.

```
Transaction class>>newWithAmount: aQuantity from: fromAccount to: toAccount
whenCharged: aTimepointOrDate
  ^self
    newWithAmount: aQuantity
    from: fromAccount
    to: toAccount
    whenCharged: aTimepointOrDate
    creator: nil
    sources: Set new
newWithAmount: aQuantity from: fromAccount to: toAccount whenCharged:
aTimepointOrDate creator: aPostingRule sources: aSetOfEntries
^self new
    setAmount: aQuantity
    from: fromAccount
    to: toAccount
    whenCharged: aTimepointOrDate
    creator: aPostingRule
    sources: aSetOfEntries
Transaction>>setAmount: aMoney from: aDebitAccount  to: aCreditAccount  whenCharged:
aTimepointOrDate creator: aPostingRule sources: aSetOfEntries
    "private"
    self require:
        [aMoney isKindOf: Money.
        aDebitAccount isKindOf: ServiceAccount.
        aCreditAccount isKindOf: ServiceAccount.
        (aTimepointOrDate isKindOf: Date) or: [aTimepointOrDate isKindOf: Timepoint].
        (creator == nil) or: [creator isKindOf: PostingRule]].
    self initialize.
    self addEntry: (Entry new
        setAccount: aCreditAccount
        amount: aMoney
        charged: aTimepointOrDate).
    self addEntry: (Entry new
        setAccount: aDebitAccount
        amount: aMoney negated
        charged: aTimepointOrDate).
    creator:= aPostingRule.
    aSetOfEntries do: [:i| self sourcesAdd: i].
    self checkInvariant.
Object>>require: aBooleanBlock
  aBooleanBlock value ifFalse: [self error: 'Precondition Violation']
Transaction>>checkInvariant
  |balance|
  balance := entries
    inject: Quantity zero
    into: [:total :each | total := total + each amount].
  self require: [balance = Quantity zero].
```

Listing 7.3   Creating a two-legged transaction.

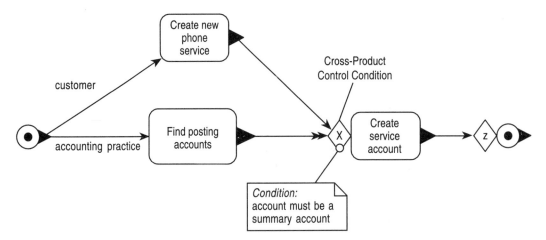

Figure 7.4   Event diagram for creating a new phone service.

This diagram uses a cross-product control condition (an extension to the regular event diagrams). The control condition is evaluated for each combination of its incoming triggers, in this case for each combination of new phone service and posting account. It invokes the create service account operation for each phone service and summary posting account in the accounting practice.

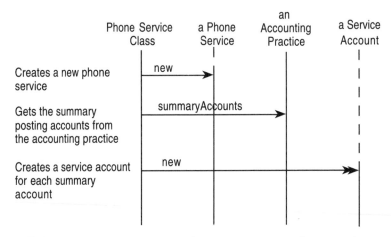

Figure 7.5   Interaction diagram for creating a new phone service.

To determine which accounts are required, the accounting practice is asked for its posting accounts, as shown in Figure 7.6 and Listing 7.5. An accounting practice can contain posting rules that reference detail accounts (although that it is not done here). Thus the posting accounts have to be filtered to keep only the summary accounts.

```
PhoneService class>>newWithAccountingPractice: anAccountingPractice customer:
aCustomer phoneLine: aPhoneLine
  ^self new
    setAccountingPractice: anAccountingPractice
    customer: aCustomer
    phoneLine: aPhoneLine
PhoneService>>setAccountingPractice: anAccountingPractice customer: aCustomer
phoneLine: aString
  |newObj summaryAccounts|
  self require:
    [(anAccountingPractice isKindOf: AccountingPractice) &
    (aCustomer isKindOf: Customer)].
  name := (aCustomer name), '#', (aCustomer phoneServices size + 1) printString.
  accountingPractice := anAccountingPractice.
  self setCustomer: aCustomer.
  line := aString.
  self createServiceAccounts.
  ^self
PhoneService>>createServiceAccounts
  "private - initializing"
  (self accountingPractice summaryAccounts) do:
    [:each | ServiceAccount newWithPhoneService: self parent: each].
```

Listing 7.4   Setting up a new phone line.

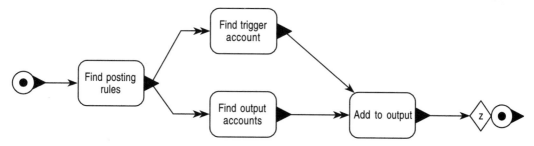

Figure 7.6   Finding posting accounts.

We want the trigger account for each posting rule and all the output accounts
for each posting rule.

```
AccountingPractice>>summaryAccounts
    ^self postingAccounts select: [:each | each isSummary]
AccountingPractice>>postingAccounts
  |answer|
  answer := Set new.
  postingRules do:
    [:each |
    answer add: each trigger.
    answer addAll: each outputs].
  ^answer
```

Listing 7.5   An accounting practice can provide its summary accounts.

7.4 Setting Up Calls

Phone calls are modeled as transactions from a network account to a basic time account. The units for phone call entries are minutes.

The following method shows the setting up of a phone service and the placement of some sample calls. Note that it is defined on a class called Scenario1, as shown in Listing 7.6. Test methods can get quite complex; thus it is good practice to put them on a scenario object (using *scenario* in the

```
Scenario1>>setupCalls
  |adams  network |
  self init.
  adams := Customer new name: 'Adams'; persist.
  theService := PhoneService
    newWithAccountingPractice: (AccountingPractice basicBillingPlan)
    customer: adams
    phoneLine: (PhoneLine new name: '617 123 1234').
  network := theService accountNamed: 'Network'.
  basicAccount := ServiceAccount findWithPhoneService: theService topParent:
                  (Account findWithName: 'Basic Time').
  Transaction
    newWithAmount: (Quantity n:'10 min')
    from: network
    to: basicAccount
    whenCharged: (Timepoint
        date: 'jan 1 1995'
        time: '13:15').
  Transaction
    newWithAmount: (Quantity n:'8 min')
    from: network
    to: basicAccount
    whenCharged: (Timepoint
        date: 'jan 1 1995'
        time: '14:25').
  Transaction
    newWithAmount: (Quantity n:'6 min')
    from: network
    to: basicAccount
    whenCharged: (Timepoint
        date: 'jan 1 1995'
        time: '19:05').
  Transaction
    newWithAmount: (Quantity n:'33 min')
    from: network
    to: basicAccount
    whenCharged: (Timepoint
        date: 'jan 1 1995'
        time: '20:20').
  ^basicAccount
```

Listing 7.6   Setting up test phone calls.

sense of a use-case, not as defined in Section 9.4) to keep them under control if no proper testing framework is available. The variables `basicAccount` and `theService` are class variables of this test class.

Using user-defined fundamental classes, such as quantity, can make creating new objects difficult. Hence quantity has a method `n: aString`, which creates a new quantity from the string. This is a personal convention that I use since `fromString: aString` can get rather unwieldy.

7.5   Implementing Account-based Firing

We use the account-based triggering scheme here (see Section 6.7.3). Each account has a method to process itself by firing all posting rules that use it as a trigger, as shown in Listing 7.7.

```
DetailAccount>>process
    self allOutboundRules do: [:j| j processAccount: self].
    lastProcessed := entries last
allOutboundRules
    "private"
    |answer|
    answer := self triggerFor.
    self allParents do: [:i| answer addAll: i triggerFor].
    ^answer
```

Listing 7.7   An account fires outbound posting rules.

Entries are held in `orderedCollection`*, with new ones added on the end. The* `lastProcessed` *instance variable keeps track of the state of processing.*

7.6   Separating Calls into Day and Evening

To separate the calls into day and evening calls, we look at each entry, consider the time on the entry, and then make a transaction from the basic time account into either the day time account or the evening time account.

A posting rule that operates on an entry-by-entry basis is quite common. We can create an abstract subtype of posting rule called an each-entry posting rule (the class `EachEntryPR`). This subtype calls the operation `processEntry: anEntry` on each unprocessed entry in the triggering account, as shown in Figure 7.7 and Listing 7.8.

The message `currentInput:` loads an instance variable to hold the service account that is being processed by the posting rule, as shown in Listing 7.9. It is accessed by private methods and is only defined within the execution of `processAccount`. A temporary, private instance variable is often

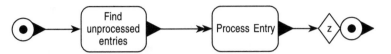

Figure 7.7   Each-entry posting rule's method for processing an account.

We use the process entry operation on each unprocessed entry.

```
EachEntryPR>>processAccount: anAccount
  self currentInput: anAccount.
  anAccount unprocessedEntries do: [:each | self processEntry: each].
  self clean.
EachEntryPR>>processEntry: anEntry
  self subclassResponsibility
DetailAccount>>unprocessedEntries
  self isUnprocessed ifTrue: [^ entries copy].
  ^entries
    copyFrom: self firstUnprocessedIndex
    to: entries size.
DetailAccount>>isUnprocessed
  "private"
  ^lastProcessed isNil
DetailAccount>>firstUnprocessedIndex
  "private"
  ^(entries indexOf: lastProcessed) + 1
```

Listing 7.8   How an EachEntryPR processes a triggering account.

```
PostingRule>>currentInput: anAccount
    "private"
    self require: [currentInput isNil].
    currentInput := anAccount.
    self setCurrentOutputs
PostingRule>>setCurrentOutputs
    "private"
    currentOutputs := Dictionary new.
    outputs associationsDo:
      [: each |
      currentOutputs
        at: each key
        put:(ServiceAccount
            findWithPhoneService: (currentInput phoneService)
            topParent: each value)]
PostingRule>>clean
    "private"
    currentInput := nil.
    currentOutputs := nil.
```

Listing 7.9   Setting up the current input and outputs.

used in such cases because posting rules in general (although not in this case) are defined as instances. Thus we cannot instantiate them for invocation of the rule. An alternative is to treat the defined posting rule instance as a prototype [2] and clone it for execution.

The `currentInput:` message also sets up current output service accounts for the same phone service as the one provided as input.

This method does not do the actual calculation and posting. Instead it is done by `processEntry:`, which is abstract and should be defined by subclasses. Thus we see three layers of subclassing here. `PostingRule` defines the basic interface and services of posting rules. The process account method on `EachEntryPR` is a template method,[2] which outlines the steps of processing an account entry by entry but leaves a subclass to actually work out how to process each entry.

For this posting rule we can define new subclass of `EachEntryPR` called `EveningDaySplitPR`. This is an example of the singleton class implementation (see Section 6.6.1). Hard-coded into this class are the appropriate accounts, which are set up at initialization, as shown in Listing 7.10.

```
EveningDaySplitPR>>initialize
    super initialize.
    outputs := Dictionary new .
    outputs
      at: #evening
      put: (Account findWithName: 'Evening Time').
    outputs
      at: #day
      put: (Account findWithName: 'Day Time')
```

Listing 7.10   Initializing the evening/day split process rule.

The splitting is done by the overriding `processEntry:` method, as shown in Figure 7.8 and Listing 7.11.

7.7   Charging for Time

Charging for both the evening and day calls follows the same pattern, as shown in Figure 7.9. Again the charges are calculated on an entry-by-entry basis, so a subclass of `EachEntryPR` is used. Two posting rules are used—one for day, one for evening. The same class, `TransformPR`, is used for both of them.

---

[2] A template method is a skeleton of an algorithm that defers some steps to subclasses [2].

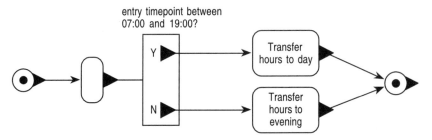

entry timepoint between
07:00 and 19:00?

Transfer
hours to day

Transfer
hours to
evening

Figure 7.8   Evening/day split process rule's method for the process entry operation.

```
EveningDaySplitPR>>processEntry: anEntry
  Transaction
     newWithAmount: (anEntry amount)
     from: (anEntry account)
     to: (self outputFor: anEntry)
     whenCharged: (anEntry timepoint)
     creator: self
     sources: (Set with: anEntry)
EveningDaySplitPR>>outputFor: anEntry
  ^(anEntry timepoint time > (Time fromString: '19:00')) |
  (anEntry timepoint time < (Time fromString: '07:00'))
    ifTrue: [self currentOutputs at: #evening ]
    ifFalse: [self currentOutputs at: #day].
```

Listing 7.11   How the evening/day split process rule processes an entry.

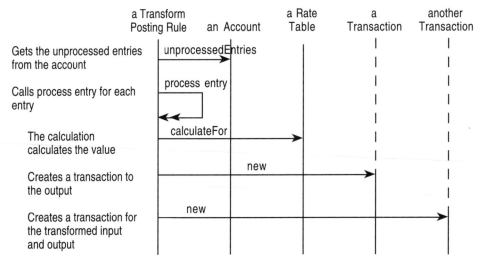

Figure 7.9   Interaction diagram for processing an account with a transform posting rule.

A special feature of this posting rule is that it is triggered by an entry in minutes but produces entries in dollars, hence the term *transform.* Its actual reaction is to generate two transactions. One transfers the minutes back to the network account, thus completing the cycle for minutes. The second generates a new transaction in the money world: from a network income account to an activity account, as shown in Figure 7.10 and Listing 7.12.

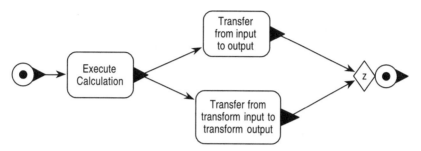

Figure 7.10   Event diagram for transform posting rule's method for the process entry operation.

```
TransformPR>>processEntry: anEntry
    Transaction
      newWithAmount: (anEntry amount)
      creator: self
      from: (anEntry account)
      timepoint: (anEntry timepoint)
      to: (self currentOutputs at: #out)
      sources: (Set with: anEntry).
    Transaction newWithAmount: (self transformedAmount: anEntry)
      creator: self
      from: (self currentOutputs at: #transformedFrom)
      timepoint: (anEntry timepoint)
      to: (self currentOutputs at: #transformedTo)
      sources: (Set with: anEntry).
TransformPR>>transformedAmount: anEntry
    "private"
    ^self calculationMethod calculateFor: anEntry amount
```

Listing 7.12   How a transform posting rule processes an entry.

The `transformedAmount` is calculated by a method object (see Section 6.6.2), specifically a rate table, such as that shown in Tables 7.1 and 7.2. The method class defines the abstract `calculateFor:` method. The rate table is a subclass that stores a two-column table of quantities to produce the kind of graded charging that the problem demands. It is implemented using a dictionary. The keys of the dictionary indicate the various threshold points, and

LENGTH OF CALL	COST
Up to 1 min	98¢
> 1 min	30¢

Table 7.1   Rates for day calls.

LENGTH OF CALL	COST
Up to 1 min	70¢
1–20 mins	20¢
> 20 mins	10¢

Table 7.2   Rates for evening calls.

the corresponding value indicates the rate that applies up to that threshold. Listing 7.13 shows how the evening rate is set up. The top rate indicates which rate applies once you get over the top threshold.

```
RateTable>>eveningRateTable
    | answer |
    answer := RateTable new.
    answer
        rateAt: (Quantity n: '1 min')
        put: (Quantity n: '.7 USD').
    answer
        rateAt: (Quantity n: '21 min')
        put: (Quantity n: '.2 USD').
    answer topRate: (Quantity n: '.12 USD').
    ^answer
```

Listing 7.13   Setting up the evening rates in the rate table object.

Listing 7.14 shows how the rate table then calculates the amount. It does this in two parts: taking each step in the rate table and adding any amount over the top threshold. There is not much point showing a diagram for this; the tables indicate what is needed from a conceptual perspective clearly enough. One particular thing to watch for with these systems is that they can handle both positive and negative numbers the same by using absolute values.

7.8   Calculating the Tax

The final posting rule shows the calculation of the tax. This rule differs from the previous rules in that it does not operate on an entry-by-entry basis. This posting rule has to look at all charges over a one-month period to assess the tax.

Another complication is that we cannot (or rather do not wish to) guarantee that the posting rule is only run once at the end of the month. Thus the posting should take into account any tax already charged for the month due to an earlier firing. This follows the principle that the posting rules should be

```
RateTable>>calculateFor: aQuantity
    | answer input|
    self require: [aQuantity unit = self thresholdUnits].
    input := aQuantity abs.
    answer := (self tableAmount: input) + (self topRateAmount: input).
    ^aQuantity positive
        ifTrue: [answer]
        ifFalse: [answer negated]
RateTable>>tableAmount: aQuantity
    "private"
    |input sortedKeys lastKey thisRowKeyAmount answer|
    sortedKeys := table keys asSortedCollection.
    lastKey := Quantity zero.
    answer := Quantity zero.
    sortedKeys do:
    [:thisKey |
    thisRowKeyAmount := ((aQuantity min: thisKey) - lastKey) max: Quantity zero.
    answer := answer + ((table at: thisKey) * thisRowKeyAmount amount).
    lastKey := thisKey].
    ^answer
RateTable>>topRateAmount: aQuantity
    | amountOverTopRateThreshold |
    amountOverTopRateThreshold := aQuantity - self topRateThreshold.
    amountOverTopRateThreshold positive
        ifTrue: [^self topRate * amountOverTopRateThreshold amount]
        ifFalse: [^Quantity zero].
RateTable>>topRateThreshold
    ^table keys asSortedCollection last
```

Listing 7.14   How a rate table calculates a value for an input quantity.

defined independently of how they are fired. This increases flexibility and reduces coupling in the model.

The `MonthlyChargePR` class is a subtype of posting rule and thus implements `processAccount`, as shown in Figure 7.11 and Listing 7.15.

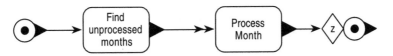

Figure 7.11   Monthly charge posting rule's method for processing an account.

This process is based on a balance over a time period, rather than each entry.

Each month is processed with `processForMonth:`, as shown in Figure 7.12 and Listing 7.16.

The final transaction is from the output account to the input account, because the activity account will be increased due to the tax liability.

```
MonthlyChargePR>>processAccount: anAccount
  self currentInput: anAccount.
  (self monthsToProcess: anAccount)  do: [:each | self processforMonth: each].
  self clean
MonthlyChargePR>>monthsToProcess: anAccount
  ^(anAccount unprocessedEntries collect:
      [:each | each whenCharged date firstDayOfMonth]) asSet.
```

Listing 7.15   How a monthly charge posting rule processes an account.

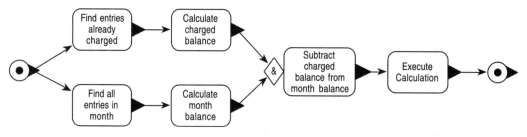

Figure 7.12   Event diagram for processing a month.

```
MonthlyChargePR>>processforMonth: aDate
  | inputToProcess totalToCharge |
  inputToProcess := (self inputBalance: aDate) - (self outputAlreadyCharged: aDate).
  totalToCharge := (self calculationMethod calculateFor: inputToProcess) -
                        (self outputAlreadyCharged: aDate).
  Transaction
      newWithAmount: totalToCharge
      creator: self
      from: self currentOutput
      timepoint: aDate lastDayOfMonth
      to: self currentInput
      sources: (self currentInput entriesChargedInMonth: aDate).
MonthlyChargePR>>inputBalance: aDate
      ^self currentInput balanceChargedInMonth: aDate.
MonthlyChargePR>>outputAlreadyCharged: aDate
      ^(self currentOutput balanceChargedInMonth: aDate) negated
```

Listing 7.16   How a monthly charge posting rule processes a month.

7.9   Concluding Thoughts

This is a very simple example, so it is difficult to draw too many conclusions
from it. The reader can convincingly argue that this problem can be tackled in
a much simpler form without all this framework stuff. The framework, however, is valuable for scalability. A real business may have dozens of practices,

each with dozens of process rules. With this structure we represent a new billing plan by an accounting practice. When we build a new practice, we create a network of new *instances* of the posting rule. We can do this without any recompilation or rebuilding of the system, while it is still up and running. There will be unavoidable occasions when we need a new subtype of posting rule, but these will be rare.

7.9.1   The Structure of the Posting Rules

Figure 7.13 shows the generalization structure of the posting rules discussed in this chapter. The abstract posting rule class has an abstract processAccount method. The subtypes each implement `processAccount`. The each entry posting rule implements this method by calling another abstract method, `processEntry`, on each entry. The further subtypes implement processEntry as needed. The day/evening split posting rule's method is hard coded, while the transform posting rule delegates to a rate table. The example shows how a

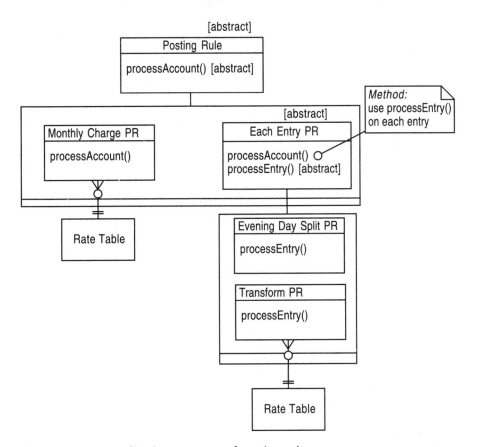

Figure 7.13   Generalization structure of posting rules

combination of abstract methods, polymorphism, and delegation can provide the kind of structure that supports a variety of posting rules in an organized structure.

This is not the only structure of posting rules we could use. Another alternative would be to combine the two steps of working out the charge into a single step. Such a posting rule would have two rate tables, one for day charges and one for evening charges, and would be responsible for both the splitting and the rate table charging.

There are no rules for deciding how to divide up posting rules. Our fundamental aim is to be able to build new practices without needing a new subtype of posting rule. We want to have as small a set of subtypes of posting rule as we can, for that will make it easier to understand and maintain the posting rule types. Yet we need these subtypes to have all the function that is required so we can put them together for new practices. We want to minimize the times when we need to build new posting rule subtypes.

Simpler posting rules result in larger practices and are usually more widely available. I tend to keep posting rules to small behaviors initially. If I see a frequently used combination of posting rules, then I might build a more functional posting rule to represent that combination.

7.9.2   When Not to Use the Framework

An alternative to using this framework is to have only one class per billing plan to handle all the behavior (day/evening split, charging, and taxing), as shown in Figure 7.14. The class would take all the entries in a month and produce a bill. There would be one such object for each billing plan.

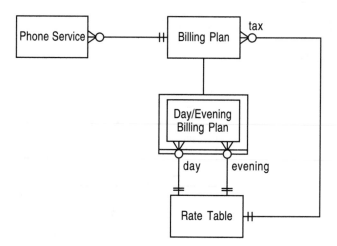

Figure 7.14   Using a billing plan.

A billing plan is simple but not as flexible.

This approach is quite plausible. Although there may be many billing plans, there are usually a few basic methods for billing that can be parameterized, much as the transform posting rule can be parameterized for many different rate schedules. Such a type, for this problem, would be parameterized by an evening rate table, a day rate table, and a taxing rate table.

The key question is how many subtypes of billing plan there are. If we can represent all the billing structures with a dozen or so subtypes of billing plan (although there might be hundreds of instances), then using a billing plan type is plausible. The accounting model's strength is that it allows you to build the equivalent of new subtypes of billing plan by wiring together posting rule and account objects. This is a powerful advantage if there is a large or frequently changing set of subtypes of billing plan.

Another way to think about it is to consider the billing plan as a posting rule that posts from the basic time account to the activity account in one step. Using accounts would still be valuable to give the history of phone calls and charges at the input and result of billing plan. We would lose the intermediate totals.

7.9.3   Accounting Practice Diagrams

A diagram often helps to visualize a complex problem. Figures 7.15 and 7.16 are suggestions (and most certainly tentative ones) in that direction. Complex practices will be helped by these kinds of diagrams. We might imagine that we could build a system by drawing a diagram and decreasing the amount of programming required and thus increase the productivity of such applications.

Practice should result in a diagram form that is simple yet conveys the key information. Figure 7.15 has the advantage of being simple, displaying the key triggering and output relationships. It does not, however, show the full flow of accounted items in the way that Figure 7.16 does. If you use these

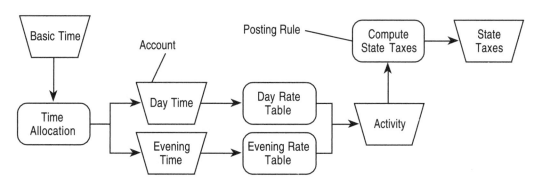

Figure 7.15   A simple way of diagramming the layout of process rules and accounts.
It shows the trigger and main output account for each posting rule but hides the full flow of transactions.

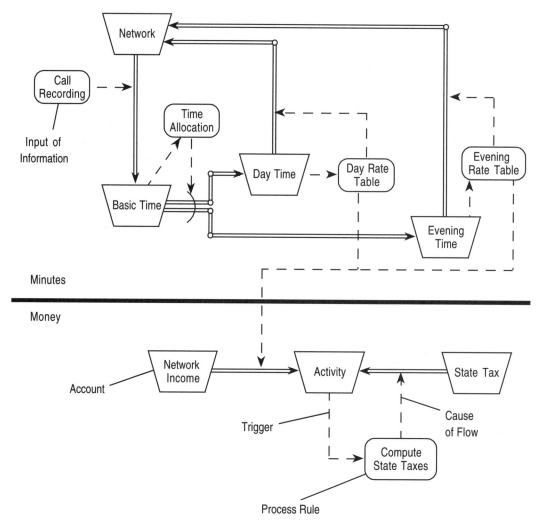

Figure 7.16   A more expressive diagram of the accounts and posting rules.

This diagram makes the flow of transactions explicit. Each posting rule is triggered by a single account and causes a number of flows. The direction of the flow shows where items are withdrawn and deposited. The diagram shows more information and is thus more complicated.

patterns, I strongly recommend using diagrams. Start with the ones suggested here and let the diagram standard evolve to one that is the most useful (and let me know what it is).

References

1. Beck, K. *Smalltalk Best Practice Patterns. Volume 1: Coding.* Englewood Cliffs, NJ: Prentice Hall, in press.

2. Gamma, E., R. Helm, R. Johnson, and J. Vlissides. *Design Patterns: Elements of Reusable Object-Oriented Software.* Reading, MA: Addison-Wesley, 1995.

3. Meyer, B. "Applying 'Design by Contract,'" *IEEE Computer*, 25,10 (1992), pp. 40–51.

8

Planning

Planning is a vital part of any large endeavor. Many managers spend most of their time developing and tracking plans. This chapter provides some basic patterns for planning. The patterns describe individual plans as well as protocols—standard procedures that can be used repeatedly.

Any action carried out within a domain can be recorded. The *proposed and implemented action (8.1)* pattern divides the possible states of an action into two key subtypes, which represent the intention and what actually happens. The end of an action is similarly divided into *completed and abandoned actions (8.2)*. An abandoned action represents a final cancellation of the action, and temporary holds on an action are represented by *suspension (8.3)*.

A *plan (8.4)* is used to hold a group of proposed actions. We discuss structures of plans that record the dependency and sequencing of a group of actions while allowing a single action to appear in several plans. The latter property is essential to choreographing multiple plans, which are one-off arrangements. A *protocol (8.5)* is used for standard plans that are repeated many times.

Carrying out an action requires resources. The *resource allocation (8.6)* pattern describes protocols for proposed and implemented actions. We consider two different kinds of resources: consumables, which are used by actions, and assets, which are used over time.

So far our discussion of plans has focused on planning and monitoring actions and has ignored the effects of the actions. The final pattern we discuss handles *outcome and start functions (8.7)*, which tie the patterns in this chapter with the observation and measurement patterns developed in Chapter 3. These functions allow us to say what we think an action has achieved (outcome), what a protocol should achieve (outcome function), and what conditions make us want to begin a protocol (start function).

Planning is a complex area, and the patterns in this chapter, even more than other chapters, are not intended to be complete. The patterns came out of the Cosmos Clinical Process Model [1], and its constructions are thus decidedly bent in directions that support health care planning. The resource side comes from unpublished discussions with the developers and users of Cosmos, and the influence of the NHS Common Basic Specification [2].

Key Concepts   Proposed Action, Implemented Action, Plan, Suspension, Resource Allocation, Asset, Consumable, Temporal Resource, Start Function, Outcome Function

8.1   Proposed and Implemented Action

The basis of any plan consists of the fundamental actions that people take. It is difficult to give any more than an outline description of what makes up an action. A plan can be coarse, consisting of large actions, or it can be fine-grained, consisting of small actions. Actions can have a range of properties, based on who, when, and where. With such coarse-grained properties it is difficult to provide more than the most generic terms of party, time reference, and location, as shown in Figure 8.1.

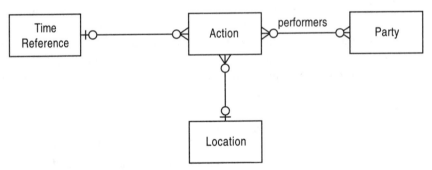

Figure 8.1   Properties of actions.

When making and monitoring plans, we must consider the many states that an action can go through. It can be scheduled, resourced, peopled, started, and completed. A state-transition diagram can record these states and how the transitions can occur. It is difficult to make any rules about these transitions. Scheduling an action and resourcing it can clearly happen in any order. A surface analysis may conclude that an action cannot be started before resourcing and scheduling. How do we deal with actions that are started before any formal decision is made to state a time for them? We could argue that such actions are scheduled a moment before they are started, but this sounds more like a management theory rationalization than a reflection of the real business process. Another problem arises with partial resourcing. Any project manager will tell you that in the real world, tasks are often begun before all the required resources are allocated. How can we reflect this situation in descriptions of action states?

The two important states of action are proposed and implemented actions, as shown in Figure 8.2. A proposed action is purely a proposal that exists in some plan. As such it can be scheduled by adding a time reference, resourced by adding parties, and located with the appropriate location. These changes can be made at any time, in any order. Once an action is begun, it is implemented. Not only is this a change in state, but also a separate implemented action object is created. This allows us to record differences between plan and implementation. By retaining the original proposed action, we can see the differences between the plan and reality. A common difference, for example, is the time reference; however, any attribute can change as planning documents finally turn into actions.

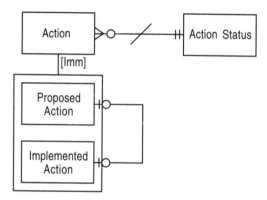

Figure 8.2   Basic structure of plans and actions.

Separate objects record the proposal and the implementation so that differences can be tracked.

Example   I decide to prepare a presentation for OOPSLA on July 1, 1997, but I don't get around to doing it until the 3rd. These actions can be represented as a proposed action with a date of July 1 and an implemented action with a date of July 3. All other attributes of the proposal are the same.

We can provide a derived action state property to make it easier to tell what state an action is in without navigating the various structures that record its state. This is not really necessary at this stage but becomes valuable as we consider additional structures later.

To retain the best degree of flexibility in recording daily actions, the links between proposed action and implemented action, as shown in Figure 8.2, are optional. Often the best laid plans gather dust without implementation, and many actions occur without any prior planning. We should resist the temptation to rationalize last-minute plans.

Example   Doctor Thursz orders a full blood count for John Smith, but the patient does not turn up for the test. This represents a proposed action without an implemented action. If the patient is rebooked for a later date, this constitutes a new proposed action.

Example   Doctor Cairns is called to attend a woman who is taken suddenly ill on a train. Here there is an implemented action but no proposed action.

8.2   Completed and Abandoned Actions

So far we have considered how actions are proposed and begin but not how they might end. Clearly actions either succeed or fail. The problem is that often we cannot determine success or failure with any certainty, especially in health care. Thus in this section we consider only two ending actions: completion and abandonment. Completion occurs when the action is carried out according to plan. Any consideration of the success or failure is left to further analysis (see Section 8.7). This definition can be too strict for domains other than health care, where success is more easily judged. The distinction between carrying out an action as expected and the action achieving its goal is still valuable.

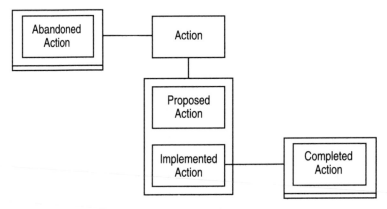

Figure 8.3   Completed and abandoned actions.

Abandonment is a complete and final cessation of the action. It can occur either before or after beginning to implement the action. Abandoning a proposed action is deciding not to begin it at all.

Example   A renal transplant provides renal function by replacing a damaged kidney with a donated working kidney. The renal transplant action is judged a success if the kidney is safely transplanted into the recipient. If the kidney is rejected later, this does not invalidate the success of the transplant procedure. The transplant procedure is still completed; it would be abandoned only if a problem occurs during the operation.

Example I chose to fly from London to Boston, expecting to arrive in Boston at 2:00 p.m. The flight is delayed, so I did not arrive until 7:00 p.m. This action was still completed, because I arrived in Boston that day. The delay I suffered meant that it was not a success. The proposed action to go to dinner that evening, however, was abandoned.

Example My car would not start, and I determined the problem was a faulty starter motor. I thus proposed and began to replace the starter motor. Just after beginning I found that the fault was actually a bad connection, and the starter motor was fine. I thus abandoned the action of replacing the starter motor, although I was not unhappy with the result!

8.3 Suspension

We can also put off actions, with the intention of continuing them later. When this occurs a suspension is linked to the action, as shown in Figure 8.4. The suspension is valid within its time period (which might be open ended). If an action continues after the end point of the suspension, the suspension still exists but is no longer suspending, and the action continues.

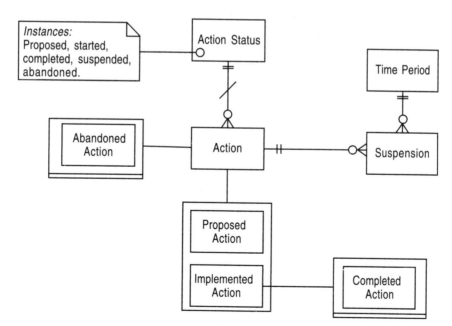

Figure 8.4 Suspension of actions.

A suspension is a temporary hold on an action.

Thus an action is suspended if it has currently open suspension. Both proposed and implemented actions can be suspended; suspending a proposed action is equivalent to postponing the start of an action.

Example A patient is on the waiting list for a renal transplant. This is represented by a proposed action of renal transplant. The patient has to wait for a kidney to become available. If the patient develops a cold while on the waiting list, the doctor must place a suspension on the patient. The transplant is not abandoned because the patient goes back on the waiting list when the cold abates. The record of the suspension is essential to explain why the doctor did not give a suitable kidney to the patient during that time.

Example I have a proposed action to wash the dishes. It is frequently suspended for long periods, but I never quite abandon it!

8.4   Plan

In its simplest sense a plan is a collection of proposed actions linked in some sequence. A sequence can be expressed in a number of ways, but most commonly it is expressed as a dependency—an indication that one action cannot begin until another completes. Plans are often described by using a dependency diagram, as in critical path analysis.

Figure 8.5 is a diagram of a dependency relationship between proposed actions. This structure is useful when the actions are always proposed as part of a single plan. In many situations, however, plans interact. When a doctor sets up a treatment plan for a patient, actions within that treatment plan are used by the nurses in setting up their nursing plans. It is not unusual for many caregivers to have plans for a patient, and it is important that these plans be properly choreographed. The structure shown in Figure 8.6 supports interaction by allowing an action to be referenced within multiple plans and for the dependencies to be drawn up between the references rather than between the actions.

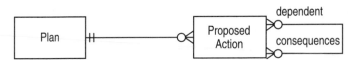

Figure 8.5   Dependencies between proposed actions.

This will only allow actions to be proposed within one plan, making it difficult to coordinate plans.

Example A doctor needs a full blood count for a patient. She checks the list of proposed actions and finds that another doctor has already proposed a full blood count as part of his plan. This is represented as the other doctor's plan having an action reference to the full blood count proposed action. A new plan can be created with a new action reference to the same proposed action.

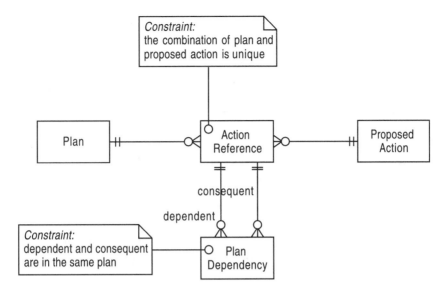

Figure 8.6   A plan consisting of references to proposed actions.

This structure allows actions to be referenced by several plans.

Example   I need to visit the liquor store to get some St. Emillion for a dinner on Saturday and Old Peculiar for a party on Sunday. The action of visiting the liquor store is referenced in both the plan for preparing for the dinner and the plan for the party. The dinner preparation's reference has a dependency where attending the dinner is the consequent and visiting the liquor store is the dependent. The party plan's reference has a dependency where beginning the party is the consequent and the visit to the liquor store is the dependent.

This notion of an action and a reference to an action within behavioral description is a common pattern in behavioral modeling. It is analogous to the definition of a subroutine and its call within another subroutine. The definition of the subroutine contains no information on how it is used within a calling program. The calling program has no knowledge of the contents of the subroutine.

The model in Figure 8.6 is a simple behavioral meta-model. A plan is a description of intended behavior, thus a behavioral modeling technique is appropriate. We can use any behavioral modeling technique. First we represent the technique by its meta-model. Then we tie the actions of the meta-model to the plan object and to the proposed actions. We should choose a behavioral model that is sophisticated without being overly complex.

Plans are always subject to change and can be replaced by other plans, as shown in Figure 8.7. The association is multivalued in both directions—as plans change, a single plan can be split up and replaced by separate plans, or several plans can be consolidated into one.

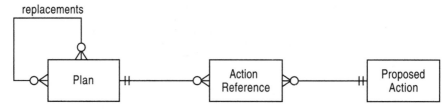

Figure 8.7   Replacement plans.

Example   I have a plan to buy bread at the Garden of Eden and cheese at Bread and Circus. I replace this by a plan to get a take-away from Jae's instead.

We can consider a plan to be a subtype of an action, as shown in Figure 8.8. Thus we can propose a plan (that is, we can plan for a plan) and monitor a plan to see if it is finished. Since planning is often quite complex, it is valuable to be able to schedule and track a plan's progress.

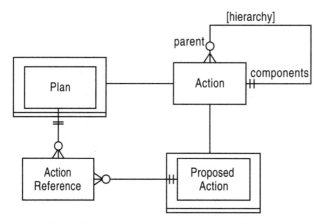

Figure 8.8   Plans as actions and compound actions.
We can plan to plan, and we can have complex actions without an explicit plan.

We can think of a plan as a way of aggregating actions. For example, a full blood count can be represented as a plan, with each component measurement as a proposed action within it. This is a very heavy-handed representation, however. The structure shown in Figure 8.8 also allows an action to be decomposed into component actions, but it allows two ways to represent actions being part of a larger action: Using the parent-component association works well for simple cases, and using a plan works well for more complex cases. We can restrict the parent-component association to a hierarchy so only the parent-component association is used for simple cases.

8.5   Protocol

An organization's standard operating procedures are common actions carried out many times in much the same way each time. We can describe these common actions, referred to here as protocols, using constructs similar to those we used for plans, as shown in Figure 8.9. Planning patterns, like other patterns in this book, can be divided into knowledge and operational levels. The operational levels describe the day-to-day plans and actions. At the knowledge level are protocols, which describe the standard procedures that guide the operational level.

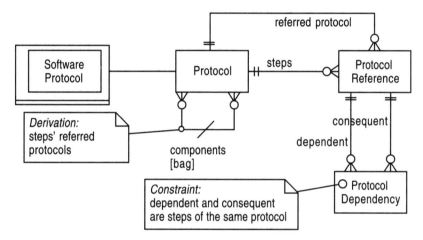

Figure 8.9   Structure for protocols.

It is a similar structure as the one for plans—a simple behavioral meta-model.

There are some interesting differences between the knowledge and operational levels in the structure. Using a hierarchic structure is much less useful at the knowledge level. Protocol can be referenced by many other protocols; it is hard to think of a case where restricting it would be useful. We can often effectively represent an action as part of another action in cases where we want to aggregate actions in a regular manner, such as the measurement as part of a full blood count.

There is no difference at the knowledge level between proposed and implemented actions, nor is there a valuable distinction between a plan and another group of actions. The components of a protocol are always a bag (since a protocol can be performed more than once within another), but the proposed actions of a plan always form a set (since you cannot do the same action twice, but you can have two actions with the same protocol).

A protocol need not be detailed with components. A protocol can be merely a name. It can be descriptions, textbook pages, Web pages, even a video of someone performing a particularly tricky surgical procedure. Protocol references can just describe components without any dependencies. Some protocols can be entirely coded into a computer, in which case they become a piece of software. (A software protocol is a protocol that is coded in software, not a protocol in the sense of a communications protocol.)

We can form actions from a complex protocol in two ways. The simplest way is to use the parent-component association. This technique works well when the component actions all take place in a well-bounded time period, and no one wants to share the component actions. We first create a proposed action for the whole protocol and only indicate the component actions if we have to specify particular properties, such as timing or resources. (If there are a lot of these particular properties, then we should use a plan.) If all actions are done by the same party at about the same time, the parent action is enough. A component action is created for each component protocol's reference; that is, a protocol carried out three times within a parent protocol would yield three component actions; any dependencies would exist exactly as in the protocol.

A plan offers greater flexibility and precision of tracking and thus is preferred when we want to monitor when and how individual protocol steps are carried out. These relationships are shown in Figure 8.10. In addition, a plan allows the component proposed actions to be picked up and shared with other plans. An important feature of plans is that, while they can copy the dependencies of the protocol, plans can also define new dependencies that might ignore that of the protocol. This ability is important in skilled professions such as health care, where we often have to override protocols to take into account the needs of individual patients. Frequently we need one-off plans, which are based on protocols but are not faithful copies.

Forming actions from a protocol will typically use plans at higher levels of the protocol, and use the parent-component association at lower levels.

8.5.1   Plans and Protocols as Graphs

We can also represent a plan as a directed acyclic graph (DAG) of proposed actions. The arcs on the graph correspond to the dependency relationships on the action references. Each plan has its own separate graph structure. We can represent this compactly as shown in Figure 8.11. This is, in essence, another association pattern in the style described in Chapter 15.

To apply this notion to a protocol, however, we do not form a DAG of the subsidiary protocols. Instead we form a DAG of the protocol references, as shown in Figure 8.12, because one protocol can appear as more than one step

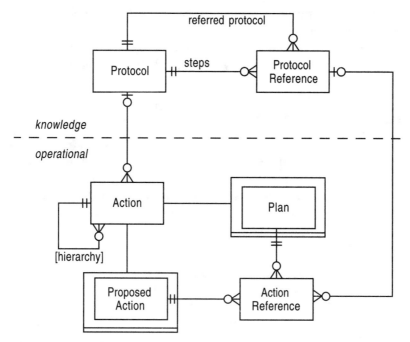

Figure 8.10   Relationships among action, plan, and protocol.

Figure 8.11   Plan as a directed acyclic graph of proposed actions.

in another parent protocol. This is specifically not the case for a plan due to the uniqueness constraint shown in Figure 8.6. The base form for a DAG association pattern thus includes the dependency types (with the constraint) together with the fact that the element in the DAG can only appear as one node in a DAG.

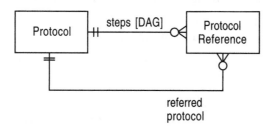

Figure 8.12   Protocol using a DAG.

If we use a graph for the plan structure we lose the ability to build the association between the plan reference and the protocol reference that is shown in Figure 8.10. Naturally we could still have the DAG version as a derived mapping; the derivation would include how to derive the graph's arcs.

8.6   Resource Allocation

The second major part of planning is allocating resources. A primary difference between proposed and implemented actions lies in how they use resources. An implemented action will actually use resources allocated to it. A proposed action will book some resources. Figure 8.13 shows resource allocation as a quantity of some resource type. Resources can only be booked by one action and used by one action.

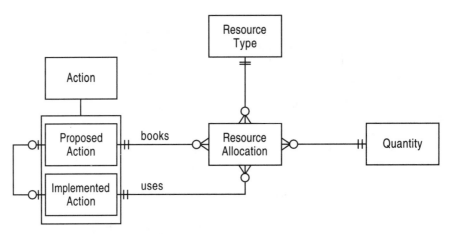

Figure 8.13   Action's use of resources.

Proposed actions book resources, and implemented actions use resources.

There are various kinds of resources. The first and most obvious is a consumable. Consumables are such things as drugs, needles, and raw materials. Consumables can be used only once and are used up by the action that uses them. Typically consumables are asked for by quantity.

Example   A resource allocation of 10 gallons of orange juice has a quantity of 10 gallons and resource type of orange juice.

Example   For a particular hip replacement operation, four units of packed red cells (blood) are booked, but only two are used. This can be represented by two resource allocations of the resource type packed red cells. One is linked to the proposed hip replacement with quantity four units; the other is linked to the implemented hip replacement with quantity two units.

Some resources are not consumed, such as equipment, rooms, and people. In no sense is a person consumed by an action (although after writing this book I wonder). However, we can say that a person's time is used up. In this case the resource type is the person, and the quantity is time. Thus my spending five hours on an action is a resource allocation of five hours of me.

This is somewhat too individual a view of resource types. Resource types, which lie at the knowledge level, more typically indicate a kind of thing rather than the thing itself. Projects that I work on demand five hours of an experienced OO modeler rather than me in particular. Although some people are sufficiently singular to be resource types in their own right, most of us mortals are merely one of many.

In planning, therefore, the requirement is stated as "We need five hours of an OO modeler." At some stage in the planning process, this is resolved by booking five hours of me, a specific instance of the resource type. This implies two levels of resource allocation: a general one where only the type is specified and a specific allocation where the individual is specified.

In Figure 8.14 the individual is referred to as an asset. Assets are classified by asset type, which is just a kind of resource type. The difference

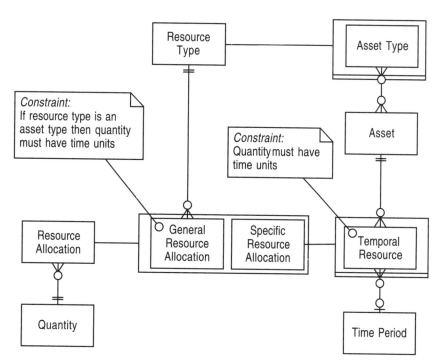

Figure 8.14   Resource allocations for assets.

Specific allocations name the individual asset used or booked. General allocations only specify the type of asset.

between a specific resource type and a general resource type is that the former links to the asset and the latter to a resource type, which for an asset would be an asset type. A temporal resource is a specific resource allocation of an asset. It can have not just an amount of time but also a specific time period. This period can be derived from the action that books or uses the temporal resource, or it can be separate.

Example   A modeling meeting is scheduled to be held in a small conference room for a couple of hours. Initially this is represented as a proposed action that books a general resource allocation. The resource type of the general resource allocation is the asset type small conference room. The quantity of the general resource allocation is two hours. At some later point the actual conference room is booked as Q9. This reclassifies (or replaces) the general resource allocation to a temporal resource of two hours of the asset Q9. If the proposed action of the meeting is booked between 2:00 and 5:00 p.m. on Tuesday, then that time period is the derived time period of the allocation of Q9. If the last hour of the meeting is to be held in the pub, then a time period of 2:00 to 4:00 p.m. on Tuesday is linked to the temporal resource.

The asset is allowed to have several asset types. This multiple classification of assets is important to represent those assets that can do several things, although not necessarily at once.

Example   If the conference room Q9 has projection facilities, it can be classified as both a small conference room and a presentation room. It cannot be booked as both at the same time by separate actions.

Specific resource allocation is less important for consumables. For example, it is usually enough to say that 10 gallons of orange juice were booked and used by an action without being more specific about which 10 gallons. With assets we usually need to be specific because there is a greater likelihood for contention between parties about use of assets.

At this point it is worth considering whether the relationships from subtypes of the action shown in Figure 8.13 should be specialized. For example, it may be reasonable to say that implemented actions can only use specific resource allocations of assets. Assuming that this is something that is required (and I'm not sure that it is in general), there are several ways of doing it. This brings up a good example of how a business rule can be modeled in different ways.

The first, and most obvious, way is to introduce a structural constraint. In this case we can use a rule such as "Implemented actions cannot use general resource allocations whose resource type is an asset type." This eager checking is an aggressive way to enforce the business rule. It says that you are not allowed to record a situation that violates the policy.

This can be too strong a way to do things, however. Sometimes it makes sense to allow a situation that violates the policy to be recorded, and to have a separate checking phase later. This lazy checking can be done by having some operation on implemented action (such as `isConsistent()`) and having that operation return true if the business rule is followed. This provides greater flexibility in handling situations where a full constraint might not be available from the beginning. The incomplete information is recorded, and a means for checking it is provided.

The great advantage of lazy checking is that it separates the resolution of the problem from the recording of the information. People recording the information can make their best attempt at the time, and then either they or a more qualified person can clear things up later. If matters can be resolved easily at the point of information capture, then eager checking is better.

Whether to allow general resource allocation of assets to implemented actions depends on the specific problem. If the needs of the domain are satisfied by knowing that it took two hours of an OO modeler without knowing which one, then general allocation of asset types should be allowed. This question may be dependent on the asset type. For example, hospital policy may dictate that all implemented allocations of consultants must be specific, although orderlies may be allocated generally.

We can use specific resource allocation with consumables if we are concerned with removing the consumable from some finite store that we have to track. In such cases we want to say that the consumable is taken from a particular holding of that consumable, as shown in Figure 8.15. Holdings can be

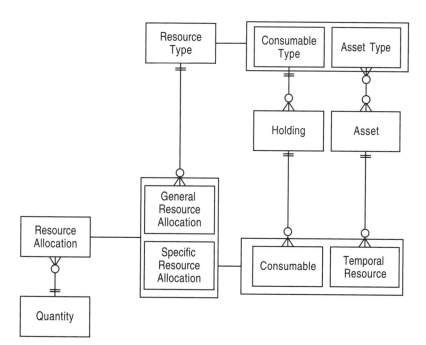

Figure 8.15   Allowing specific allocations of consumables.

organized in various ways, depending on the resource tracking process, which I am not considering here. However, it is worth saying that a holding can be seen as an account and a resource allocation as an entry, following the approach described in Section 6.14.

Resource allocations can also be used by protocols to describe the resources needed for a protocol to be carried out. In this case we use general resource allocations.

Example To make chapati (Indian bread) you need ¼ cup of flour, ⅛ cup of water, ¼ tablespoon of oil, and a pinch of salt. This can be represented as four general resource allocations.

8.7   Outcome and Start Functions

In this section we use concepts developed in Chapter 3 to consider reasons why we form a plan and how we can gauge its success.

Plans are initiated by observations, which, of course, can be hypotheses or projections. Similarly their outcomes are observations linked to the actions within the plan, as shown in Figure 8.16. Like many aspects of observation, the outcome link is dependent on the eyes of the performer. Thus some parties may not see an observation as the outcome of an action while others would. We would record this situation by having more than one observation by different performers.

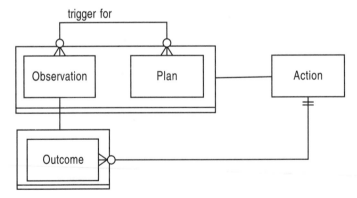

Figure 8.16   Links between observation, plan, and action.

Example John Smith came to his doctor with the classic symptoms of diabetes: weight loss, thirst, and polyuria. The doctor creates a plan triggered by these observations. The plan includes a proposed action to carry out a blood glucose measurement.

Example After experiencing poor sales, a company decides to improve the sales force's commission and to cut prices. Some analysts might say that the improved sales were the outcome of the increase in commission, others might say the improvement was the outcome of the cut in prices. Separate observations would be made by each group, with links to different actions.

Note that observations are a subtype of actions. They can be scheduled, timed, have performers, and be parts of plans. Their additional behavior is that they identify an observation concept or measure a phenomenon type.

A similar set of linkages appears at the knowledge level using start functions and outcome functions, as shown in Figure 8.17. A start function contains information on conditions that are likely to trigger the use of a protocol. Following the example of associative functions, the model records the observation concepts and protocols used as arguments to the start function but does not specify how they are combined. The intention is for different kinds of start functions to have different methods for combining them.

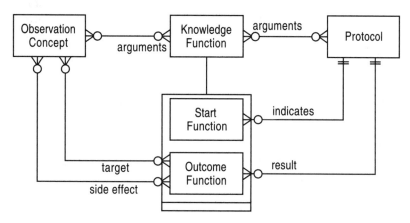

Figure 8.17   The use of start and outcome functions at the knowledge level.

Start functions indicate the conditions for beginning an action, and outcome functions indicate the targets and side effects.

Example   The protocol add oil is indicated by a start function with an argument of low oil level.

Example   Beta-blockers are a treatment for hypertension and angina but should not be used if the patient has asthma. This leads to three start functions, all of which indicate beta-blocker treatment. (Beta-blocker treatment is a protocol with a resource allocation of the resource type beta-blocker.) Two start functions, one with the argument hypertension and one with the argument angina, have a simple body with no processing, which is a straightforward indication. The third has the argument asthma and is a body of logical negation. (We could have a contra-indication subtype of start function, but it all really depends on the way the arguments are processed.)

Outcome functions operate similarly. Again the input is a combination of protocols and observation concepts. The result is two sets of observation concepts. Some observation concepts represent the target use of the protocol, that is, the effects that represent the purpose of the protocol. The other observation concepts are the side effects. A protocol can have many results. This may reflect other protocols or observation concepts that the patient might have at that time. These are introduced as arguments inherited from the knowledge function.

Example Decreasing prices have an outcome function with a target of increased market share and a side effect of reduced revenue per unit sold.

Example The protocol liver transplant has an outcome function with a target of good liver function and side effects of organ rejection and biliary stricture (narrowing of the bowel duct). The start function can also include information on the likelihoods of these conditions arising. Separate outcome functions might exist with the same target and side effects but with arguments representing diseases that affect the procedure. These separate outcome functions indicate different likelihoods for the target and side effects due to presence of the disease arguments.

References

1. Cairns, T., A. Casey, M. Fowler, M. Thursz, and H. Timimi. *The Cosmos Clinical Process Model*. National Health Service, Information Management Centre, 15 Frederick Rd, Birmingham, B15 1JD, England. Report ECBS20A & ECBS20B <http://www.sm.ic.ac.uk/medicine/cpm>, 1992.
2. IMC. *Common Basic Specification Generic Model*. National Health Service, Information Management Centre, 1992.

9

Trading

This chapter looks at the buying and selling of goods and at the value of these goods with respect to changing market conditions. Using the experience of building a trading system for a bank, the chapter looks at buying and selling from both angles, where the bank buys and sells the same goods. The bank has to understand the value of the net effect of these trades in different circumstances.

Each trade is described by a *contract (9.1)*. The contract can either buy or sell goods and is useful for businesses that need to track both directions of deals. We can look at the net effect of a number of contracts by using a *portfolio (9.2)*. We design portfolios so we can assemble them easily to select contracts in different ways. We give the portfolio a separate object, the portfolio filter, to define the selection criteria. The portfolio filter defines an interface that can be implemented by various subtypes. This construction provides flexibility for simple and complex selection criteria. It is a useful technique for defining collections in a flexible manner.

To understand the value of a contract, we need to understand the price of the goods being traded. Goods are often priced differently depending on whether they are bought or sold. This two-way pricing behavior can be captured by a *quote (9.3)*.

In volatile markets, prices can change rapidly. Traders need to value goods against a range of possible changes. The *scenario (9.4)* puts together a combination of conditions that can act as a single state of the market for valuation. Scenarios can be complex, and we need a way to define their construction so we can use the same scenario construction at different times in a consistent manner. Scenarios are useful for any domain with complex price changes.

This chapter is based on a project to develop a foreign exchange derivatives trading system for a major bank.

Key Concepts   Contract, Portfolio, Quote, Scenario

9.1   Contract

The simplest kind of financial deal is that of buying some instrument from another party. The instrument can be stock, a commodity, foreign exchange, or any other commonly traded item. A basic starting point is the model shown in Figure 9.1. This model has a contract that is a deal with another party, referred to as the counterparty, involving some amount of an instrument. Only a single instrument is shown, although strictly speaking all trading involves two instruments—one instrument being traded for another. For most markets one instrument is always the currency prevailing in the market. The price is thus represented as a money object. Money is a subtype of quantity (see Section 3.1) whose unit is a currency.

In foreign exchange markets the instrument is the exchange rate. This might seem odd, but really all instruments are exchange rates. A contract to sell stock on the Dow is really a contract to exchange stock for dollars. In most cases it is easier to represent this by saying that the instrument is exchanged for the currency of the price, but for exchange rates it is better to have both currencies on the instrument and let the price be a simple number.

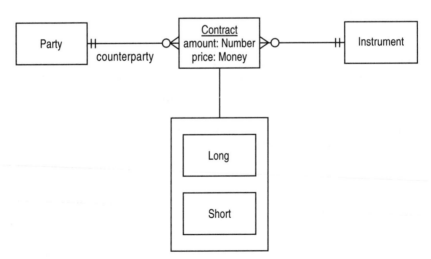

Figure 9.1   Simple model for a contract.

The amount of the instrument is traded with the counterparty. Long and short are terms for buy and sell, respectively. The single counterparty limits the contracts that can be represented.

The terms *long* and *short* are the terms traders use for buy and sell, respectively. (Computer people are not the only ones with strange jargon!) Figure 9.1 shows the difference between long and short with subtyping notation. An alternative is to have a Boolean attribute isLong. Either method is acceptable, but I prefer the explicitness of Figure 9.1 in conceptual modeling. Subtyping and a Boolean attribute are equivalent in conceptual modeling; subtyping does not imply subclassing. In an implementation modeling technique (when subtyping does imply subclassing), Figure 9.1 is not appropriate unless the behavior of the long and short differ (and possibly not even then). An interface model can go either way. Section 14.2 describes how this transformation can be made to preserve the same interface whether subclasses or flags are used.

Example   Megabank sells 1000 shares of Aroma Coffee Makers stock to Martin Fowler at $30. This is a short contract whose counterparty is Martin Fowler, the instrument is Aroma Coffee Makers stock, the amount is 1000, and the price is $30.

Example   Megabank sells 2 million US dollars (USD) for 1 million British pounds (GBP) from British Railways. This is a long contract in which the counterparty is British Railways, the amount is 1 million, the price is 2, and the instrument is GBP/USD. Alternatively it could be a short contract in which the amount is 2 million, the price is 0.5, and the instrument is USD/GBP.

Example   Northeast Steel sells 10,000 tons of steel to Chrysler. For Chrysler this is a long contract with a counterparty of Northeast Steel. The instrument is steel, in which case the amount changes to a quantity to allow 10,000 tons to be represented. (An alternative is to allow the instrument to be tons of steel, but that is less flexible for other quantities.)

This style of model is good for capturing deals done between the host organization and other parties. Often, however, deals are done internally within the host organization, such as between the options desk and the commodities desk. These internal deals are used in the management of risk. A common example is a deal to offset the risk of an option (called a hedge). Such internal deals raise the question of who is the internal party. The model shown in Figure 9.2 presents a more flexible way of answering this question. Two parties are shown on a contract: the long (buyer) and the short (seller). In

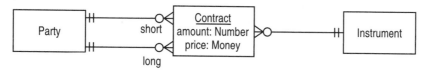

Figure 9.2   Indicating buyers and sellers by separate relationships.

Having two parties supports internal deals, completely external deals, and dealing with different parties within the host organization.

this kind of representation, the options desk and the commodities desk are represented as separate parties. If the options desk does an option with an external party and hedges it with a deal with the commodities desk, then the options desk would be a party to each contract. If the options desk were the long party in the option, it would be short in the hedge contract.

Figure 9.3 represents a similar situation in a slightly different way. Again the use of two relationships allows internal deals to be represented. However, here there is a notion of primary party and counterparty rather than long and short. The host bank party is always the primary party when doing a deal with an outside organization. In internal deals the choice between primary party and counterparty is arbitrary, although by convention the primary party is usually the one that initiates the deal. The subtype of long and short is the nature of the deal as seen by the primary party.

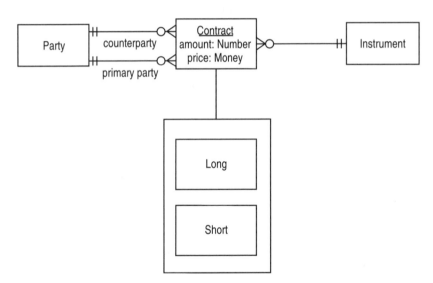

Figure 9.3   Counterparty and primary party.

This is less concise than Figure 9.2 but can better support the traders' view.

On initial analysis the model shown in Figure 9.3 looks less valuable than the model shown in Figure 9.2 because it adds an extra pair of subtypes without any great advantage. Certainly a data modeling view would reject this on the basis of a more complex data structure. The important issue, in terms of OO modeling, is interface. Is it more useful to provide operations that ask for primary and counterparty and the contract as long or short, or is it more useful to have a long and short party? It may be that the model shown in Figure 9.4, which essentially provides both interfaces, is the best. The deciding factor is what is most useful to the users of the concepts. For our example system, the Figure 9.3 model was more meaningful to the traders than that of Figure 9.2 and proved more useful in constructing software, although the Figure 9.4 interface was ultimately provided.

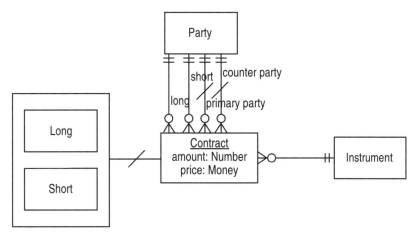

Figure 9.4   Using four party mappings.

This covers all points of view by deriving the duplicate elements.

Modeling Principle   *When more than one equivalent set of features can be provided, pick the one that the domain expert is most comfortable with. If the domain expert feels that both are very valuable, show both and mark one derived.*

The choice of what to make derived in Figure 9.4 is quite arbitrary. We could equally well make the long or short mapping derived. The model should not constrain the implementor who can use either kind of implementation. It could be argued that you could make nothing derived but simply use rules (such as, if the contract is short, then the short party is the same object as the primary party). I prefer to show some derivations to make the interrelationships explicit, but ultimately it is more a matter of modeling taste.

Modeling Principle   *Marking a feature as derived is a constraint on the interface and does not affect the underlying data structures.*

A consequence of the models shown in Figures 9.2–9.4 is that contracts can be recorded that do not involve the host bank. We can avoid this by forcing at least the primary party to be a party of the host bank. Alternatively we can ask the domain expert if holding these deals would be useful. Salespeople often like to record deals that their customers have made with other banks because it gives them information on their customers' possible risk profiles and allows them to sell a contract to improve matters. Here the flexibility of the model supports new business capabilities.

An open issue is the relationship between a contract in this trading model and a transaction in one of the accounting models from Chapter 6. A trade can be seen as a transaction that, for example, withdraws 1000 shares of Aroma Coffee Makers stock from a Megabank account and deposits them in a Martin Fowler account, while transferring the appropriate amount of money in the opposite direction. Both trades and transactions are useful, but for different purposes. More modeling needs to be done to explore their interrelationships.

9.2 Portfolio

We rarely consider contracts alone, especially when we are managing risk. Typically a bank will look at a group of related contracts and assess their joint risk. This might be the contracts dealt by a single trader, the contracts in a particular instrument, the contracts with a particular counterparty, or some other combination.

In essence a portfolio is a collection of contracts, as shown in Figure 9.5. Portfolios and contracts can be valued by pricing them according to some scenario. A scenario is a representation of the state of the market, either real or hypothetical (we will discuss scenarios in more detail in Section 9.4). The value of a portfolio is essentially the sum of the values of the underlying contracts.

Figure 9.5   Introducing portfolios.

A portfolio is a collection of contracts that can be valued as a whole.

A key question lies in the cardinality of the mapping from contract to portfolio. Whether a contract can sensibly lie in more than one portfolio depends on how we create and use the portfolios. If a portfolio is a trader's book, then a contract lies in the portfolio of the trader who is managing the deal. This, however, does not allow all trades with a particular counterparty to be considered together. Thus there seems to be an advantage in allowing a contract to lie in many portfolios. Portfolios can thus be built to manage risk according to different perspectives.

Using portfolios in this way raises another question, however. Suppose we need to form a portfolio that contains all contracts done with a particular counterparty. We could build an application that would search all contracts and assign them to portfolios. A better way, however, is to get the portfolio to assign contracts. We can give a portfolio a Boolean method, which takes a contract as an argument as shown in Figure 9.6. The portfolio then consists of all contracts for which the Boolean method evaluates to true. This allows us to construct portfolios that can select any combination of properties of a contract and then carry out the management functions of a portfolio on this derived set.

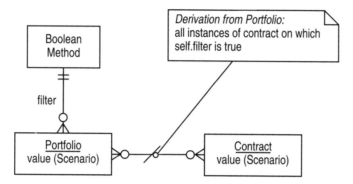

Figure 9.6 Dynamic portfolios with filters.

This allows portfolios to be described implicitly by properties of the contract.

Modeling Principle *If a set of objects can be formed with various criteria, a portfolio should be used.*

Allowing portfolios to have methods so that they can form themselves with contracts is a powerful notion. It means that there is no need to choose a single structure to consider groups of contracts. Various structures can be used, in an ad hoc manner. Once such a structure is defined, it can be remembered as used in the future and its contents regularly updated. The structure can be defined at any time, long after the original contract was put together. In effect we are making a query, and the resulting collection of objects becomes an object in its own right.

How is the Boolean method implemented? In general the method can be any block of code that returns true or false when given a contract as an argument. Smalltalk programmers can see that assigning a single argument block as an instance variable of portfolio would provide the desired capability. C++ programmers can use roughly the same principle, although it is more tricky since C++ needs a compiled function. This is the same problem as the individual instance methods discussed in Section 6.6.

In the abstract the Boolean method might be the best approach, but in practice a simpler method does as well. Portfolios are commonly formed from a number of properties of contracts, including counterparty, dealer (the primary party), instrument, and dates of the deal. We can combine these attributes into a particular contract selector object, as shown in Figure 9.7. A contract selector is not as general as a Boolean method and can only handle a limited range of filtering. However, it is easy to set up; the user can configure it easily with a suitable user interface. If we use a contract selector to handle most of the portfolios needed by the user, we can considerably reduce the amount of programming required.

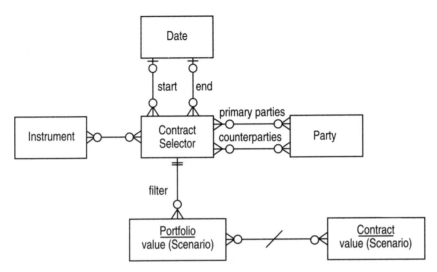

Figure 9.7 Contract selectors.

Note that this is an example of a parameterized method (see Section 6.6.4). It cannot select all possible portfolios, but it can cover most portfolios used in practice more easily than the completely general case.

Example A portfolio consists of all deals involving Aroma Coffee Makers stock sold to John Smith. This portfolio has a filter with Aroma Coffee Makers stock as an instrument and John Smith as a counterparty.

We are not forced to choose between contract selectors and Boolean methods for our filters. We can have the best of both worlds by using the model shown in Figure 9.8. This model abstracts the interfaces of both the Boolean method and the contract selector into a single, abstract type—the portfolio filter. This allows us to use the contract selector for simple cases and use a range of hard-coded filters for more complex situations. We can easily add other portfolio filters. This is an example of the strategy pattern [1].

Modeling Principle *When making a process a feature of a type, the process should be given an abstract interface so that the implementation can easily vary by subclassing. A purely hard-coded implementation is one subclass, various parameter driven approaches are others.*

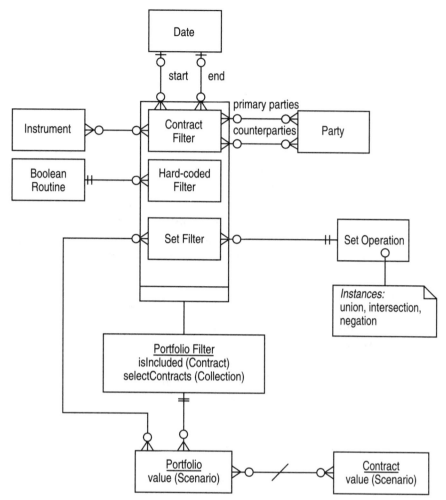

Figure 9.8 Provision of several portfolio filters.

This model provides both flexibility to handle the complicated cases and simple parameterization for the simple cases. It is a combination of strategy and parameterized implementations (see Section 6.6).

The select operation on the portfolio filter takes a collection of contracts and returns another collection of contracts. For each contract in the input collection, the select operation evaluates isIncluded and, if true, adds it to the result. Subclasses of the portfolio filter override isIncluded to provide their specific behaviors. A portfolio may use isIncluded to check individual contracts.

I should add a word about the naming of portfolio *filter* and contract *selector*. People I've worked with found the distinction between the terms quite valuable in practice. A selector selects objects of the type it is named after; thus a contract selector is used to select contracts, and it returns a collection of contracts. A filter selects some other type on behalf of its named type and is designed to be used with its named type. Hence a portfolio filter selects contracts for a portfolio. By sticking to a consistent naming, it is easier to remember the responsibilities of these two kinds of objects: The filter is only a selection mechanism, but the portfolio adds additional behavior, such as producing an overall value. In addition, the portfolio is referred to by other parts of the system, while the filter is only used for selection purposes.

Portfolios can be transient or persistent. Transient portfolios are filled on demand. The filter is specified, and all instances of the contract are checked to see if they match the filter. Once a client has finished with the portfolio, it is discarded. Persistent portfolios are created in the same way but are not discarded. When new contracts are created, they are checked against existing persistent portfolios. If they match the filter, they are added to the portfolio. Any processing based on the portfolio must then be updated, ideally incrementally. Persistent portfolios provide much faster query performance but slow down creation of contracts and use up storage. An essential modeling principle is that users should be unaware of whether portfolios are transient or persistent. Portfolios should switch from one to the other without requiring any action by the user. This requires that a new portfolio filter be checked against any existing persistent portfolio filters. If a matching one exists, then the existing portfolio should be referenced rather than a new portfolio created.

Portfolios are useful in many domains. The essential characteristic of a portfolio is that of an object that encapsulates a selection mechanism for choosing a group of objects of some type. The portfolio acts as a basis for some further summary processing. This processing can be a client object, as in this chapter, or it can be built into the portfolio itself.

Example   A car manufacturer can develop portfolios of produced cars for summarizing production and fault data. Filters can select cars according to their plant, model, shift of production, or some date range.

Example   Public health is a significant branch of health care that deals with the health of populations of patients. We can select populations according to a range of characteristics: age, where they live, observation concepts that apply, and so on. These populations can be defined by filters, and then observations can then be made about them, such as the average peak flow rate for people who smoke more than 20 cigarettes a day. (The population is a portfolio of people where the filter is smokes more than 20 cigarettes a day.[1])

---

[1] The filter on the cigarette is a different matter.

9.3   Quote

Anything traded on a financial market has a price. That price, however, is not usually a single number. Two numbers are quoted: the price to buy (the bid) and the price to sell (the offer). We can model this using a pair of numbers to represent the prices, as shown in Figure 9.9.

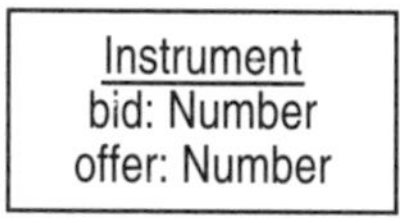

```
Instrument
bid: Number
offer: Number
```

Figure 9.9   Representing the price through two numeric properties.

An instrument can be valued using numbers or money objects. Typically stocks are valued using money but exchange rates have numbers. A quote behaves the same in either case. (We can think of a quote as a parameterized type.)

Although two numbers are common, they are not always used. Sometimes the quote is a single price, which represents the mid-value of the price. A single price is quoted with a spread—the difference between the bid and the offer. On other occasions we may see only a bid, or only an offer. This affects the way the quote is displayed. In foreign exchange markets an exchange rate such as USD/GBP might be quoted as 0.6712/5, which indicates a bid of 0.6712 and an offer of 0.6715. If only a bid is present, the quote is shown as 0.6712/; an offer-only quote appears as /0.6715.

Any object that may have two-way pricing—such as exchange rates, commodities, and so on—requires a number of behaviors as shown in Figure 9.10. Pulling these behaviors out into a separate quote object, as shown in Figure 9.11, provides all behaviors needed for two-way pricing. Anything that has a quote as a price requires a quote property.

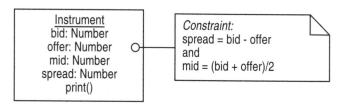

Figure 9.10   Behaviors required to support two-way prices.

A quote becomes a fundamental type and as such can best be represented as an attribute in those modeling methods that distinguish between attributes and object types. It is important to remember that an attribute does not represent the data structure, merely the presence of suitable operations.

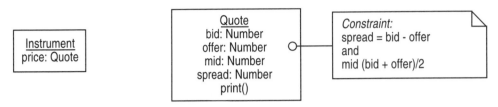

Figure 9.11   Using a separate quote object.

This is a good approach since it brings the particular responsibilities together into a simple reusable concept.

Example   The USD/GBP rate is 0.6712/6. The instrument is USD/GBP. This instrument has a quote with a bid of 0.6712, an offer of 0.6716, a mid of 0.6714, and a spread of 0.0004.

Example   A CD exchange sells used full-price CDs for $12 and buys them for $8. The bid is $12, the offer is $8, the mid is $10, and the spread is $4. The instrument is a full-price classical CD (even for a Chopin nocturne).

Modeling Principle   *When multiple attributes interact with a behavior that might be used in several types, the attributes should be combined into a new fundamental type.*

Two-way prices are common, but sometimes one-way prices are used. Modeling one-way prices is somewhat tricky. One alternative is to allow the price either to be a quote or a number. This is nearly impossible in strongly typed languages such as C++. Even in Smalltalk the client of stock is forced to determine what kind of object the price returns before doing anything with it.

An alternative is to make the quote a subtype of the number. This can work because quotes can respond to arithmetic operations, but it still forces the client to be conscious of the differences whenever manipulating stock prices, other than for printing. In C++, where number is not a built-in type but real and integer are, this method should not be used unless a number class is provided.

Another alternative is to make number a subtype of quote. Conceptually this has a definite appeal. Numbers are just simple quotes, and it is not too difficult to consider that every instance of a number is an instance of a quote, with identical bid and offer. (A similar argument can be used to say that number is a subtype of complex number.) Although the argument has conceptual merit, it falls down with an interface model. For a number to be a subtype of a quote, it must inherit the complete interface of the quote. A quote is only useful for a few domains, while a number is useful in almost every domain. Subtyping from a quote means that the quote is used in all domains, including many where the quote's behavior is not useful. A quote must be designed so it has visibility to number, and not the other way round.

Modeling Principle   *A generalization should not be used where the supertype is in a narrow domain and the subtype is widely used.*

At this point we should consider what commonalities exist between quotes in their two-way and one-way forms. Two alternatives exist: Either a one-way quote is treated as a quote, with the bid equal to the offer, or it is an error to ask for a bid or offer on a one-way quote. The former points to the presence of an abstract quote, as shown in Figure 9.12, while the latter avoids any such generalization. In the first alternative the client can treat the one-way and two-way quotes with the same behavior and not be concerned with differences. However, this can lead to inaccuracies because the client cannot be sure of dealing with the bid of a two-way quote. A type test operation (`isTwoWay` or `hasType ('TwoWayQuote')`) is needed so that the client can make the test. With no abstract quote, these inaccuracies cannot occur, but the client must use the type test every time an operation is invoked to know whether the operation is safe to use.

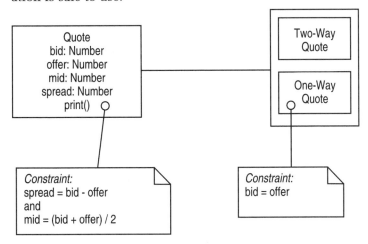

Figure 9.12   Abstract quote with subtypes.

One-way prices are treated as a special case of two-way prices.

The decision hinges on how often it is acceptable to ignore the difference between two- and one-way quotes. If it is almost never acceptable, then it is best not to have an abstract quote type. However, if it is frequently acceptable (which practice suggests it is), then I would strongly encourage the use of an abstract quote type. It is important to note that using the abstract quote never requires more effort by the client than not using one. It saves effort when the distinction is not required.

Modeling Principle   *If the difference between two similar types is often ignored, then an abstract supertype can be used. If the distinction between them is usually important, then an abstract supertype should not be used.*

Modeling Principle   *If an abstract type never needs more effort for a client to use it, then it should be provided.*

The abstract quote subsumes all the behavior of the subtypes because there is no additional operation or association on the subtypes. Typically we do not use subclasses to implement the subtyping of an abstract quote, especially since such a fundamental object usually uses containment in C++. An internal flag in a quote class is a more likely implementation, especially since we often need to par a two-way quote (that is, turn it into a one-way quote) and vice versa, which requires dynamic classification.

An implicit quote can be either a buy or a sell, in which case two-way prices are not needed. Only when both buying and selling are required are two-way quotes needed.

Sometimes we want to represent the price of a contract as a quote. Often when counterparties ask the price for a contract, they do not specify the direction; in that case the trader replies with a quote. By holding on to the quote, the trader remembers what the spread was when the contract was quoted. The actual amount charged can easily be derived from the direction of the contract and the quote.

9.4   Scenario

The price of an instrument is never constant; otherwise, the stock markets of the world would be much less interesting places. We need to be able to show how prices can change over time and to keep a history of those changes. We can do this by placing a timepoint on the quote, as shown in Figure 9.13, or by placing a timepoint on the relationship between the instrument and the quote, as shown in Figure 9.14. The difference between the two methods is small but significant. In the former, the quote is responsible for both its two-way nature and its time-dependent behavior. In the latter method those responsibilities are separated. Since I see a quote as a fundamental type that should kept as simple as possible, I prefer to use the approach shown in Figure 9.14.

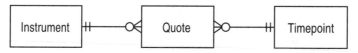

Figure 9.13   Adding a timepoint to a quote.

The timepoint indicates at what time the quote is correct for the instrument.

In these models, finding the closing prices for a market involves taking all the stocks within that market and looking for the latest quotes for each stock. Another alternative is to treat this collection of quotes as an object in its own right—a scenario, as shown in Figure 9.15. The scenario represents the state

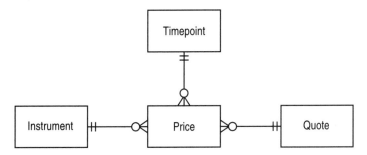

Figure 9.14   A price made for a stock at a particular time.

This separates the two-way behavior (quote) from the notion of a value for an instrument at a timepoint (price).

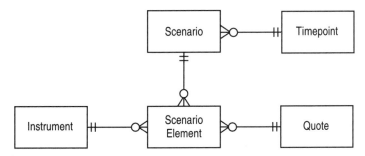

Figure 9.15   Scenario

This allows a group of prices at a single time to be treated as a single object.

of the market at a certain point in time, and the elements within the scenario represent the prices at that point.

If we only want to capture the published prices of a stock exchange, then a scenario seems to add little to the picture. It is easily generated by looking at the timepoints in the nonscenario model. The important question here is where the trader gets prices. One source is the exchange's public quotes. For those that manage funds of stocks, another consideration is possible future prices. Much of the effort of fund managers and traders goes into managing the risks of their portfolios as market conditions change. This risk management involves looking at alternative situations and considering their effects on prices of assets.

Example   A fund manager is managing a portfolio of stocks. She is concerned with the possibility of a fall in oil prices, which would boost the prices of many stocks but decrease the price of others, such as oil companies. This manager wants to look at several falls of differing magnitudes and consider how they affect a portfolio. Each of these falls leads to a different scenario.

Example A production manager is assessing likely production costs for cars. The costs of raw materials and labor are instruments concerned with pricing. Several scenarios can be constructed with different likely values for these instruments.

The above examples are hypothetical cases that show the strength of the scenario approach. The scenario object provides a base to pull together all the factors in a hypothetical case so that different cases can be compared easily.

We also need to consider markets that do not have a single publisher for a price, such as the foreign exchange market. In such cases we need to add the party that is publishing the price to the model. Figures 9.16 and 9.17 show earlier models with publishing parties added. Both the scenario and non-scenario approaches are effective, and again the need for hypothetical scenarios for risk management is the deciding factor.

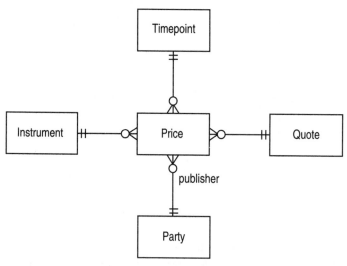

Figure 9.16   Model in Figure 9.14 with a publishing party.

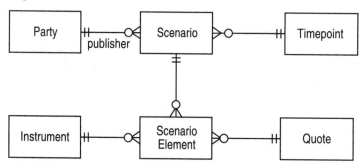

Figure 9.17   Model in Figure 9.15 with a publishing party.

Using a publisher is one more reason to use a scenario.

Example   An import/export merchant considers the prices of goods in a number of European countries. We can describe these prices by forming a scenario where the instruments are the goods he is interested in trading. By looking at the differences between these markets, using two-way prices, he can look for opportunities where the price difference is greater than the cost of transporting the goods (a process referred to as arbitrage).

Modeling Principle   *Scenarios should be used when a combination of prices or rates should be considered as a group.*

9.4.1   Defining How to Build a Scenario

Where do prices come from? In some cases this can be a simple question, for instance, when prices are published by an exchange. In other cases, particularly when there are hypothetical scenarios, more complex schemes might be used.

In broad terms we can see three origins of a price: publication by some body that is widely quoted in the market, calculation from other prices or market characteristics, or the opinion of an individual trader or team of analysts. The first case, shown in Figure 9.18, is the most straightforward. Instructions are required to source the relevant information. Typically these instructions come from a source, such as Reuters, that tells where to look for information (for example, "Page 3, second column of the row starting *IBM*").

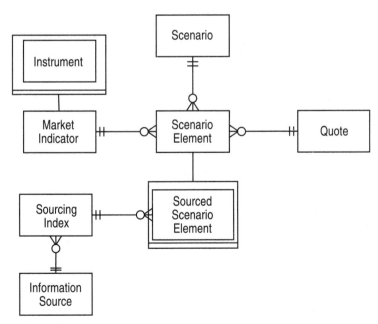

Figure 9.18   Sourcing a scenario element.

This model describes where a particular element comes from.

In effect, using a published price makes the quote for a sourced scenario element derived. Rather than asserting the quote for a sourced scenario element, we derive it using the sourcing index. There is thus an argument for making the link to a quote a derived link. This can be done safely if the link can never be asserted, as when a trader records a hunch. Asserting the quote can cause problems because sometimes the quote can be asserted and sometimes derived. One way out of this is to use a notation for hybrid or optionally derived relationships (see Odell [2], page 56). This seems to take the derived issue too far. I tend to notate according to the most common case and describe what happens precisely in the supporting documentation.

Example   An analyst looking at prices for mail order goods can treat each company as an information source. The sourcing index can be a page number in a catalog. There can then be a separate scenario for each retailer, or an overall scenario can be built that combines all retailers. Rather than asking for the price of an instrument, questions such as lowest price and average price of some instrument are supported.

Figure 9.18 introduces market indicator as a supertype of instrument. This reflects the fact that scenarios can contain things other than instruments. For derivatives, an important part of the pricing approach is the volatility of an instrument—a number that indicates how much the value of the instrument is changing. This volatility is not an instrument that can be traded, but it is recorded in a scenario in the same way as an instrument. Hence a market indicator includes volatilities, as well as all instruments.

Example   Foreign currency markets have many market indicators that are not instruments, including interest rates on the various currencies and the volatility of an exchange rate—an indication of how much the exchange rate is changing.

Example   An analyst looking at prices for mail order goods is interested in the increase in jeans prices. Jeans price increase becomes a market indicator but not an instrument. Jeans are both a market indicator and an instrument.

Calculating scenario elements is also straightforward. The key is to accept that the algorithm for calculating the price can be an object in its own right. A simple example of this is cross-rates used in foreign exchange. If we know the exchange rates for USD/DEM and for USD/GBP, then we can calculate the exchange rate for GBP/DEM as (USD/DEM) / (USD/GBP). We can represent this by having a cross-rate scenario element, which we model by having a subtype of scenario element that references other scenario elements for the numerator and denominator of the cross-rate, as shown in Figure 9.19. The quote for the cross-rate scenario element is then derived from the quotes for the denominator and numerator scenario elements.

Note that the denominator and numerator are expressed as scenario elements rather than market indicators. If we are just expressing cross-rates as

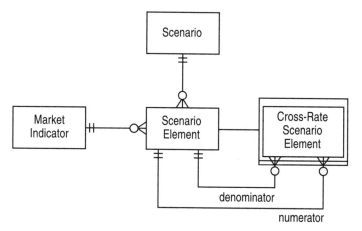

Figure 9.19   Calculating scenario elements by cross-rates.

This can be used to determine a third element from the ratio of two known elements.

described above, then referencing the market indicators seems the most sensible (USD/GBP is a market indicator). However, the whole point of providing scenarios is to allow us to post several different prices, under different assumptions, for the same market indicator. Referencing the scenario element allows us to focus on which of these prices we are to use. There might be two USD/DEM figures: one from Reuters and one from LIBOR. By referencing the scenario elements, we are able to indicate which one we want.

Example   A trader is a specialist on the French franc. She determines the exchange rate between Dutch guilders (NLG) and French francs (FFR) by cross-rates using the German mark (DEM). She does this by creating a cross-rate scenario element. The market indicator for this scenario element is NLG/FFR. For the numerator she uses the NLG/DEM rate quoted by Reuters; that is the scenario element for the instrument NLG/DEM in the Reuters scenario. However she does not get the DEM/FFR rate for the denominator from Reuters; instead she uses her own scenario (built on the basis of her own specialized knowledge). Thus she forms the cross-rate from scenario elements in different scenarios.

The kind of approach used for cross-rates can be used for a number of common calculations, where new kinds of calculations are supported by new subtypes of the scenario element. Figure 9.20 shows a generalization of this structure. In this case the calculated scenario element has a list of scenario elements as arguments and a formula. The formula represents the algorithm for the calculation, which uses arguments provided to it by the arguments on the calculated scenario element. For the cross-rate the formula is `arg[1] / arg[2]`. The actual arguments are provided by the calculated scenario element. This allows a single formula to be reused by several calculated scenario

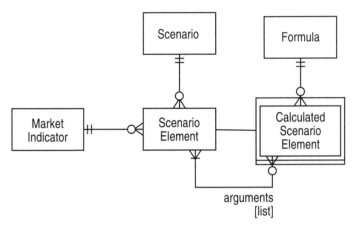

Figure 9.20   A more general approach to calculated scenario elements.

The formula can be a spreadsheet-style formula based on the arguments. It supports a range of arithmetic combinations of scenario element.

elements. The cross-rate for GBP/DEM uses the formula with arguments <USD/DEM, USD/GBP>, and the GBP/JPY cross-rate uses the arguments <USD/JPY, USD/GBP>. Note the importance of providing the arguments as a list rather than the usual set for multivalued mappings. The position is essential for the formulas to be correctly written.

Example   The price change for jeans is calculated by a calculated scenario element that takes the difference between prices of jeans in this year's scenario and last year's scenario.

We can implement the formulas in several ways. One way is to hard-code formulas in the implementation language. Since common formulas (such as cross-rates) are widely reused, hard-coding is not a disadvantage in this case. If the number of formulas is small and does not change too often, this is the best approach. Even if a new formula is added every month, this would be fairly easy to control even for a complex system. We can use a more sophisticated approach if we want to give the user the ability to add formulas. We can build an interpreter [1] that recognizes a simple range of formulaic expressions. This technique is familiar to any user who has used spreadsheets. We could provide an interactive formula builder, but any user who can build a formula can probably type a spreadsheet-like formula. The interpreter [1] thus does not have to recognize all possible formulas. It is perfectly all right to have some formulas built by the parser and some hard-coded. The software for scenario elements does not care how a formula is built but is concerned with providing arguments to the formula that generate the calculated quote. Following the best principles of object-orientation, interface is separated from implementation. (For further discussion on this see Section 6.6.)

Modeling Principle   *To make a process a feature of a type, the process must have an abstract interface so that the implementation can easily vary by subclassing. A purely hard-coded implementation is one subclass; various parameter driven approaches are others.*

The interaction diagram shown in Figure 9.21 reveals some useful points about how this behavior might work. First note how the formula is given a list of quotes as input, rather than a list of scenario elements. This is mildly arbitrary, but providing the same thing as input as is returned as output is a useful policy to follow. Without this, coders can quickly get confused about the type of things they are dealing with. This, of course, assumes that the arithmetic operations are all defined with a quote, which would be a natural place to deal with two-way price arithmetic. In this case we can set up the formulas so that they work on anything that supported arithmetic, not only quotes.

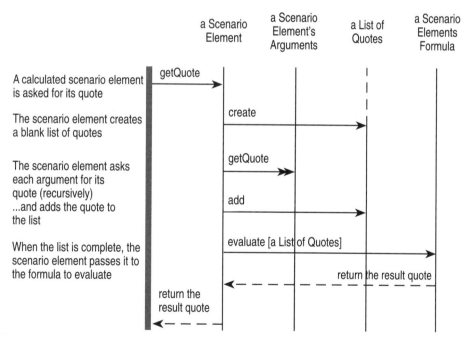

Figure 9.21   Interaction diagram for calculated scenario elements.

The behavior is naturally recursive in that the getQuote operation calls getQuote on all the arguments, potentially resulting in a long chain of calculations. This, like many recursive structures, is very elegant (but difficult to show on an interaction diagram). In practice, however, it can lead to quite a number of redundant calculations. A caching policy for calculated quote values is needed to prevent unnecessary recalculation caused by repeated calls of `getQuote` to the same object. As with any cache, of course, we have to ensure that the cache is properly updated when a source value changes. We can use the arguments mapping in the reverse direction to reset all dependent scenario elements.

Modeling Principle   *When information can be retrieved from an information source or calculated from other available figures, an abstract interface with sourcing and calculation as subclasses should be provided.*

References

1. Gamma, E., R. Helm, R. Johnson, and J. Vlissides. *Design Patterns: Elements of Reusable Object-Oriented Software.* Reading, MA: Addison-Wesley, 1995.
2. Martin, J., and J. Odell. *Object-Oriented Methods: A Foundation,* Englewood Cliffs, NJ: Prentice-Hall, 1995.

10

Derivative Contracts

To fully understand this chapter, you will need to read Sections 9.1 and 9.2 first. Derivative financial trades [3] are gaining an increasingly prominent role in trading. A derivative trade is one whose value depends on another security's value. The simpler forms of derivatives have been around for quite a while; for example, stock options were first traded on an organized exchange in 1973. Since then, more and more exotic variants of derivatives have appeared. They are valuable to investors because they reduce the risk that comes from changing prices. However, when they are not properly controlled, derivatives can be dangerous: Recently, in several famous cases, organizations have lost spectacular amounts of money on ill-managed derivatives.

Modeling derivatives brings out many useful aspects of modeling because derivatives form a natural generalization hierarchy—one that is more interesting than the usual examples of plants and animals. The purpose of this chapter, therefore, is to explore some of the problems of this kind of generalization hierarchy using derivatives as examples.

We begin by introducing the simple derivatives: *forward contracts (10.1)* and *options (10.2)*. Forward contracts introduce the notion of tenor, which leads to a discussion of why date calculations are more complicated than adding up days. Options present a couple of awkward modeling areas: handling the trader's definitions of calls and puts, and the relationship between an option and the underlying contract.

A more complex type of derivative, the combination option, can be seen as an aggregation of simpler options. Subtyping from options with the composite pattern is not always effective; this leads to the *product (10.3)* pattern. This pattern is based on the difference between the seller's and trader's views of the deal and can be applied to regular trading as well. It also serves as an example of how generalization is often the first method we think of using but is not necessarily the best.

With subtyping we must ensure that the subtype's behavior is consistent with that of the supertype. Using barrier options as an example, we will explore how subtyping and state charts interact with *subtype state machines (10.4)*.

If we have a portfolio of options, we can choose to have a browser that highlights pertinent details, depending on the kind of option. This leads to a situation where there are *parallel application and domain hierarchies (10.5)*. The two hierarchies are awkwardly coupled. This pattern poses a problem with several solutions, none of which is all-powerful.

Key Concepts   Forward Contract, Tenor, Option, Product

10.1 Forward Contracts

The contracts discussed in Section 9.1 are simple and involved in immediate deals. Most markets involve a range of more complex deals. The simplest of these is the forward contract. With a normal contract, often referred to as a spot contract, delivery occurs as close as possible to the date on which the contract is traded. Delivery usually occurs in a couple of days. Forward contracts are agreements to do a deal some time in the future. For example, a company is due to receive a tanker full of oil in two months. The company will have to pay several million dollars for this oil. However, if the company is German, its normal financing is done in marks. If the dollar/mark exchange rate changes significantly in the next two months, the company could find itself having to pay more marks than it expected, which could be a significant problem. Of course, the company would also gain from a favorable change in exchange rates; but the uncertainty is not good for the company. To allay this uncertainty, the company could choose to buy several million dollars in a forward contract exchange rate deal, paying an agreed amount of marks now for delivery of dollars in two months. The price is offered by the bank who is carrying out the deal based on the market's perception of where the dollar/mark rate is likely to go in the next couple of months. Such a deal is said to have a tenor of two months (as opposed to a tenor of spot).

A forward contract is quite easily captured by holding separate trade and delivery dates for the contract, as shown in Figure 10.1. A spot deal will have suitably close trade and delivery dates, while a forward contract deal will have these dates separated by two months. A subtype is not needed to show this, although we can add one for clarity.

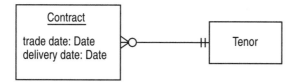

Figure 10.1   A contract that can support forward contracts.

The tenor is based on the difference between trade and delivery dates.

Example Aroma Coffee Makers agrees on January 1, 1997 to buy 5000 tons of Brazilian coffee from Brazil Coffee Exports. Delivery is set for October 20, 1997, and the price is set at today's price.

Example I buy an airline ticket for travel in three months, paying the price currently quoted for the journey.

An important consideration when discussing forward contracts is the tenor of the contract. The tenor is the period between the trade date and the delivery date, in our example two months. Prices are generally quoted on the market with a particular tenor in mind, and the tenor is an important part of the contract's consideration. However, the tenor is not simply the duration between trade and delivery dates. If our two-month contract is traded on May 4, the delivery date will not be on July 4, simply because the 4th of July is a holiday in the United States. Holidays have a big impact on how these dates are calculated. Assuming July 4 does not fall on a weekend, a two-month contract dealt on May 4 will take delivery on July 5. Note that if for some reason Germany had a holiday on July 5, the delivery date would be shifted forward another day. The contract still has a tenor of two months, even though its delivery date is the same as a contract with a delivery date of two months and one day. Note that this behavior is required for spot contracts as well: a deal done on a Thursday will be delivered on a Monday (unless it is a holiday) even though spot is taken as two days. Hence Figure 10.1 includes trade date, delivery date, and tenor.

In this kind of structure, the calculation of the delivery date is not something that can be done by the trade date and tenor alone. Without considering holidays, we can determine the delivery date by a simple calculation between date and tenor. However, the market holidays have to be taken into account. This means that the market has a date calculation routine that allows it to adjust for holidays, as shown in Figure 10.2. This consideration of holidays is an important feature in many areas, where the concept of working days becomes important. It is usually not possible to determine working days globally because holidays vary from country to country, or possibly with even greater granularity. Individual sites may also have local holiday conventions that will affect working day calculations.

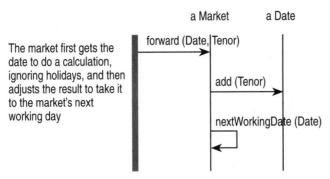

The market first gets the date to do a calculation, ignoring holidays, and then adjusts the result to take it to the market's next working day

Figure 10.2   Getting the market to calculate dates.

Date calculations often need to be delegated to another object when working days need to be calculated.

Example   A company needs to make a payment to an employee within five working days from June 30,1997. If it is a US company, this is by July 8 (skipping over weekends and July 4); for a UK company it is July 7.

Modeling Principle   *Date calculations are often affected by holidays, which need to be skipped over. Holidays vary from country to country and often by the organizations involved.*

10.2   Options

For our German oil company, a forward contract is a valuable tool for reducing the risk of an exchange rate change that would cause them to pay more for their oil. But the company does run the risk of losing out should the exchange rate change in their favor. Financial directors essentially have to bet on the exchange rate movement. If they think the mark will go up, they should buy on the spot market; if they think it will go down, they should buy forward contracts. Options reduce this risk. An option gives the buyer the right to buy dollars at a prearranged exchange rate if the holder wishes. Thus, if the mark goes down, the oil company can exercise its option and buy the dollars at the prearranged price; if the dollar goes up they can ignore their option (let it expire) and buy on the spot market. The bank charges a premium to the oil company to sell them the option, so the bank now manages the risk. Since the bank handles many such deals, they can offset the risks of various deals against each other. Figures 10.3 and 10.4 describe the behavior of an option.

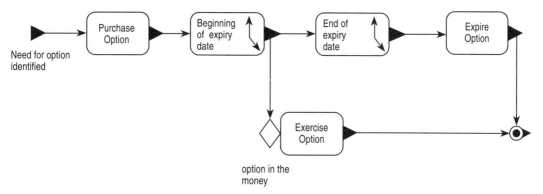

Figure 10.3   Event diagram for the process of using an option.

An option can only be exercised after the start of the expiration date and will only be exercised if it is "in the money," that is, if exercising the option is a better deal than a spot trade at the current price.

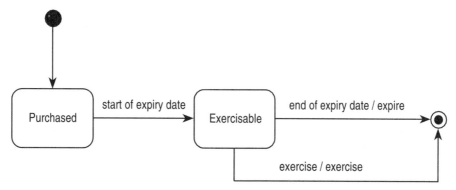

Figure 10.4   Harel state chart to illustrate how an option behaves.

The option can only be exercised on its expiration date (a "European" option).

Many features of the option are similar to that of a normal contract. Like a normal contract, options have counterparties and trade dates. Other features of the option include the expiration date, the amount of premium, and date the premium is delivered.

Thus we can consider an option to be a subtype of a contract, as shown in Figure 10.5. A key feature of the option structure is the polymorphic operation value(Scenario). The value of a spot contract is easy to understand because it is simply the result of applying the spot exchange rate in the provided scenario to the amount of the contract. Options are rather more complex to value, to put it mildly. The most common technique is Black-Scholes analysis [3]. An explanation of this is beyond the scope of this book, except to point out that as far as the caller of this operation is concerned, it is a single operation. The complexities of the mathematics can safely be hidden within the operation.

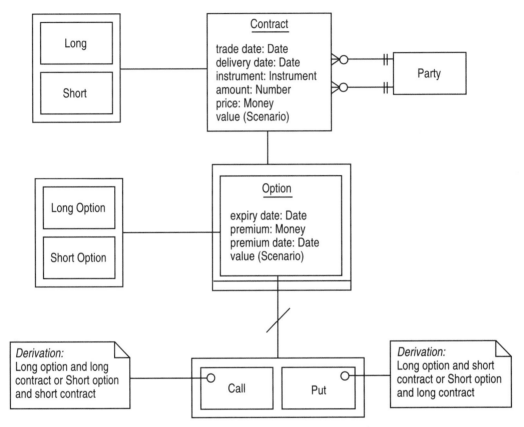

Figure 10.5   Structure of an option.

Call *and* put *are terms derived from the longs and shorts.*

10.2.1   Longs, Shorts, Calls, and Puts: Representing a Tricky Vocabulary

The question of longs and shorts does need discussion. In Section 9.1 we explained that a contract can be long (buy) or short (sell). For options, however, we find that there are four possible choices. We can sell an option to sell money, sell an option to buy money, buy an option to sell money, or buy an option to buy money. The long/short choice still exists on the contract, but it is supplemented by a further long/short choice on the option. The trader's vocabulary includes the terms *call* and *put*. A call is an option to buy (that is, a long contract), while a put is an option to sell (a short contract). Naturally we can buy or sell a call, or buy or sell a put. Representing this language is somewhat tricky, as well as confusing.

If I sell an option to buy yen, then the counterparty can buy yen from me at the expiration date. The difference between this and a forward is that the counterparty can choose not to. If I buy an option to sell yen, then the position is the same, but the control over exercising the option is now mine. Either way, I am (potentially) short on yen, hence the contract is short. In the former the option is also short, while in the latter the option is long. In the first case traders would say they are selling (short) a call, and in the second they would say they are buying (long) a put.

One way of looking at this would be to say that we could replace the long/short description of a contract by call/put. But this does not really work because we do not use the terms *call* and *put* on contracts that are not options.

Another possibility is to use the terms *long* and *short* for options only to indicate the state of the option rather than the contract. Thus the first example above would be a short call and the second a long put. This might make sense to a trader but would be apt to confuse any software. When evaluating risk, the position of the amount of the contract is important, and in the above examples both are short. Hence we need to be able to ask the direction of the contract (which defines the position), the direction of the option, and the call/put. So the two examples are (short contract, short option, call) and (short contract, long option, put). Clearly one of these can be derived from the other two. The diagram indicates that call/put is derived. The derivation is a reminder that one is derived rather than any direction to an implementor of what is actually stored or calculated in the implementation.

Representing language like this is always a bit of a battle, particularly when it seems unnecessarily illogical. The important thing is to represent the fundamentals in a logical manner. These fundamentals may be part of the domain expert's terminology or invented during the modeling process (but if they are invented, the domain expert must be comfortable with them). The rest of the terminology can then be derived from these fundamentals.

Modeling Principle   *Derived markers should be used to define terminology that is derived from other constructs on the model.*

Modeling Principle   *Marking a feature as derived is a constraint on the interface. It does not affect the underlying data structures.*

Example   On June 1, 1997, I am given an option to buy 200 shares of Aroma Coffee Makers on January 1, 1999 at a price of $5 per share. This is an option with a trade date of June 1, 1997, an instrument of Aroma Coffee Makers stock, an amount of 200, delivery and expiration dates of January 1, 1999, a premium of $0, and a price of $5. I will gain shares, so the contract is long (with respect to me), and the option is also long (since I hold it); it is thus a call.

Example   When I make a reservation for a flight, I am being given a call option on the ticket. The expiration date of the option is the date the reservation must be ticketed.

Another concern is the interaction between delivery date and expiration date. For an option, the delivery date can be computed if the expiration date is known (delivery date = expiration date + spot). The reverse is not true, however (due to the interference of holidays). This means that, for options, delivery date is a computed mapping. The important point here is that the interface does not change: There is still an accessor for delivery date; however, the information is stored. There are two alternatives to describe this situation: We can note (typically in the glossary) that for options the delivery date attribute is overridden and calculated from the expiration date according to the formula. Another option is to describe the formula as a constraint on the option type. Both are perfectly reasonable and the choice is a matter of taste. It is entirely up to the implementor what code and data structure to use.

10.2.2   To Subtype or Not to Subtype

The structure shown in Figure 10.5 is not the only way to handle options; another choice is shown in Figure 10.6. The difference between the two structures is how the optionality is added to the contract. In Figure 10.5 we add it by subtyping. In this scheme an option is a kind of contract with additional properties and some variant behavior. In Figure 10.6 we may say that an option has a base contract often referred to by traders as the underlying of the option. There is at least some notion of containment here, especially in the fact that we would not be likely to ask the contract to value itself if it was an underlying to an option. Similarly the delivery date would be dependent on the option's expiration date.

The choice between the two structures is not easy. Both have elegant qualities. The Figure 10.6 model separates the notion of option and contract with a definite notion of underlying. One disadvantage of this scheme is that a single contract is represented by two objects. It is easier to alter Figure 10.6 to handle compound options (options where the underlying is an option). With so little choice between them, we can easily end up getting bogged down. Prototyping can sometimes clarify the situation but not always. When alternatives like this present themselves, it's a good idea to use the simpler approach and then change to the more complicated one later if necessary. With this case, however, it is arguable which is the simpler. When it is this close, I trust the domain experts' instincts by asking them which *feels* best. We will continue to use Figure 10.5 as the basis for further discussion.

Modeling Principle   *When faced with alternative approaches, choose the simplest first and change to a more complex one as needed.*

Modeling Principle   *When there is little to choose between modeling alternatives, follow the instincts of the domain expert.*

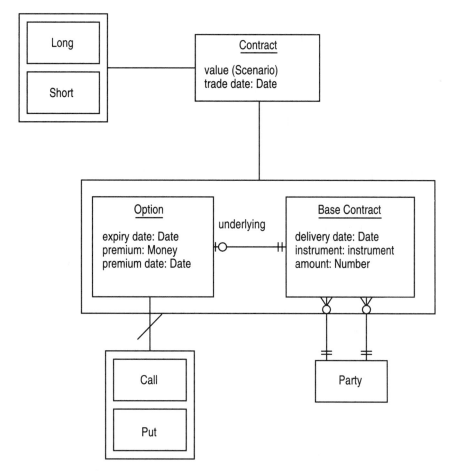

Figure 10.6   The separate object approach to options and contracts.

Both this and Figure 10.5 are reasonable alternatives, although this chapter builds on Figure 10.5.

10.3   Product

Derivative trades have long been considered somewhat risky, mainly because of the complex mathematics required to evaluate risk. The Black-Scholes equation [3], which serves as the building block for much of the evaluation process, is a second-order partial differential equation. Even with an engineering background, these animals still give me the willies.

The most spectacular example of the pitfalls of derivatives trading is the collapse of Britain's venerable Barings Bank. According to current reports, the primary cause of the collapse was dealing in a particular kind of derivative called a straddle—an example of a combination option. Combination options can be seen as a composite of other options. It seems appropriate to discuss this section with straddles as an example.

The concept of a straddle is in fact very simple. You have a holding worth some $70 million, depending on prices, and you are concerned about any large change in its value over the next three months. Either going up or down will cause a problem. To avoid the problem, you can buy a call and a put, both with a price of $70 million and an expiration in three months. Let's assume the premium on each of these is $2.5 million. If the price goes up, you exercise the call and you gain the value of the holding at the new price, less $70 million and the $5 million total premium. Thus if the value of the holding rises above $75 million you are happy. Similarly if the value falls below $65 million you are happy. The worst thing that can happen is that the price stays steady, in which case you lose the $5 million premium. The attractiveness of a straddle comes from a fixed risk that covers an otherwise very wide range of movement. Naturally a very volatile instrument can result in a higher premium for the straddle, but if you are trying to reduce your risk in a volatile environment, this can be a very useful product.

If you are the seller, of course, you are faced with a more tricky prospect: You can lose an unlimited amount of money if the price moves a large amount. This is indeed what caused a certain bank to lose its barings. Again, the bank should have used other trades to hedge this risk.

In modeling this straddle we should immediately note that it is composed of two options that are constrained by their prices, dates, direction, and instruments. Figure 10.7 shows a straddle modeled as a subtype of an option. As a combination option it can have components, with the constraint on the straddle defining the precise characteristics. Other subtypes of combinations would be used for other common cases: spreads, strangles, and the like.

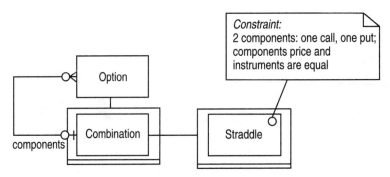

Figure 10.7   Modeling straddles as subtypes of options.

A straddle is a combination of a call and a put.

Use of the subtype confirms that a straddle is a kind of option and has the same behavior as its supertype. This raises a question, however. Some behavior can be safely inherited, such as the ability to value itself and the trade date. We can think of the premium as the sum of premiums of the component options. But what about the price? For a straddle, the components are all priced the same, so we could consider it to be the price of the straddle. Another common combination, however, is the spread. As previously mentioned, a spread is two options, but both options are the same direction (that is, two calls or two puts) at different prices. What is the price in this case? Going back to the straddle, is it a call or a put?

Figure 10.8 shows one way of dealing with this problem. Those attributes that can make sense at both levels can be put on an option, while the awkward attributes are placed on a conventional option. This helps to some extent but begins to fail as we recall that price was defined on the contract not the option, and that there are combinations (such as covered calls and protected puts) that combine options with regular contracts. Again, the generalization could be manipulated, but one wonders what could safely be put on the supertype.

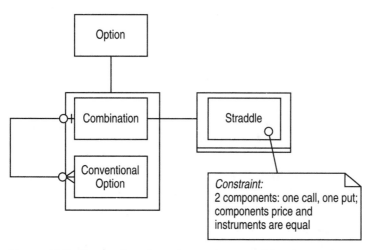

Figure 10.8   Separating the subtypes into combination and conventional.

These concerns are enough to raise a serious question about using composition and subtyping together. The main problem is that, when managing risk, traders do not actually concern themselves with combinations. A combination is nothing more than the component contracts. We consider its risk the same as if the contracts were sold to separate counterparties in the same portfolio. It is the customer and the salesperson who form the combination and think of the contracts as a combination. Once the combination is dealt it behaves no differently than any other contract.

This leads us to the model shown in Figure 10.9. Here the salesperson's view is explicitly separated from that of the risk manager. The risk manager sees contracts, which are assembled into a product by a salesperson. The straddle is now a particular kind of product. This allows us to reconsider the behavior of the contract and move the sales-related behavior to the product while leaving the risk side of things to the contract. This includes the parties to the product who are generally irrelevant to risk management (unless exposure to a particular party is being considered). Since contracts must have a product (due to the mandatory relationship), a contract can still find its parties by collaborating with its product (but see the discussion in Section 10.3.1).

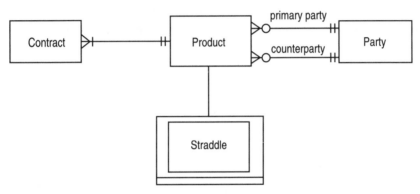

Figure 10.9   Introducing the product.

The product reflects the perspective of sales. In risk analysis the way in which contracts are combined as products is ignored.

In considering whether to subtype, we need to ask two questions. The first is whether all the features of the supertype are really inherited by the subtype. An immediate subtyping, such as is shown in Figure 10.7, should be reviewed against all the features of the supertype, including features of supertypes of the supertype. It is easy to forget this and be led down a dangerous path. This analysis will lead to refactoring the generalization hierarchy, and this refactoring may not be trivial. The second question we need to ask is, does the domain expert really consider the subtyping to hold? In our example the domain expert resisted subtyping, preferring the Figure 10.9 model. Later on, the Figure 10.8 style did reappear but has not, so far, seemed compelling enough to change the model (and the framework that implements it).

Modeling Principle *Subtyping should be used only when all the features of the supertype are appropriate to the supertype and it makes sense conceptually to say that every instance of the subtype is an instance of the supertype.*

This leaves an interesting question as to whether it is worth putting some explicit generalization structure on the product to represent the various kinds of combinations, as shown in Figure 10.10. Clearly it is not for risk calculation purposes. It is useful, however, for creating new products of this form. Indeed the deepest examples of this kind of generalization are likely to lie at the application and presentation layers (see Section 12.3) where specific presentations are required for pricing and deal capture of combinations. In such situations a shared definition in the domain model is very valuable, even if the definition is currently used only in sales work. More sophisticated analysis of trades may require an understanding of how these combinations are defined.

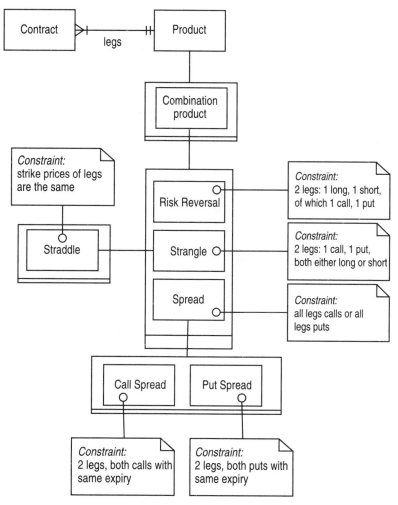

Figure 10.10   The common combination products.

This is a good example of a hierarchy based on constraints. The contracts linked to a product are called the legs of the product.

Example   A client has a large holding in Aroma Coffee Makers stock and is concerned about the movement in stock price over the next 6 months before he can sell it. He might buy a straddle around the current price of $5. To the trader this product is broken down into two separate options.

Example   I wish to buy 7000 shares of Aroma Coffee Makers. The trader is not able to find a single other party who wishes to sell the exact amount. He can find one party to sell 2000 shares and another to sell 5000 shares. I have one product with the trader to buy 7000 shares. The product consists of two contracts for each trade.

Modeling Principle   *The product/contract split should be used whenever the customer sees a single deal that is broken into several deals by the trader.*

The key difference between a product and a contract is that the product represents the customer's intention while the contract refers to what actually gets traded between the counter and primary parties.

10.3.1   Should a Product Always Be There?

One of the consequences of the model in Figure 10.9 is that noncombinations are represented by a single contract and a single product. The product is adding little to the picture (other than the separation of responsibilities between sales and risk management).

Another possibility is not to make the link to product mandatory. In such a scheme only a combination has a product. Simpler contracts have no product link. A contract has links to a party, but they are derived when a product is present. The disadvantage of this scheme is that it handles responsibilities inconsistently. A contract is responsible for handling the relationships with a party, except when it delegates the responsibilities to a product. This inconsistency can lead to a great deal of confusion. For that reason I prefer to use the model in Figure 10.9.

Traditional data modelers would come to the same conclusion from a different route. Normalization leads them not to wish to duplicate the links to party and thus choose a model like Figure 10.9 (although it might get altered for performance reasons in a physical model). The object-oriented argument is different because it focuses on having clear responsibilities, yet both arguments share an underlying theme: Conceptual simplicity leads us to having the minimum of base[1] associations. In OO development this principle leads us to clearly separated responsibilities, and in relational data modeling it leads us to 14th normal form (or whatever the number is these days).

Modeling Principle   *Do not duplicate base associations that have the same meanings. Following this principle leads to types with well-separated responsibilities.*

---

[1] We can have as many derived associations as we like.

Modeling Principle   *Be consistent in the allocation of responsibilities. Be wary of a type that sometimes is responsible for something and sometimes delegates that responsibility. (This behavior may be correct but it should always be questioned.)*

10.4   Subtype State Machines

Although many common derivatives can be represented as combinations of options, this is not uniformly the case. A barrier option can either appear or disappear when the price of the instrument, as quoted on some agreed market pricing (such as a Reuters page), reaches a particular limit. Thus an option could be bought to buy (call) 10 million yen at a price of 90 JPY/USD, which would knock-in at 85 JPY/USD. This option behaves differently than a standard one. Effectively the option cannot be exercised unless the exchange rate falls below 85 JPY/USD before the expiration date. If it does fall below this barrier, then the option is knocked in and will remain exercisable whatever happens to the price between that date and the expiration. If the price never falls below the barrier level, then the purchaser can never exercise. (Barriers can also be knock-outs, in which case they can only be exercised if the exchange rate does not pass the barrier.)

This different behavior can be expressed by a modification of the state chart for a barrier, effectively replacing it with the one shown in Figure 10.11. The event diagram for using it is shown in Figure 10.12.

The only structural change is the addition of the barrier level to the option, which does work well as a subtype of option since it provides a change in behavior and adds a new feature (the barrier level).

10.4.1   Ensuring Conformance of State Charts

The state chart presents an interesting issue in its own right. We can replace the state chart shown in Figure 10.4 with that of Figure 10.11, providing the different behavior of the barrier subtype. However, this raises a question: Are we allowed to do that? Most methods stress the importance of being able to substitute a subtype for a supertype; this is reflected in object diagrams by only allowing us to add associations, not remove them. Many textbooks do not mention what rules govern state diagrams with subtypes. Shlaer and Mellor [6] indicate that state diagrams can only be placed at either a supertype or a subtype. However, if all subtypes share a common portion, that may be placed at the supertype to ease maintainability (splicing). Rumbaugh [5] indicates that subtypes can (usually) only add orthogonal state diagrams.

The best discussion of how subtyping and states work is given by Cook and Daniels [1], who devote a whole chapter to subtypes and state diagrams. They stress the principles of design by contract [4], which can be summarized

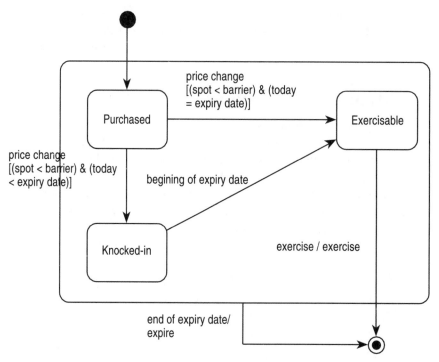

Figure 10.11   Harel state chart for a knock-in call.

If the instrument's price never passes the barrier, the option cannot be exercised. After the price has passed the barrier once, it does not matter what other changes occur.

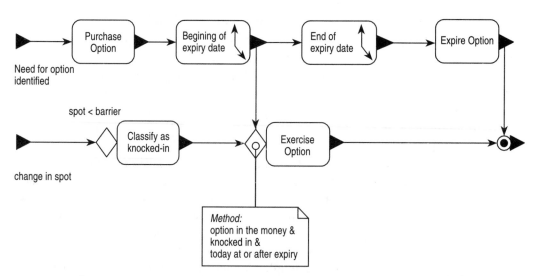

Figure 10.12   Event diagram of the process of using a knock-in option.

by saying that a supertype's state chart can be extended in two ways: either by adding an orthogonal state chart or by taking a supertype's state and splitting into substates. Supertype transitions can be modified only by redirecting them to substates of their supertype's state.

Applying these guidelines to the option state models, we see a number of problems. The first lies in the treatment of the start of expiration date event. In Figure 10.4 (the option diagram), this causes a transition from purchased to exercisable, but in Figure 10.11 (the barrier diagram), the transition comes from the new knocked-in state. The end of expiration date event has a similar problem: Figure 10.4 shows it transitioning from the exercisable state only, while Figure 10.11 has it transitioning from any state.

The first question comes from considering what an object should do if it receives an event that is not in a state in which we can do anything with it. The object can either silently ignore the event or raise an error. Some general policy should be stated to interpret how to deal with this; for example, Cook and Daniels advise [1] explicitly listing events in which an object is interested. Any events that normally would be silently ignored if there were no defined transition are listed as allowable events. This resolves what would happen should the Figure 10.11 (barrier) diagram receive a start of expiration date event while in the purchased start. If start of expiration date is an allowed event, it will just ignore it.

However, this is still not entirely consistent with the supertype. Figure 10.11 shows that when the start of expiration date event is received, a purchased option changes to exercisable. Looking at this in contract terms, the change to purchased is part of the postcondition of start of expiration date. We cannot weaken this postcondition in the subtype, only strengthen it. To have a knock-in call as a subtype of an option, we must replace both state charts with those shown in Figures 10.13 and 10.14.

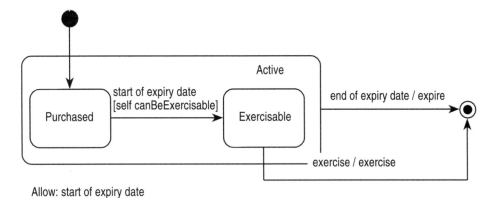

Allow: start of expiry date

Figure 10.13   Modified state chart for option to allow Cook and Daniels conformance with knock-in calls.

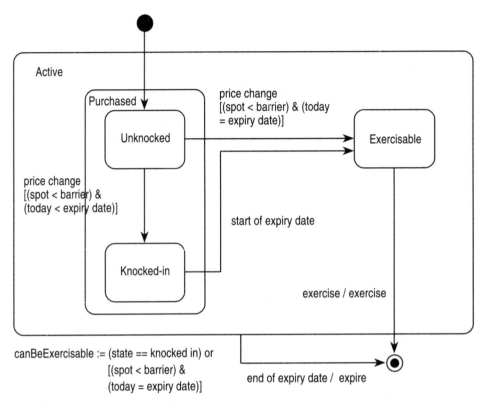

Figure 10.14   Modified state chart for knock-in calls to support conformance with Figure 10.13.

To provide conformance, these diagrams reflect two changes. The first is to generalize purchased and exercisable into an active state. We can then redirect the end of expiration date event from here. The second modification is to add canBeExercisable as a guard on the start of expiration date event. This operation is a way of saying that the start of expiration date does not always lead to the exercisable state. For regular options canBeExercisable is always true. Subtypes of an option can override it for other behavior.

Figure 10.14 shows how this override occurs for knock-in barriers. We introduce substates of purchased to indicate whether the barrier has been knocked-in or not. We then split the source of the start of expiration date transition and weaken the guard to show the unguarded transition. Since we have allowed start of expiration date on the supertype, the barrier can ignore start of expiration date when unknocked.

10.4.2   The Problems with Using Conformance

Having gone through this exercise of gaining conformance, we should stop and ask ourselves a few questions about the process. In my judgment Figures 10.4 and 10.11 represent simpler and clearer expressions of behavior than Figures 10.13 and 10.14. Thus, although we have gained conformance (at least according to the Cook and Daniels definition), we have lost comprehensibility. In addition, modeling the knock-in call caused us to change the supertype diagram. It was perfectly good as it was—we only changed it because we needed a different state chart that forced us to construct a conforming subtype state chart. This implies that a new subtype can force us to change supertype state charts, unless we are clever enough to produce a remarkably flexible supertype state chart. Unfortunately I don't think I'm that clever, so subtyping is going to be fraught with difficulties.

One solution to these difficulties is to recast the generalization hierarchy to avoid needing to worry about conformance. We assumed that a knocked-in call would be a subtype of an option, each with their own state chart, as shown in Figure 10.15. Another approach is to treat an option as an abstract type without its own state chart and create a conventional option subtype to hold the Figure 10.4 state chart, as shown in Figure 10.16. This avoids having to worry about the conforming state charts, allows the more natural state charts, but does introduce a separate type. It is also more consistent with the guidelines of Rumbaugh and Shlaer and Mellor, who do not discuss conformance between state models.

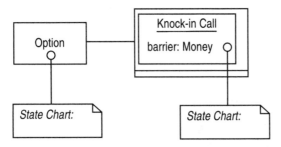

Figure 10.15   Knocked-in call as a subtype of an option.

This is the natural approach, but how are the state models related?

Design by contract says that subtypes must satisfy their supertypes' postconditions. However, that does not necessarily imply that the postcondition on start of expiration date should include the transition to the exercisable state. If we choose not to include it as part of the postcondition, then the

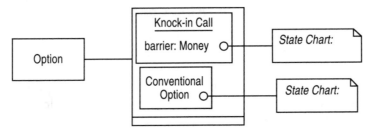

Figure 10.16   Creating a conventional option type.

This can make it easier to cope with the state models, but it is not as natural.

original diagram is acceptable. The important thing is that start of expiration date should be allowed in all cases; whether it causes a transition or not is undefined.

This is, in fact, an example of a wider issue in using design by contract. Often people say that the postconditions of an operation should define all changes to the observable state of an object. This principle is often advocated by the formal methods community but is not true for design by contract. The postcondition merely specifies the state that must hold at the end of the operation. We can always indicate that nothing must change other than what is specified, but that is not assumed in the approach.

Indeed subtyping makes such a restrictive postcondition dangerous. The whole point of subtyping is that the supertype cannot predict all the extensions that subtypes might make. Using an overly restrictive postcondition cripples the flexibility offered by subtyping. Postconditions define aspects of the object's observable state that must be true. Thus any other changes can occur providing they don't violate the explicit clauses of the postcondition.

Modeling Principle   *The effect of generalization on state charts is not well understood. It is important to ensure that all events on a supertype can be handled by the subtype. Any state chart that can be subtyped must allow unknown events.*

Modeling Principle   *A postcondition defines a condition that must be true of the object after the operation. Other changes that are not mentioned by the postcondition can take place.*

10.5   Parallel Application and Domain Hierarchies

Faced with a portfolio of various contracts, a trader might like to look at a list of the contracts together with important information about them. Such a list would show each contract on one line. The information shown on the line would vary depending on the kind of contract. The columns might be long/short, trade date, strike price, call/put (options only), expiration date (option only), barrier level (barrier only), knock-in or knock-out (barrier only).

In this scheme some columns in the table are only relevant for certain subtypes of the option. This adds a certain amount of complexity to the problem. What we cannot do is assume that some browser line class asks each contract for each relevant attribute. Such an approach would not work because the browser line class cannot ask a nonoption for its expiration date, since by definition a nonoption does not have one.

A first stage in laying out a design is to use the layered structure discussed in Chapter 12. In using this the portfolio, browser and browser line types are application facades operating as shown in Figure 10.17. The portfolio browser's subject is a portfolio, the browser line's subject is a contract. Neither portfolio nor contract have any visibility to the portfolio browser or browser line, since the latter types lie within the application tier and domain types have no visibility to application types (see Figure 12.6).

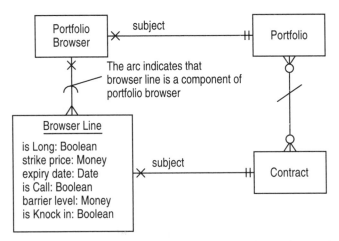

Figure 10.17   A portfolio browser and its relationship to the domain model.

A portfolio browser and browser line are application facades.

This structure allows a browser line to have attributes for all the columns required by the interface. As far as a presentation programmer is concerned, each line has these attributes, which may be nil. If an attribute is nil, then that implies a blank space in the browser's table. The problem lies in the link between the browser line and the domain model.

The browser line knows it is dealing with a collection of contracts. Unfortunately it needs to ask for information that is only defined on certain subtypes of the contract. If a browser line asks a nonoption for its expiration date, it will get an error. Several strategies can be used to deal with this interaction: type checking in the application facade, giving the supertype an encompassing interface, using a run-time attribute, making the application facade visible to the domain model, and using exception handling.

10.5.1   Type Checking in the Application Facade

In this strategy the browser line is responsible for dealing with the problem. Before each request to the contract, a type check is made on the contract to ensure that the request can be issued safely, as shown in Figure 10.18. In C++ this takes the form of a type check, followed by a downcast, followed by the request.

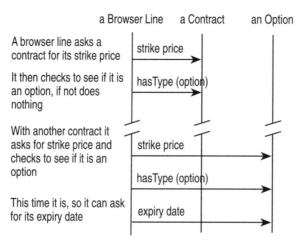

Figure 10.18   Interactions for type checking in the browser line.

The type is checked before an operation is called that is only defined on the subtype.

This strategy has a number of disadvantages. The browser class, in the face of many subtypes of the contract, becomes quite complex. Furthermore any changes in the contract hierarchy causes changes in the browser. Of course, if the change is a new subtype that introduces a new column to the browser, then such a change would be required in any case, driven by a presentation change.

The degree of type checking that this scheme implies can be reduced by a couple of approaches. We can use a subclass of browser line for each subtype of contract. We can use a type check to instantiate the correct subclass of browser line to do the job. Another approach is to use the visitor pattern [2]. Although these approaches are preferable if the degree of type checking is excessive, they still require the browser line (and its subclasses) to know about the contract hierarchy.

10.5.2   Giving the Supertype an Encompassing Interface

The essential problem is that it is an error to ask a contract for its expiration date. One solution is to add all of the subtype operations to contract. Contract would naturally reply with a nil for all of these, but the relevant subtypes could override that operation to provide their value.

This approach has many problems. It becomes impossible to tell what is a truly legal operation on a contract and what is really an error. Compile-time type checking is defeated because it cannot tell which is which. Each time a subtype is introduced, contract's interface must be altered. Thus I'm not a fan of this approach.

10.5.3   Using a Run-Time Attribute

Run-time attributes provide a very flexible system of adding attributes to types without changing the conceptual model. When implemented they allow attribute changes without recompilation during the execution of the system.

The basic model for contracts is shown in Figure 10.19, or preferably Figure 10.20, which uses a keyed mapping (see Section 15.2). All contracts have a number of terms, and each receives a term type. In this example each attribute of the contract and its subtypes (strike price, is call, barrier level, and so on) would be term types. If a contract is asked for a term, it replies with the value object if there is a term. In this way it is not an error to ask for a nonoption's expiration date.

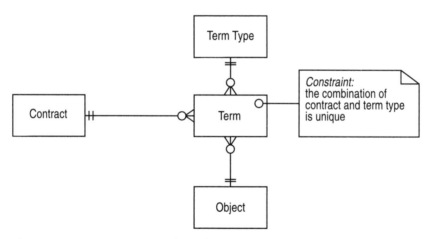

Figure 10.19   A run time attribute for contract.

This way asking a nonoption for a property only defined on option would not cause an error.

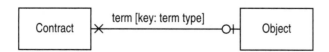

Figure 10.20   Figure 10.19 using a keyed mapping.

Of course, this model allows a nonoption to be given an expiration date by accident. This can be prevented in a couple of ways. The first is to use a knowledge level (see Section 2.5), as shown in Figure 10.21. The other is to treat the term type as a derived interface. Both the model attributes (those on contract and its subtypes) and the term type interface are provided. Updates are only provided through the model attributes.

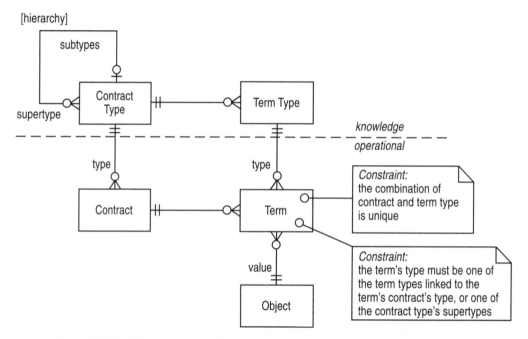

Figure 10.21   Using a knowledge level to control the placing of terms on contracts.

This would stop terms from being placed incorrectly on contracts but can only be checked at run-time.

Using run-time attributes does provide flexibility but it comes with significant disadvantages. First, using term types makes the interface of a contract and its subtypes harder to understand. As well as looking at the operations defined on the type, the user of a contract must also look at the instances of the term type, and indeed which instances are valid. Second, attribute types cannot be type checked at compile time, removing a very important advantage of compile-time checking. This does not matter for the browser line, since the whole point is to relax any compile-time checking, but it does matter a great deal for other parts of the system. A third disadvantage is that the basic language mechanisms are being subverted. The compiler is not aware of what is going on, and language features, such as polymorphism, must be hand-coded by the programmer. Also, run-time attributes do not perform as well as model attributes.

Many of these disadvantages can be mitigated by providing both interfaces. Those parts of the software that know about attributes at compile time can use the model attributes, and the browser can use the run-time attributes.

10.5.4   Making the Application Facade Visible to the Domain Model

In this approach the responsibility for loading a browser line is given to the contract that browser line is summarizing, as shown in Figure 10.22. Since control is now in the contract, or its subtype, it can load the browser line with the correct values for that subtype. The browser line supports all necessary information for the application, and the contract or subtype knows what is applicable for that subtype.

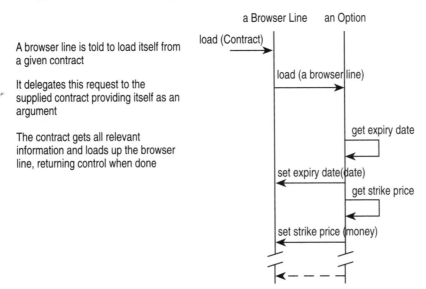

Figure 10.22   Interactions for contracts loading browser lines.

The browser line must be visible to the contract, which violates the usual visibility rules between domain and application tiers.

The advantages of this approach include the fact that the interaction is much simpler because no type checking is required, and a more complex interface is not needed for the contract. In addition, adding a new contract does not require the browser line to change, unless there is a corresponding change in the presentation. All that is needed is a new overriding operation to load the browser line.

The biggest disadvantage lies in the breaking of the visibility rules between application and domain tiers that are discussed in Chapter 12. This can be avoided by placing the browser line in its own package, as shown in Figure 10.23. In this way the dependency from the domain model is limited to only the browser line type. Visibilities may be further reduced by splitting the browser line type into two. The presentation for the browser and the contracts use very different interfaces to the browser line. The browser line can be given its own browser line facade in the browser facade package. This facade has a simple interaction with the browser line. In this case the visibility from the browser presentation to the browser line package can be removed.

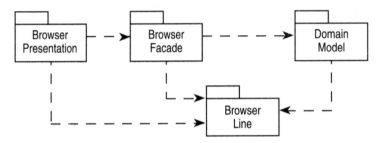

Figure 10.23   Visibilities for a browser line package (based on Figure 12.6).

The browser line package is a special case between the application and domain tiers.

Another disadvantage arises from the possibility of several browser applications that may have slightly different needs. Each application would need its own browser line, which would all need to be known by contract. The splitting of browser line can help here. One browser line facade would be created for each application, all of which would use the single browser line package. Adding new kinds of browsers thus would not alter the contract's responsibilities unless a new feature were added to the browser line.

The fact remains that any new feature required of the browser line requires modification of the entire contract and all its subtypes. This is the fundamental trade-off between putting control in the browser line as opposed to putting control in the contract. If new contracts are added more frequently than features are added to the browser line, then we should put control in the contract. However, the change to the normal pattern of visibility is not to be taken lightly. Unless new contract subtypes occur significantly more often than changes in the browser line, I would not put control in the contract because many new subtypes in the contract would themselves imply new features to the browser line.

10.5.5   Using Exception Handling

Of course all of the above ideas are based on the idea that it is a bad thing to ask a nonbarrier for its barrier level. With the right environment, however, this is not such a problem. If making a request of an object results in a run-time error and that error is made manifest through an exception, then the browser line can simply catch the exception and treat it as a nil. The browser line should check that the exception is actually a result of the receiver not understanding the request and not some other, more worrying error. It also assumes that it is possible to send a message to an object for which the receiver does not have an interface. This is where a lack of type safety becomes an advantage, coupled with the exception handling features now present in the newer implementations. Smalltalk can always be used in this way, since it is untyped. Type safety can be bypassed in C++ by using a downcast.

References

1. Cook, S. and J. Daniels. *Designing Object Systems: Object-Oriented Modelling with Syntropy*. Hemel Hempstead, UK: Prentice-Hall International, 1994.

2. Gamma, E., R. Helm, R. Johnson and J. Vlissides. *Design Patterns: Elements of Reusable Object-Oriented Software*. Reading, MA: Addison-Wesley, 1995.

3. Hull, J.C. *Options, Futures, and Other Derivative Securities* (Second Edition). London: Prentice-Hall International, 1993.

4. Meyer, B. "Applying 'Design by Contract,'" *IEEE Computer*, 25, 10 (1992), pp. 40–51.

5. Rumbaugh, J., M. Blaha, W. Premerlani, F. Eddy, and W. Lorensen. *Object-Oriented Modeling and Design*. Englewood Cliffs, NJ: Prentice-Hall, 1991.

6. Shlaer, S. and S. J. Mellor. *Object Life Cycles: Modeling the World in States*. Englewood Cliffs, NJ: Prentice-Hall, 1991.

11

Trading Packages

To fully understand this chapter, you will need to read Chapters 9 and 12 first. Developing large information systems presents particular challenges. The fundamental way to deal with a large-scale system is to decompose it into smaller systems. This requires some form of architectural modeling, as discussed in Section A.5.

The first organizing tool of any information system is the layered architecture discussed in Chapter 12. This architecture identifies many of the package divisions of the system. In a larger system, however, the domain model becomes too large for a single package. This chapter looks at how we can split a large domain model. The concepts of package and visibility (see Section A.5) are again deployed as the basic tool for the division. The trading concepts of Chapter 9 provide the examples.

The first pattern looks at how to organize the models of scenarios and portfolios. The main problem is that of *multiple access levels to a package (11.1)*. A risk management application uses scenarios to get the information needed to value portfolios. Another application needs to set up and manage scenarios. Both applications need access to the scenario types, but they need very different levels of access. Different clients needing different interfaces is a common problem. Solutions include allowing a package to have multiple protocols and using different packages.

The relationships between contracts and parties raise the problem of *mutual visibility (11.2)*. Three solutions suggest themselves: a one-way visibility between contract and party, putting them both in the same package, or putting them in separate mutually visible packages. All three solutions have significant disadvantages.

The final pattern explores *subtyping packages (11.3)* by considering how to position the derivatives discussed in Chapter 10 onto the package structure. This pattern illustrates that subtypes can be placed in a package separate from their supertypes with visibility from the subtype to the supertype.

11.1   Multiple Access Levels to a Package

Portfolios are constructed from contracts using market indicators as descriptions. Scenarios are used independently to develop prices for market indicators. Portfolios and contracts need to use scenarios to value themselves, but scenarios do not need any knowledge of portfolios and contracts, as shown in Figure 11.1.

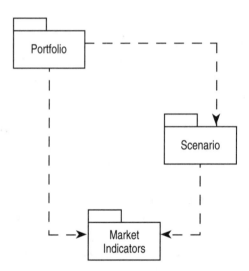

Figure 11.1   An initial picture of package visibilities.

To carry out valuations, a portfolio only requires the price of a market indicator. The portfolio package does not need to know how the scenario is set up. Thus, although the scenario element type needs to be visible to the portfolio so the getQuote message can be sent, there is no need to see the subtypes with the definition of how the quote is formed. Indeed we can go further and say that even the scenario element is not useful to the portfolio. A better approach would be to present the interface to the portfolio as shown in Figure 11.2. This interface has a keyed mapping (see Section 15.2) on the scenario, which takes a market indicator as an argument. Since no other properties of the scenario element are important, the interface for the portfolio package is simple.

Figure 11.2 An interface for the scenario package that hides scenario elements.
This is the best interface for the portfolio package, which does not need to know about scenario elements.

This approach requires two different types of scenario package: one for the interface to portfolio and another for setting up scenarios. Thus something more than a simple assignment of types to packages is needed. The immediate and obvious approach is to divide the types in the scenario package into public and private types in the package. Public types are those visible to other packages that have a visibility into the scenario package (such as portfolio). Private types are only visible to types within the scenario package. In this case the scenario is a public type and the scenario element is a private type. This logic can be extended to operations. Public operations can be public within a package and public to other packages. Although this represents a fine degree of control, it can be too difficult to maintain. The art of good visibility design is to choose a degree of visibility that is fine enough to be useful but not so fine as to make the portfolio a nightmare to manage. (Things that are difficult to manage tend not to be managed, which leads to out-of-date, useless models.)

One problem with this approach is that users need software to set up and manipulate scenarios. This requires components at the application logic and presentation layers, as discussed in Chapter 12. Thus the model must include a scenario management application package that is separate from the scenario package. Figure 11.3 shows the addition of a scenario management application package and a risk management application package. This approach would not work with the public/private approach described above, however, because the scenario management application requires the private types of the scenario package. Although both portfolio and scenario management require visibility of the scenario package, they need different types of visibility.

One solution to this problem, proposed by Wirfs-Brock [1], allows a package to have more than one protocol.[1] In our original pattern, we set up a protocol as a set of operations; however, it is quite reasonable to make it merely a set of types to allow simpler control of visibility. Using separate protocols results in a diagram such as Figure 11.4, in which the scenario has two protocols: The one used by the portfolio permits only the small protocol, while the scenario management application uses the deeper protocol. The protocols are shown by semicircular ports on the package box. (I'm only showing ports on packages with more than one protocol.)

---

[1] Wirfs-Brock uses the term *contract*, which is confusing in this example, so I use *protocol*.

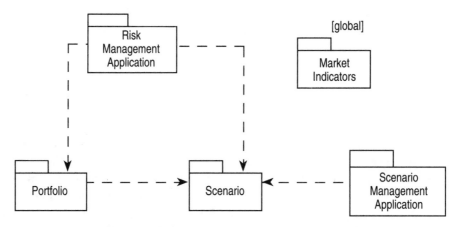

Figure 11.3   Adding application packages to Figure 11.1.

The problem with this is that the scenario management application needs a much larger interface to the scenario package than the portfolio package needs.

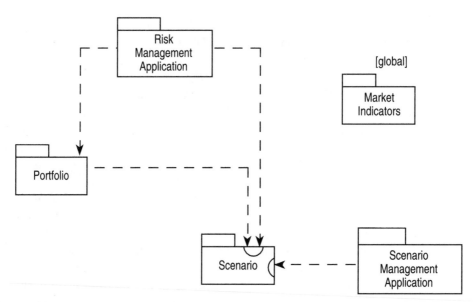

Figure 11.4   The packages of Figure 11.3 with protocols.

Each protocol implies a separate interface.

Using separate protocols is one way to deal with the multiple visibility issue. Another is to introduce an extra package, as shown in Figure 11.5. The scenario element and its subtypes are moved from the scenario package into the scenario structure package. The scenario package contains only the scenario type and its simple associations. The portfolio package has visibility

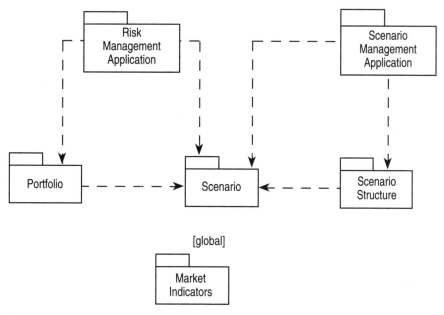

Figure 11.5   Using an extra package for the scenario structure.

only into the scenario package, while the scenario management application sees both the scenario and the scenario structure package. We can define new scenarios with the extra visibility.

A question that might occur to the attentive reader is whether the scenario needs to have visibility to the scenario structure. Responding to a request for a quote requires use of the internal structure. An intriguing aspect of inheritance and polymorphism manifests itself in these visibilities. The scenario package can contain a scenario class that defines the interface required by all packages with visibility to the scenario. However, this scenario class need not implement all of the interface (and thus is abstract). We can place a second scenario class in the scenario structure package that implements the interface. This second scenario class has full visibility to the contents of the scenario structure. Any scenario object used by another package is an instance of the scenario structure's scenario class, but those clients of the class do not realize it. All they see is an object that conforms to the interface of the scenario package's scenario class. It may be worth providing a notation to show where this kind of subclassing occurs across package boundaries, although I don't use one.

So when an object in the portfolio package sends a message to a scenario, it is actually sending a message to an instance of the concrete scenario class that lies in the scenario management package. However, the caller thinks it is calling an instance of the abstract scenario class that lies in the scenario package. An object can send a message to an object in a package it cannot see, providing the called object is a subclass of a class in a package the calling object can see.

A consequence of this is that visibilities do not reflect compilation or load dependencies. Although the scenario structure is not visible to the scenario, the scenario needs the scenario structure to function (strictly speaking, it is dependent on some package that implements the interface). The scenario structure contains the concrete subclasses of the scenario without which the scenario package cannot work.

Although two different scenario classes are needed in this scheme, they may conform to a single scenario type. In this case a new subtype is provided to allow access to the internal structure of a scenario for applications such as scenario management. It is possible to have a single type, however, when other types do not need to call special features only present on the subtype.

11.2 Mutual Visibility

Adding packages for contracts and parties raises more complex issues. With scenarios and portfolios, separate packages were used for two reasons. First, scenarios and portfolios seem to be separate lumps of the model. They are themselves complex sections that seem to make a unit of labor. Second, we do not need any knowledge of portfolios to construct a model of scenarios. The second reason is the strongest because it leads to the visibility relationships shown in Figure 11.1.

It is reasonable to conclude that contracts can be put together and modeled without a knowledge of portfolios. Contracts can be recorded independently of the dynamic structure of the portfolio used to group them together for risk assessment purposes, as shown in Figure 11.6.

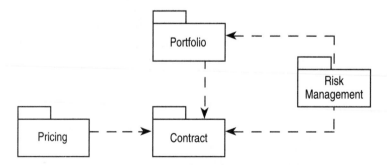

Figure 11.6   Packages for portfolio and contract.

The risk management application needs both packages, but the pricing application only needs to know about contracts.

The relationships between parties and contracts are a greater problem. We can make an argument for placing a party in its own package. A number of applications might look for information about parties without wanting to know anything about the deals being carried out with them. A common party package might hold common information about parties used by many dealing systems, rather like a contact database. Thus we can conclude that a party package is valuable.

What would be the relationship between the party and contract packages? It would be valuable for a party to tell which contracts were dealt with it, and for a contract to tell who the parties for the contract were. This implies mutual visibility between a party and a contract, as shown in Figure 11.7. But mutual visibility may cause problems in a package model. On the whole we try to design package models with a layered architecture and simple lines of visibility. Many people believe such an architecture should never have cycles in visibility relationships, because a cycle breaks the rule of clear layers. Mutual visibility is the simplest case of a cycle.

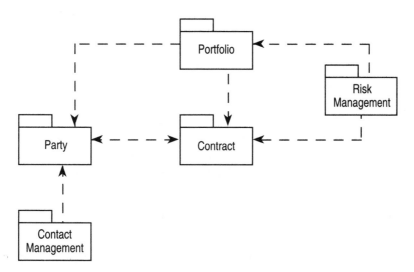

Figure 11.7   Separate party and contract packages.

Some applications need only one of either the party package or the contract package, but both of these packages need each other. This can imply mutual visibility. If mutual visibilities are unacceptable, we can choose a single direction or combine the packages.

To remove mutual visibility we must either alter the features of party or contract so that only one knows about the other, or combine them into a single package. Each alternative has trade-offs.

The benefit of restricting the visibility between the party and contract types to one direction is that it decreases the coupling between the two types (and their respective packages). If we remove the mappings from party to its contracts (making the association one-way) we can work on the party package without needing to know anything about contracts. This reduces the coupling (the party is no longer coupled to the contract), which is an advantage. However, a user who wants to know which contracts a particular party is the counterparty for must look at every contract and use the mappings to the party to form the set. Thus we have reduced the complexity for the developer of the party package but increased the complexity for the developer of any application that needs to use both types. There is no absolute right answer here; we have to look at the trade-offs in each direction and decide which choice is the lesser burden.

Modeling Principle   *The decision between a one-way and two-way association is a trade-off between less work for the developers of the types involved (by reducing their coupling) and convenience for the users of the types.*

Assuming we decide in favor of the two-way association, our only route to eliminating the mutual visibility is to combine the party and contract packages. This is not free of disadvantages, however. In Figure 11.7 we can see the contact management package only needs to know about parties, not contracts. Combining these two packages would remove this information. Contact management would be forced to have greater visibility than it needs to have.

This situation leads me not to ban mutual visibilities or other cycles. Certainly cycles should be reduced to the minimum. Eliminating them completely, however, leads to either forcing the trade-off between one-way and two-way associations or large packages whose clients do not need all the visibility that is implied.

Modeling Principle   *If a package only needs visibility to part of another package, consider splitting the latter package into two mutually visible packages.*

Figure 11.8 shows another example of this situation. The product (see Section 10.3) is added in its own package. The preceding arguments lead to the mutual visibilities among product, party, and contract. This leads to fairly coupled domain model packages. The application packages, however, need to see only parts of the picture, and each application package has slightly different needs. The three mutually visible packages allow us to be clear on these needs.

Another way of doing this puts protocols on packages. Then the party, product, and contract packages are combined and three separate protocols are provided to correspond to the old packages. Applications then select the protocols in the same way that they select the packages shown in Figure 11.8.

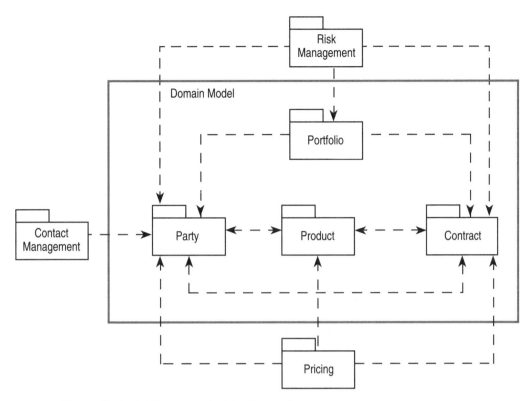

Figure 11.8   Adding a product to the package.

Again different application needs may be served by mutually visible packages.

To summarize, when types are naturally closely coupled, we have three options. We can decouple the types by making the associations one-way (but this makes it harder for the user of the types). We can put them into a single large package (but this means that any user of the package has visibility to the whole package, even if only part of it is needed). We can have two mutually visible packages (but this introduces cycles into the package structure). If you have protocols on packages, you can have one big package with separate protocols.

11.3   Subtyping Packages

Visibility is easiest to consider with subtyping. The subtype always needs to see a supertype, but we should avoid the reverse. Hence we add combinations, options, and barriers (described in Chapter 10), as shown in Figure 11.9.

We should also avoid mutual visibility between a subtype and its supertype. The whole point of subtyping is to allow a type to be extended without

Portfolio

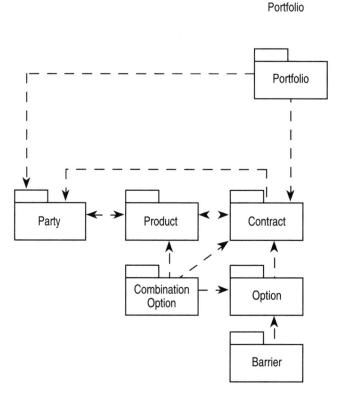

Figure 11.9   Adding various kinds of options.

Subtypes need visibility to their supertypes, but not vice versa.

the supertype being aware of it. If we design types with supertypes knowing about their subtypes, then future specialization is likely to be more difficult because we have built assumptions about subtyping into the supertype. Any effort to remove such dependencies is repaid in later enhancements. Designing supertypes correctly usually requires experience in designing a few subtypes first, so it is better not to fix the supertype until a few subtypes have been put together.

11.4   Concluding Thoughts

Visibility always implies trade-offs. To restrict visibility reduces the ease with which the model can be navigated. With lots of one-way visibilities, getting around the model can be rather like getting around a city with lots of one-way streets. Two-way visibilities make navigation much easier, which means less code to write and maintain. Such visibilities come at a price, however. The more bits of the system see each other, the more difficult it is to control the effects of change in the model. Restricting visibility cuts down this interdependence.

Different OO modelers make this trade-off differently. Some restrict visibility to a great extent, using techniques such as one-way associations and visibility graphs on types. I find this too restrictive. I consider visibility at the package rather than the type level. The architecture presented in Chapter 12 separates a system into basic layers. Within the domain tier, further visibility restrictions can be used, but this is seldom simple. I prefer this approach, however, because of my experience with information systems. Other kinds of developments merit different trade-offs.

Most projects do not consider package architecture in any great detail. Often only the basic layers of the architecture are in place, if anything. This results in disadvantages to the project concerned and makes it difficult to assess the value of a properly enforced architectural model. Only more practice will allow us to further understand the trade-offs discussed here.

If developing a package architecture is complex for one project, the complexity increases tenfold when we try to integrate information systems for a large organization. Large organizations are plagued by multiple systems that cannot communicate. Even if the hardware and software are beaten into shape, such integration is defeated by the difference between the concepts that underlie the systems. One generally recognized solution is to do enterprise-wide modeling. The problem with this approach, however, is that it takes too long. By the time it is done, if it ever is, the effort is usually discredited and out of date. I believe that there is an upper limit to the size of chunk of modeling that can be tackled in one go, and this is linked to delivering useful systems that justify the expense of modeling within a reasonable period of time. A more opportunistic approach needs to be taken to integrating them. For this task I believe that packages and visibilities are necessary tools. They are not sufficient for the task, and I will not pretend to know what else is needed. Such enterprise-wide integration is still little understood and, like many people, I have only learned what not to do!

References

1. Wirfs-Brock, R., B. Wilkerson, and L. Wiener. *Designing Object-Oriented Software.* Englewood Cliffs, NJ: Prentice-Hall, 1990.

Support Patterns

Analysis Patterns discuss problems in analysis, and some models that can deal with them. Support patterns address problems in building computer systems around the analysis patterns. In Chapters 12 and 13 we consider the architecture for a client/server information system and how such a system can be layered to improve its maintainability. Chapter 14 looks at how conceptual models can be implemented, suggesting common patterns to turn analysis patterns into software.

Finally Chapter 15 is more abstract, examining modeling techniques themselves and how advanced modeling constructs can be viewed as patterns. This gives us a better basis for extending modeling methods to support particular needs.

12

Layered Architecture for Information Systems

The analysis patterns in this book will be of great value to developers of corporate information systems. Information system (IS) development involves more than an understanding of a domain, however. A world of many users, databases, and legacy systems must be accommodated. This chapter discusses architectural patterns for information systems. An architectural pattern describes the high-level division of a system into major subsystems and the dependencies among the subsystems. An information system architectural pattern divides the system into layers (or tiers). Architectural patterns are useful on their own, but they also show how the analysis patterns fit into a wider context. Chapter 13 describes a technique for using the patterns in this chapter.

The early days of object technology did not focus much on IS development. The main problem is that large volumes of often complex information must be shared by many people. Although this information is shared, different users have different needs. Providing common information that can also be locally tailored is a primary goal of large information systems. Furthermore, a great deal of flexibility is required to meet constantly changing information needs. Most information systems are dominated by maintenance, which primarily involves coping with changing information demands. The main advantage of object technology in these environments is not in the speed of building new systems but in reducing the maintenance burden [3].

The most fundamental issue in developing a modern information system is understanding the underlying software architecture. A broad picture of the software architecture that is suitable for information systems must precede any discussion of which techniques to use or what process to consider.

Most IS developments tacitly assume a *two-tier architecture (12.1)*, which follows from mainframe interactive systems and is common in client/server developments today. Despite its wide use, the two-tier architecture has many shortcomings due to the tight coupling of the user interface to the physical data layout. The *three-tier architecture (12.2)*, also called the three-schema architecture, addresses this by putting an intermediate layer between the user interface and the physical data. This domain tier closely models the conceptual structure of the problem domain. Object technology is particularly well suited to three-tier approaches, and the domain tier can be placed on either client or server machines.

Next we turn our attention to applications, which manipulate the objects of the domain tier and display information on the user interface. These two responsibilities can be used to split the application into *presentation and application logic (12.3)*. The application logic can be organized as a set of facades on the domain tier, one facade for each presentation. This division has many advantages, and the application facades can be used to simplify client/server interactions.

Database interaction (12.4) can be handled in two ways. The domain tier can be responsible for accessing the database, which handles its own persistence. This works well for object-oriented or simple relational systems. When there are complex data formats or multiple data sources, an additional data interface layer may be required.

This chapter is based on various experiences, in particular the Cosmos project of the UK National Health Service and a derivatives trading system for a London bank.

12.1   Two-Tier Architecture

Most interactive IS development is organized, at least roughly, along the two-tier principle, as shown in Figure 12.1. A two-tier architecture divides the system into a shared database and several applications. The shared database sits on a server that has the disk space and processing needed to cope with heavy demands. The database contains the data required by a significant portion of the enterprise, structured to support all the needs of that portion. (For large companies a single corporatewide database is infeasible, so a database will take only a portion.) The database is designed and maintained by a database group. Although the term *database* is used here, it should be remembered that data is often stored in flat files (most commercial data still is on flat files such as VSAM). As such *database* can refer to any data source.

Applications are developed for specific local uses. Traditionally CICS/COBOL was used, but more recent efforts have used 4GLs and the popular application development tools Powerbuilder and Visual Basic. These tools

Applications   Database

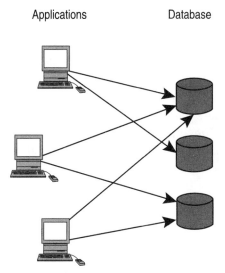

Figure 12.1   Two-tier architecture.
Applications directly access databases.

provide sophisticated features for developing GUI systems, and a good Windows interface is generally demanded by PC users who are used to such capabilities on their spreadsheets and word processors. Applications are usually built on a case-by-case basis. Any new data capabilities required are requested of the database group.

The two-tier architecture has some advantages. Most organizations have data that needs central control and consistent maintenance. Applications that interpret this data need much less centralized control. Much IS work involves presenting some existing data in a new and meaningful manner.

There are also many disadvantages of the two-tier architecture, most of which are inherent in current technologies. The idea that all data is shared and all processing is local is broadly true but a gross simplification. Many processing aspects of an enterprise are shared. Databases, whether SQL or older, are unable to provide a computationally complete language. The data is also unencapsulated, leaving a lot of integrity control in the hands of the application programmer. This makes it difficult to change a database structure that already has many applications running against it. These problems are reduced by stored procedures that can provide support for processing and encapsulate data.

Databases are often unable to give a true representation of the enterprise. This is due to the lack of modeling constructs, which are common in conceptual modeling techniques but are still a long way from support in everyday databases. Flat files and hierarchic databases have well-known limits on data structure. The current standard for new development, relational databases, also suffer from the high cost of joins. Data models that are true to underlying business semantics are usually highly normalized and need reorganization for performance to be reasonable.

The data for an application is also unlikely to be on one database. Databases, even if organized sensibly at the time of creation, are usually not so coherent after a few years of business changes and corporate reorganizations. The two-tier architecture requires the applications to know which databases hold which data, as well as the structure of the data in each database, which may be quite a distance from the semantics of this data.

12.2   Three-Tier Architecture

A better architecture has in fact been around for a very long time. The three-schema architecture was proposed back in the 1970s [4]. This provides a three-tier approach, as shown in Figure 12.2: external schema, conceptual schema, and storage (internal) schema. The storage schema is the database design, and the external schema is the applications; the new layer is the conceptual schema, which I refer to as the domain tier. This represents the true semantics of the enterprise. It should ignore the limitations of data storage structures and data location.

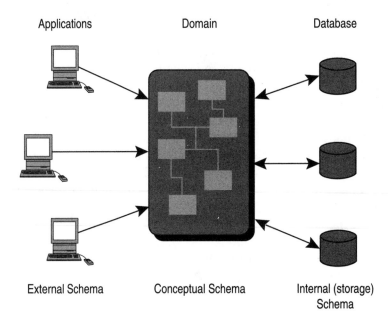

Figure 12.2   Three-tier architecture.

The main advantage of the three-tier approach is that it allows applications to be described purely on the semantics of the domain. They do not have to be concerned with the physical location and structure of the data but can look instead at a logical picture that removes these dependencies. This also frees the data administrators to change the physical structure and location without breaking existing applications.

The three-tier architecture is widely approved but rarely implemented. The principal reason for this is the difficulty of using it with existing technology. There are tools for data storage and for application development but not for implementing a domain tier. The most useful development is the logical data model, which is generally seen as a necessary first step in database design. This allows designers to consider enterprise semantics before committing to a physical design. As such the modifications for physical design could be made in an informed manner.

The stress on data is significant. Most practitioners consider the domain tier to be a logical data model. They might do process modeling, but it is usually considered separately by application developers. However, this view is not shared by all data modelers. A strong school of semantic data modelers view data modeling as very comparable with object-oriented modeling because it embraces subtyping and derived data, ties processes to objects, treats processes as data, and embeds processes within the semantic model.

With the development of object-oriented techniques, the domain tier can begin to come to the fore. Objects represent a very good way to implement domain tiers. They support encapsulation, complex structural relationships, rules, processes, and all the things considered by advanced semantic modelers. Reusable class libraries (or, better still, frameworks) are also at the heart of the domain tier. The key reusable objects of an enterprise are those that describe the domain—the framework that implements the domain tier (hence the term *domain framework*). Thus object modeling and domain tier development coincide very effectively.

Implementation issues are somewhat more complex, but the basic principle still works very well: If the domain tier is expressed as an object-oriented model and implemented as a domain framework, then applications can be written against this domain framework. This provides the separation between applications and databases that is so sorely needed.

12.2.1 The Location of the Domain Tier

In a client/server world an important question is where this domain tier should sit. A two-tier approach places application software on the client (desktop machines) and the data on various data servers. With the domain tier we have two basic choices: We can place the domain tier on the clients, or we can introduce a new layer of processors, which is the domain server and consists of one or many networked machines.

Client-based domain frameworks allow us to concentrate development on client machines, simplifying our systems support. Introducing a new layer of machines may well be a new headache for many shops and provides another set of machines and systems to maintain. The domain tier is provided as a set of libraries to application developers of client systems who can then write application code as necessary.

One problem with a client-based domain tier is that we may need to do a lot of data selection and processing on the client. This forces us to use powerful client machines. As desktop machines become ever more powerful, this becomes less of a problem, but we cannot assume such power. Technology pushes us to ever smaller machinery; some users want to use palmtops and PDAs, which can limit processing. Often it is easier to upgrade servers when more processing power is required.

Available software fits quite well with a client-based approach. Smalltalk, generally the most useful language for IS applications, requires a user interface tied into the domain tier, although "headless" Smalltalks that run on a server without a user interface are beginning to appear.

The domain tier is easier to control and update in a server-based domain tier. If the domain tier is on the clients, then any revision needs to be sent out to each client. Software updates on a server can be handled in a much more straightforward pattern. This control also extends to support of standing data, particularly those items that involve how data is accessed.

We need to consider concurrency issues. It is interesting that IS applications probably use more concurrency than any other style of software yet worry about it least. This is due to the powerful transaction model that is usually handled very well by a database, freeing the application programmer from most concurrency headaches. As the domain tier is introduced, we have to ask ourselves where the transaction boundary is to be. We can place it either in the data servers or in the domain tier itself. The logical place is the domain tier, but this requires us to build in transaction control features—a tricky business. Such placement also encourages the server-based domain tier, since a commit across many clients is pragmatically beyond current technology. I never encourage clients to build their own transaction control systems; that task is outside the scope of most IS developments.

OO databases provide a solution to this problem. The major concern in IS communities with OO databases is trusting the corporate data to a new technology. OO databases have responded to this by providing gateways to traditional database products. In this approach an OO database can act as the transaction control mechanism without necessarily storing any data itself. Over time some data, particularly the complex and connected data that an

OO database can manage so well, can be moved to the OO database. However, key corporate data can stay in more traditional places as long as the developers like. The important warning here is that there is little information on multiuser performance for OO databases. Many of the dramatic performance improvements quoted for OO databases are based on small, single-user databases. Anyone using an OO database, even if only for transaction control, should benchmark before committing to the database.

If only a single OO database is used, then the data storage layer is effectively collapsed into the domain tier. This is permissible provided that this is an effective architecture and that extensions to the system to support other databases can be done in such a way that these other databases are provided behind the domain tier so that they are not visible from applications.

12.3   Presentation and Application Logic

The three-tier architecture provides some very important benefits. Much attention has been lavished on how the domain tier can be constructed, and a good portion of OO modeling is directly applied to this key layer. Little, however, has been said about applications. Applications are built by assembling the reusable components in the domain tier, and there are guidelines for this task as well, although they are often not described in any detail.

Typically in today's environment a programmer develops an application within a GUI environment, which is built on the domain tier. This requires knowledge of the GUI environment and of the domain tier, and a complex domain tier can make the learning curve quite steep. Programming in many graphics environments (such as Visual C++) can also be pretty daunting.

Consider a relatively simple example of a financial institution that has a portfolio of derivative contracts between US dollars (USD) and Japanese yen (JPY). Such an organization is concerned with managing the risk associated with such a portfolio. Several factors can affect this risk, including the spot exchange rate, the volatility of the exchange rate, and the interest rates of the two currencies involved. To consider this risk, the analyst wishes to look at the price of the portfolio under various combinations of these different factors. One way of doing this is by using the grid shown in Figure 12.3. The analyst picks two variables to analyze, sets various values for these, and sees a matrix that shows the value of the portfolio under the combinations of values.

What are the processing tasks and how should we divide them between the application and domain tiers? One fundamental task is that of determining the value of a derivative contract, a complex process typically handled by Black-Scholes analysis [2]. This process would be widely used by any system in a derivatives trading environment, so it would be placed in the domain tier. Another common task is the valuing of many contracts together in a portfolio,

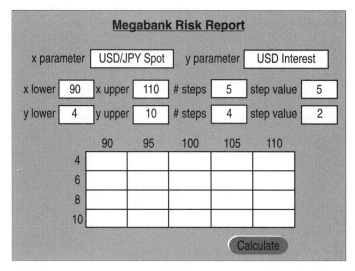

Figure 12.3   An example application to manage derivative risk.

which is usually placed in the domain tier. The next task is to build a grid of values from the parameters (upper, lower, step size, number of steps) in the grid. This task is unique to this risk report screen so logically should be part of the application tier, together with the code that builds and controls the GUI.

The task of building the matrix is quite involved and requires a closer look. It involves setting the various parameters, keeping them consistent, and then using the parameters to build the grid of values. This process can and should be separated from the display on a GUI screen. Thus I recommend splitting of the application tier into two: a presentation tier and an application logic tier, as shown in Figure 12.4.

The responsibilities of the two tiers are quite easy to separate. The presentation tier is responsible for user interface only. It handles windows, menus, fonts, colors, and all positioning on screen or paper. Typically it uses a user interface framework such as MFC or MacApp. It does not do any calculations, queries, or updates to the domain tier. Indeed it does not need to have any visibility to the domain tier. The application logic tier does no user interface processing whatsoever. It is responsible for all accesses to the domain tier and any processing other than user interface processing. It selects information from the underlying domain tier and simplifies it into the exact form that the presentation requires. The complex interrelationships of the domain tier are thus hidden from the presentation. Furthermore, the application logic tier performs type conversion. The presentation will typically deal only with a small set of common types (integer, real, string, and date, plus the collection classes used in the software). The application logic provides only

Presentation   Application   Domain   Data Source
                    Logic

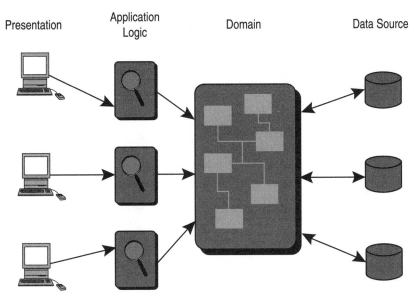

Figure 12.4   Splitting up the application tier into presentations and application logic

these types and is responsible for converting the underlying domain types into these types and interpreting any updates requested by the presentation.

A useful way of organizing the application logic tier is to develop a series of *facades*. A facade [1] is a type that provides a simplified interface to a complicated model. We can prepare a facade for each presentation. The facade has a feature for each element on the corresponding user interface. Each presentation thus has a simple interface to the domain model that minimizes any processing for the presentation other than the user interface. (Chapter 13 discusses a technique for designing these facades).

Figure 12.5 shows how this organization works for the risk report screen mentioned above. We need two classes: a risk report presentation and a risk report facade. The presentation creates the layout of the screen and manages the user's interactions with it. The facade provides an underlying structure that mimics the presentation. It has operations to get and set the parameter, upper, lower, number of steps, and step size for the x and y coordinates of the grid. The facade contains the rules necessary to ensure proper consistency among these values (such as the invariant `xUpper - xLower == xNumberOfSteps * xStepSize`). It also provides a method to return the answer grid. Ideally this returns a single matrix using a general matrix class. (If for some reason this is neither available nor desired, then the facade provides operations to get particular cells, but a reusable matrix class, essentially a new kind of collection, is usually the best solution.)

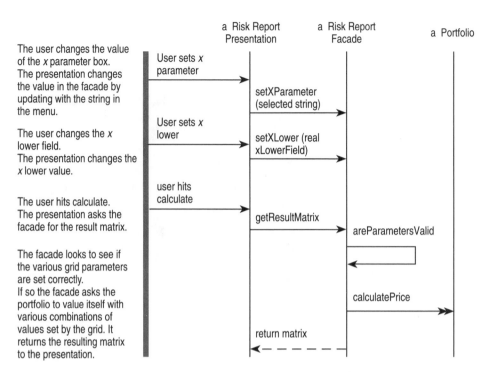

Figure 12.5   Interaction diagram summarizing collaborations between presentation, facade, and domain tiers.

The `getResultMatrix` method on the facade looks to see if enough information has been provided by the presentation (if not, it can add defaults) and then asks the domain tier to value the portfolio with the various combinations of parameters. The domain tier puts the results into the matrix and returns it to the presentation.

Setting of parameters is an example of using type conversion. Various objects can be placed as parameters in this list, including USD/JPY spot, USD/JPY volatility, USD interest rate, and JPY interest rate. (The list depends on the currencies of the contracts in the portfolio.) The facade provides appropriate strings to the presentation, translating from the types in the domain tier (see Section 13.5). The facade typically provides a list of such strings for the presentation to place in its pop-up menu. The presentation can then select a string. The facade correlates the selected string to the underlying domain objects (a dictionary handles this nicely). In this way the user interface is completely insulated from the domain model.

In this situation the visibilities between the domains are defined as shown in Figure 12.6. Visibilities flow only from presentation to application logic to domain tier. This line of visibility is valuable because it insulates the

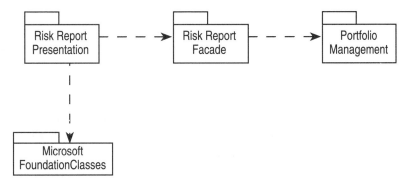

Figure 12.6 Visibilities between presentation, facade, and domain categories.

domain tier completely from the applications that rely on it. A problem can occur, however, if the presentation needs to be automatically updated when a change occurs in the domain model. One option is for the presentation to poll at regular intervals, but this can get quite messy. A better option is to use the observer pattern [1]. This allows the facade and presentation to be automatically updated without breaking the visibility rules.

12.3.1 Advantages of the Presentation/Application Logic Split

Layering is a good idea in principle, but it does have some disadvantages: the extra work is required to build the layer, and a performance penalty can be incurred in using it. The important question is, are the advantages worth the costs?

One advantage comes from the different styles of programming involved in the two layers. GUI programming can be very complex, requiring a knowledge of GUI frameworks and how to use them well. If new GUI controls are required, programming becomes even more complex. On the other hand, GUI development can be quite straightforward if we have a good GUI screen builder, allowing us to draw controls on the screen and make event handlers that would typically be relayed as calls to the application facade. In either case development organizations can use GUI specialists who need to know little about the domain model. Similarly the facade programmers need know nothing about how the GUI system works, they concern themselves with getting the right interactions with the domain types. Thus we see that there can be GUI developers who understand the user interface environment but need to know nothing about the domain model, and facade developers who understand the domain model but do not need to know about GUI development. The presentation/application logic split separates different required skills, allowing developers to learn less in order to make a contribution.

The split allows multiple presentations to be developed from a single facade; this is particularly useful when customized screen or paper layouts containing the same information are required. When tools are used for screen and report building, this allows a quick turnaround for new presentation styles.

The facades provide a good platform for testing. When facade and presentation are combined, the base computation can only be tested via the GUI, requiring manual testing (or GUI testing software for regression testing). When these are separated a test harness can be written for the facade's interface. This leaves only the presentation code that needs to be tested by using more awkward tools. The separation of testing reinforces the point that the two layers can be built separately, although the presentation must be defined before the facade can be built.

12.3.2 Stretching Facades in Client/Server Environments

The facade is valuable as a focal point for client/server interactions if the domain tier is based on the server. A useful technique in these cases is to "stretch" the facade across the client and the server, placing a facade class on both the client and the server. When the user opens a presentation, the corresponding facade is opened on the client side. The client facade passes the request onto the server facade. The server facade goes through the creation process, pulling information out of the domain classes. When all the information for the facade is complete, the server facade sends all information for the facade over to the client. Since the server and client facades can be in different object spaces, a series of private communications between the two facade classes can occur. The user can then interact with the presentation, which will update the client facade with each modification. These modifications are not passed onto the server facade until the user commits the modifications. At that point the modified facade object is passed back to the server, and the server facade then updates the domain tier, as shown in Figure 12.7.

The point of stretching a facade is that it allows a single point of reference for client/server interaction. If a client facade (or a presentation) accesses the server domain classes directly, we will see many calls required across the network to populate the client. These network calls can be a significant overhead on performance. The facades can have methods to build a single transfer packet and interpret such a packet into the facade's data. We can then pass all information in a single network call.

The various responsibilities of the facade can be split between the client and server classes. Only the server facade needs the responsibilities for interacting with the domain model. Both classes need to be able to send and receive information to the other. Ideally only the client facade needs the operations to support the presentation. In practice, however, I find it worthwhile to

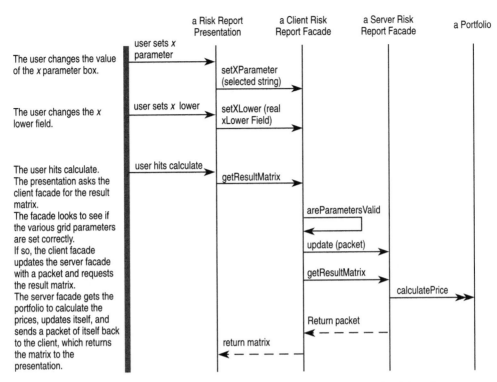

The user changes the value of the *x* parameter box.

The user changes the *x* lower field.

The user hits calculate. The presentation asks the client facade for the result matrix.
The facade looks to see if the various grid parameters are set correctly.
If so, the client facade updates the server facade with a packet and requests the result matrix.
The server facade gets the portfolio to calculate the prices, updates itself, and sends a packet of itself back to the client, which returns the matrix to the presentation.

Figure 12.7 The interaction diagram of Figure 12.3 using stretched facades.

give the two classes the same interface to make testing easier (that is, they are the same type). Both sides require load and save operations. The client facade implements these operations by communicating with the server facade, and the server implements them by communicating with the domain model.

12.4 Database Interaction

We need to think carefully about how to integrate databases and legacy applications into this structure. The simplest case is when an object database is used. In this case the straightforward approach is to simply integrate the database into the domain tier. The object database then provides facilities for persistence, transaction management, and other features that no enterprise programmer should have to worry about.

Few applications, however, are that simple in an IS shop. Many IS organizations are distrustful of object databases and are reluctant to place critical data in them. This is partly because of their newness but also because of their complexity. Relational tables are relatively easy to dissect if something goes wrong. Object databases, with rampant disk pointers, are much more difficult.

Even if object databases were a confident choice for new development, there is still the issue of existing data. Even relational databases, despite their current position as the proven technology for database development, have not yet reached the position of managing the majority of corporate data. The vast majority of corporate data lies on hierarchical databases, flat files, and the like. Object systems must interact with these systems, taking feeds as necessary, dealing with the fact that many systems have to be accessed to get an integrated picture. There are two broad approaches we can use: letting the domain model interact with the data sources or using a database interface layer.

12.4.1 Linking the Domain Tier to Data Sources

Let's consider the simple case of a stand-alone system that needs to use a relational database for data storage. We can design the relational database specifically to support the domain model. We should design the domain tier first and base the database schema on that. For all but the simplest systems, it is not possible to simply take each object type in the domain model and turn it into a relational table. Despite their name, relational databases have a problem relating data because computing joins is time-consuming. A good relational design thus should denormalize significantly to get good performance. The domain model provides a starting point for the database design, but the database design needs time to be done well. The resulting database schema can look quite different from the original object diagrams.

The obvious way to link the domain tier to the database is to have the domain classes know how to build themselves from the database. Classes can have load routines that pull data out of the database and use this to create and knit together the framework. It is important that applications not get involved in this behavior. When an application requests an object, the domain tier should look to see if it is in memory. If not, it should get the object to create itself off the database. The application should not need to know how this interaction is occurring.

An exception to this procedure occurs when applications need a particular data configuration to work on, and that data can be pulled from the database in one step at the beginning, thus improving performance. In this case it can be useful for the domain tier to offer application-specific load requests that give the application a chance to let the domain tier know what it is about to be asked for. To some extent this compromises the principle that the domain tier should not know what applications use it, but the performance gains can be compelling in some circumstances.

12.4.2 Database Interface Tier

The direct link between the domain tier and the database does have some significant problems. It can complicate the domain classes excessively by giving them two independent responsibilities: providing an executing model of the business and pulling data from a database. The code required to interact with the database can be quite substantial, bloating the classes excessively. If data has to be pulled from multiple databases and feeds, then this problem becomes critical.

An answer, of course, is to add another layer—a database interface tier, which is responsible for loading the domain tier with data from the database and for updating the database when the domain changes. This tier is also in charge of handling feeds and other legacy interactions.

In many ways the database interface tier is very similar to the application logic tier. In both cases a facade is provided to a complex domain tier to cope with a less powerful representation. This facade selects and simplifies the object structure and performs type conversion to the simpler external type system. Again, the domain tier should be unaware of the various views that can be taken of it. Typically the database interface classes are based on the data source with which they are working. A database interface class can be constructed for each table in a relational database, or each record type in a feed. Class libraries to support database interaction often support this kind of correspondence.

The biggest difference between this tier and the application logic tier lies in the initiation of activity. With the user interface, the user's action causes the presentation to initiate the activity. Since the presentation has visibility to the application logic, then it is straightforward for it to call the application logic. The initiation of activity follows the line of visibility. However, this is not the case with the database interface. The domain tier begins the process by wanting to save itself, but we do not want the domain model to see the database. Thus the initiation of activity is opposite to the desired visibilities. One solution is to use the observer [1] again, but that could well lead to a very high degree of message traffic.

An alternative is to extend the architecture with an interface broker, which is visible to the domain tier. This broker provides a very small interface, which allows only messages that initiate the database interface. These might typically be calls as general as `loadMe(anObject)` and `saveMe(anObject)`, which pass on all responsibility to dealing with the request to the database interface tier. The broker's responsibility is to then pass this request onto a class in the database interface that can best handle the request. Thus if we have spot contracts held in one database table and conventional options held in another, the interface broker first interrogates the object to find which it is and then passes the request onto the appropriate database interface class, as shown in Figures 12.8 and 12.9.

The advantages of this layering are similar to the advantages of layering elsewhere. Again, responsibilities are split in a useful manner, separating the data interface from the enterprise model. Table formats or feeds change can be

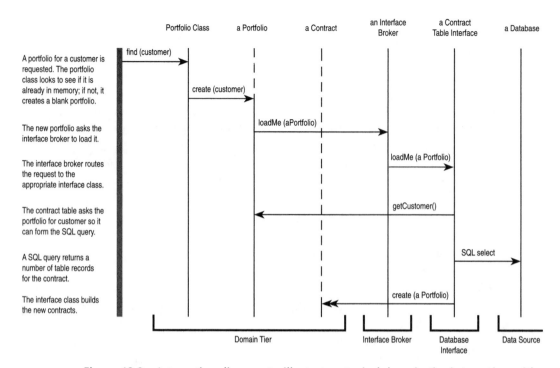

Figure 12.8 Interaction diagram to illustrate a typical domain tier interaction with a data source.

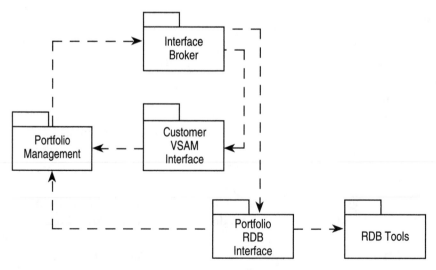

Figure 12.9 Categories for database interface tier.

done without altering the domain model. This is particularly important when table formats are outside the control of the project team or when it is likely that the data structure can change to help with performance. The greater the volatility of these sources, the more important it is to use an intermediate layer.

Access to different databases can require different tools and skills. Specialized class libraries exist to interface to database products. A knowledge of SQL and of the specific database format may be required. Other databases (multidimensional, hierarchical) have their own interfaces and structures to learn. Separating this interaction out, particularly if there are many different data sources, allows team members to concentrate on areas where their skills are strongest.

12.5 Concluding Thoughts

Building large IS systems in a client/server environment is still a difficult activity with many pitfalls. Many of these lie in using a two-tier architecture, which works well for small systems but does not scale well. A three-tier architecture improves matters considerably and is well supported by object technology. Table 12.1 provides brief descriptions of the three tiers.

TIER	DESCRIPTION
Domain	A direct model of business objects applicable to the whole domain. Independent of individual applications and data sources.
Application logic	A selection and simplification of the domain model for an application. Contains no user interface code but provides a set of facades of the domain tiers for the user interface. Converts from rich domain tier types to the types required by a presentation.
Presentation	Performs the formatting of information from the application facade into a GUI or paper report. Is only concerned with user interface, and has no knowledge of underlying domain tier.
Data interface	Responsible for moving information between data sources and the domain tier. Will provide a simple interface broker for the domain tier to issue requests. Has visibility of both the domain tier and the data sources. Will be divided into subsystems based on the type of data sources used.

Table 12.1 Summary of layers and their purposes.

Splitting the application tier to separate application logic from the user interface is a valuable technique. Its advantages include the reuse of application logic for different GUIs, ease of testing, performance management for client/server systems, and support for more specialized development staff. An intermediate layer is also useful for data access, particularly when there are many complex data sources.

Some classes must be used by all tiers. This includes common fundamental types (integer, date, quantity), collections, and also some domain specific fundamental types.

References

1. Gamma, E., R. Helm, R. Johnson, and J. Vlissides. *Design Patterns: Elements of Reusable Object-Oriented Software.* Reading, MA: Addison-Wesley, 1995.
2. Hull, J.C. *Options, Futures, and Other Derivative Securities* (Second Edition). London: Prentice-Hall International, 1993.
3. Kain, J.B. "Measuring the return on investment of reuse." *Object Magazine*, 4, 3 (1994), pp. 49–54.
4. Tsichiritzis, D.C., and A. Klug. "The ANSI/X3/SPARC DBMS framework: report of the study group on database management systems." *Information Systems*, 3 (1978).

13

Application Facades

To fully understand this chapter, you will need to read Chapter 12 through Section 12.3 first. In Section 12.3 I explained how applications can be split into presentation and application logic. Presentations contain all user interface logic, and the application logic provides a set of custom facades for the presentation. These application facades are responsible for selecting and arranging all information for a presentation.

We can define and build application facades by using a fairly standard technique described in this chapter. (Uncharacteristically, this chapter does not contain patterns.) This technique can be considered an addition to object-oriented methods.

An application facade looks much like any other type: It has attributes and operations. All of the attributes, however, are derived from the domain model. Models are given based on a health care example (13.1). The contents of a facade (13.2) are defined by a number of methods that are attached to each attribute. These methods describe how the attribute is retrieved, how it is updated, how a set of legal values can be found, how it can be validated, and how a default value can be obtained.

Some common methods (13.3) can be used in many application facades, so they can be moved into domain models. Application facades also contain operations (13.4), which can be local to the facade or delegated to the domain model. User interface frameworks will not usually be aware of the many interrelated types in the domain model, so the application can perform type conversions (13.5), creating more primitive types that the user interface can understand. An application will often contain multiple facades (13.6), which can be described using a structural model.

I have used this technique on several projects, including the UK National Health Service and a trading system for a London bank. It was designed specifically for facades in the application logic tier. It can also be used for facades in other circumstances, including database interaction.

13.1   A Health Care Example

Application facades are best understood from a fairly complex and abstract domain model. Figure 13.1 shows such a model whose basic structure is based on the Cosmos model designed for health care [1]. Further explanation of many of the ideas can be found in Chapter 3, and it may be worth reading that chapter before continuing with this chapter.

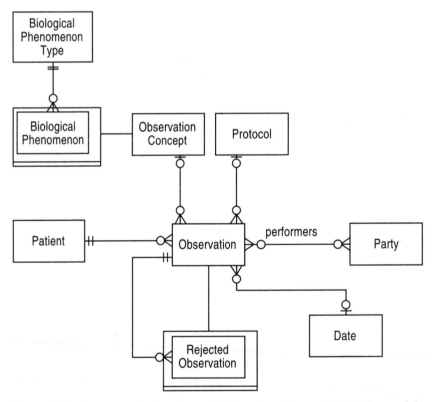

Figure 13.1   An example domain model from health care. This is the model on which the domain tier is built.

Consider an example from a hospital information system, which needs to record information on each patient gathered from all parts of the hospital so that it can keep a complete medical record for each patient. The range of information that can be recorded about a patient is vast. To reduce the bulk of the model, an abstract approach is used, as shown in Figure 13.1.

The model describes all the information that can be recorded about a patient in terms of biological phenomenon and biological phenomenon types. For example, there is a biological phenomenon type of gender with biological phenomena of male and female, and there is a biological phenomenon type of blood group with biological phenomena of A, B, A/B, and O. To say that a patient has a blood group of O, we use an observation that links the patient to the appropriate biological phenomenon. We can also indicate other appropriate information about the observation, such as who did it (the performer), when it was done (the date), and how it was done (the protocol). If it is later found to be wrong and the correct blood group is A, then we reject the original observation and replace it with a new one. This is necessary so that a full record of a patient can be held.

Such a model can handle a wide range of cases. The blood transfusion department, however, has simpler and more focused needs. It merely wishes to record a set of attributes for a patient. For example, consider the registration of a blood donor. Attributes of a blood donor include name, blood group, and date of last donation. The name is straightforward since this is directly linked to the patient type. The blood group and last donation date, however, require more complex processing, as we shall see below.

13.2   Contents of a Facade

Each application facade consists of a reference to the domain model (referred to as the subject of the facade) and a number of attributes that represent the information for the user of the facade, as shown in Figure 13.2.

An application facade is opened with a particular object in the domain model as the subject. This subject acts as the starting point for all the manipulations that are done by the facade. When we define the facade, we define the type of the subject. For the blood transfusion registration example, the subject would be `patient`. The user of the facade never accesses the subject directly but treats the facade as a logical window on the subject.

Each attribute in the facade then acts as a logical attribute of the subject. Each attribute should have its type defined, and this type should correspond to a type on the domain model. Similarly we can define operations on the facade. In the case of blood donor registration, we have a donor facade as follows:

> **Application facade:** donor
> **Subject:** patient

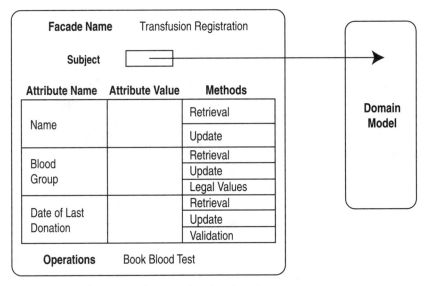

Figure 13.2   The parts of an application facade.

Attributes:
name: string
blood group: biological phenomenon
date of last transfusion: date
Operations:
book blood test

We then define a series of methods for each attribute on the facade. These methods describe how information is translated from the domain model into the facade and how the facade updates the shared information. There are various ways of defining these methods. One is to use an English sentence, which would be easy to understand but could result in ambiguity. At the opposite end of the spectrum is a formal approach such as predicate calculus, which is appropriate if everyone understands it. In between lie various forms of structured English.

13.2.1   Types of Methods

The retrieval method defines how data is obtained from the model to fill the attribute. We can consider this method to be a query over the model, starting at the subject. A retrieval method can be very simple; for example, the registration name can correspond to the name of the patient. But retrieval can become rather complex. The blood group of the patient requires finding all nonrejected observations of the patient whose biological phenomenon's biological phenomenon type is blood group. Similarly the last donation date is found by taking all procedures whose protocol is blood donation and returning the date of the latest one. Read-only attributes will not have any other methods.

The legal values method provides a set of legal values that can be used for validation checking. Often (as for name) there is no finite set of legal values; the type is enough for validation. For blood group, however, something more sophisticated is called for: the type of the attribute is the biological phenomenon, but only biological phenomena whose biological phenomenon type is blood group are allowed. Thus the legal values are supplied by a query that returns the set of biological phenomena A, B, A/B, and O. As well as being useful for validation checking, these values can be used to fill a menu or list on a user interface.

The update method is the one that requires the most powerful techniques. Even if the retrieval method is simple, the meaning of an update can vary widely. Again the name object provides a simple case where the attribute of a patient is updated. Changing the blood group is more complex, so we need to create a new observation that is linked to the biological phenomenon supplied by the attribute. The old observation is rejected and linked to the new object to show which object rejected it. In addition we can supply some implied information. For example, a change in the blood group will always be supplied by the transfusion unit, and the unit always uses the same protocol, so we can add this information to the record automatically by making the logged-in physician the performer of the procedure and by using the standard protocol. Obviously we have to be careful about how much information can be implied in this way, and that information should be echoed back to the user.

A validation method may be required if either the legal values or the attribute type are not enough to check validity. A validation rule that is context specific to the facade needs to be supplied. For example, the last donation date may need to be earlier than today and later than the currently held value.

The default method is used when a new record is being created, as opposed to an existing one updated. To reduce complexity, we usually assume that creating a new record is the same as updating a blank record. The user can then fill in the attributes, and exactly the same validation methods are applied as are used for updating. The default method indicates what information should be supplied if the user is starting with a blank record. It is formed in much the same way as a retrieval method.

Some attributes will not have a single value but a list of values. In this case there are two update methods: one for adding an item and one for deleting an item. The retrieval method returns a collection, which can be a set or a list. If the collection is a set, then ordering criteria is specified to indicate the order in which the values are displayed. Usually this is the standard ordering criteria based on numbers or strings. Table 13.1 summarizes the various methods discussed here.

METHOD NAME	DESCRIPTION
Retrieval	Value according to domain model
Legal Values	Allowable values if less than the type
Update	How to update the model for a change in value. For multivalued attributes both add and delete updates have to be specified.
Validation	Used to test new values, only necessary if more complex then legal values
Default	Initial value to be used on creating a new object from a facade

Table 13.1   Summary of methods.

13.2.2   Sample Methods

Table 13.2 shows an example of how these methods might be worded, taken from the blood donor example given above. The rules have not been expressed in a formal notation (and are thus ambiguous) but are written in a pseudo-SQL manner, which has proven to be a reasonable compromise between rigor and ease of understanding.

13.3   Common Methods

In applications that use facades, we see many methods that have a similar structure. The blood group attribute is an example of a very common case in the medical record model. The blood group methods retrieve a particular biological phenomenon of a particular biological phenomenon type for a patient, where it is assumed that a patient only has one biological phenomenon of that type. In asking for the blood group we ask "Which biological phenomena of type blood group does this patient have observations for?" There are many cases (such as a patient's gender) where this kind of method exists. Therefore it makes sense to have a general service that can hold not only the common access and updating cases but also all the processing for special cases (such as when a patient has inconsistent observations).

We can incorporate such services into the domain model as operations or computed mappings on the patient. In our blood donor example, this would lead to an operation

```
valueOf (aBiologicalPhenomenonType): aBiologicalPhenomenon.
```

ATTRIBUTE	METHOD NAME	METHOD BODY
Name	Retrieval	`subject.name`
	Update	`Change subject.name`
Blood Group	Retrieval	`subject.observations. biological phenomenon where biological phenomenon. biological phenomenon type = 'Blood Group'.`

	Update	`oldObs:= All subject. observations where subject. observations. biological phenomenon. biological phenomenon type = 'blood group'.`
		
		 `Create new observation (newObs) where newObs. patient = subject, newObs. biological phenomenon = new Blood Group, and newObs. rejected observations = oldObs.`

	Legal Values	`All biological phenomena with biological phenomenon type = 'blood group'`
Date of Last Transfusion	Retrieval	`the latest subject. observations. date from those subject. observations with protocol = 'blood transfusion'.`
	Update	`Create new observation with patient = subject, protocol = 'blood transfusion', and date = Date of last transfusion`
	Validation	`new Date of last transfusion later than old Date of last transfusion`

Table 13.2   Sample methods for a facade.

Note there might be a corresponding update operation on patient that would also subsume the application facade's update method.

Moving application facade methods into the domain model is useful in two ways. First, they provide a higher-level interface to the facade, easing development of application facades. In particular this means that common code to handle these kinds of attributes can be held once in the domain model and not duplicated in many application facades. The second virtue of this approach is that it provides a good route for optimization. The fact that the code is common enough to be held in a shared method implies that it will be executed frequently. It thus makes a good target for optimization. This can be particularly important when the OO system provides navigational as opposed to declarative queries.

Clearly not every application facade method should be moved to the domain model. The value of application facades is that they separate what is local to one context from what is necessarily shared. Each facade method that moves into the domain model increases the complexity of the domain model. Thus the designer must be suspicious of moving facade methods to the domain model and only do so if the benefits outweigh the increased complexity that will occur.

13.4   Operations

Just as any other object type, application facades contain both data and process. The methods discussed in Section 13.2.1 are private methods on the facade that manage the mapping between the application facade and the domain model. Public methods also exist to allow access and update of the facade's attributes.

Additional operations within the application facade are not simply manipulations of attributes. These operations should be declared separately and typically involve some complex processing. It is useful to consider whether these operations are local or shared, as shown in Figure 13.3. A shared operation is used across the organization, while a local operation is only used by that application. If the operation is shared, then it should be implemented within the domain model attached to the most appropriate shared class. The shared operation should ignore any facades and operate solely on shared objects. The operation on the facade should then simply pass the call onto the shared operation, providing the necessary arguments and interpreting the returned values for use within the facade.

A local operation, however, should not be placed in the domain model but implemented within the local model. It would not use structures and operations of the domain model, relying instead on the attributes and operations of the application facade. In this way a clear separation is maintained between local and shared code.

Note that the distinction between local and shared operations is purely an issue of conceptual sharing of the code. It does not affect the implementation concerns of, say, a client/server environment. Depending on that environment, local operations can be run on a server or shared operations run on a client. The distinction is based solely on whether the operations are conceptually shared or not. Shared operations are heavily reused and must be maintained more carefully, in the same way as the rest of the domain model. Local operations can be dealt with purely within the facades. They are reused only if the facade they are part of is reused.

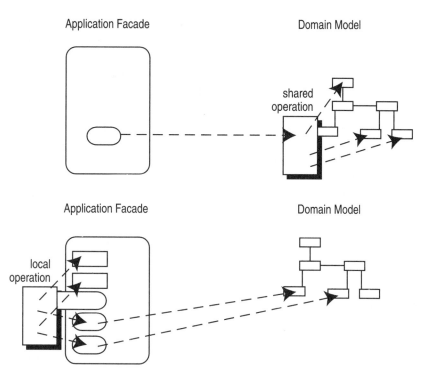

Figure 13.3   Operations in application facades.

A shared operation is implemented within the domain model and accesses the structures and services of the domain model. The facade provides a reference to that operation, while a local operation is implemented within the facade and only accesses the attributes and operations of that facade.

13.5   Type Conversions

One difficulty with using OO systems is the complexity of moving objects around a network, particularly when moving from one object space to another. This problem occurs when information needs to move either from one OO system to another with different object IDs, or from an OO to a non-OO system. In these cases we can move only information about the object, not the actual object. One solution is to use a proxy designed to translate calls made on the proxy to calls on the original object. This system works well where both client and server are part of a distributed database, but many systems have PC clients connected to database servers, where any calls on an object become expensive network calls.

This is particularly important when the non-OO systems involved do not have an understanding of objects and messages. Information must be transferred by using a lower-level representation, such as ASCII strings. In this case it is necessary to transform object information into a string, send it over the network, and decode it back into objects.

We can use facades to help simplify network access, controlling the translation to strings and allowing the application to take a large slice of information in one go. We do this by holding the attribute values as strings, as shown in Figure 13.4. The links to the objects can be maintained by holding a lookup table in the class portion of the facade. The lookup table maps from the strings to the database objects, making validation and updating easier. The table can be implemented with a dictionary, where the keys are the strings and the values are the database objects. The set of keys can be used for

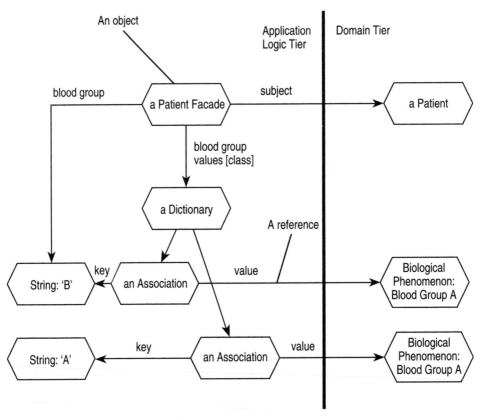

Figure 13.4 Example objects for type conversion.

The application facade has a reference to its subject in the domain model. For its attributes it stores strings and sends strings to the presentation. It also has a link (static or via its class) to a dictionary that associates the strings with the underlying domain objects. (For clarity only two blood groups are shown here.) It has a dictionary for each attribute that needs this kind of type conversion.

loading menus or validation purposes. When an attribute is changed the table can convert it to an object for replacement in the database. Since the table is held in the class portion of the class, it is only held once. It also only needs to be refreshed if a change is made to the available options: This change is usually infrequent.

Thus the blood group attribute has a corresponding dictionary, `BloodGroupValues`, in the class portion. This dictionary has keys of the strings 'A', 'B', and so on, with the objects in the database as values. On retrieval the blood group is translated to a string (using a name function or by the dictionary) and stored in the attribute. When updated the new string is used as a lookup to the dictionary, and the corresponding value is used for the update in the database.

When we use this approach we should describe facade attributes as having internal and external types. The internal type is the type within the domain model, while the external type is that provided to the presentation. In the blood group example, the internal type is `Biological Phenomenon`, while the external type is `String`.

13.6   Multiple Facades

Application facades do not usually appear alone but rather in groups. An application consists of a number of presentations and their corresponding facades. These components can be linked in two ways. The first method is to have the facade contain components, as in a table. For example, a history of transfusions, each with its place and date, can be displayed as a table within an overall blood donor presentation. The second way is to allow the user to navigate from one presentation to another. For example, a user looking at a screen of blood test information can open a separate screen to look at details of the blood sample used for the test.

The structural model shown in Figure 13.5 illustrates how these facades are related. I use aggregation to show information displayed in the same presentation (such as a table) and regular associations for information displayed by opening a different presentation. Similarly I use unidirectional associations to reflect the paths that the user can take in opening one presentation from another.

Using a structural model is very helpful, but it is important to remember that the style of modeling is different. In the domain model we should avoid duplicating responsibilities, particularly when it comes to holding information. For this reason we could use a different notation to stress the different heuristics. On the whole, however, I think the extra notation adds too much complexity.

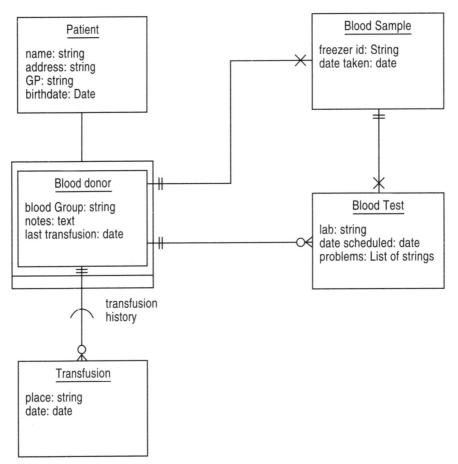

Figure 13.5   An example diagram of application facades.

The types shown are external types (see Section 13.5). The model indicates we have a blood donor presentation that shows all the information on the patient presentation with additions. It also shows a table of transfusions. The user can navigate to a separate presentation that shows a list of blood tests. From the blood test presentation, the user can navigate to the appropriate blood sample presentation, from which the user can navigate to the blood donor presentation.

The other kind of relationship between facades, which can be very important, is a subtyping relationship. A patient facade might already cover a lot of general information required for patients. The information required for donors would include this information and add to it. Thus the donor facade is truly a subtype of the patient facade: All attributes of the patient facade are present in the donor facade, and the donor facade can respond to all patient facade messages.

In many ways the structure of the facades is driven by the structure of the presentations that the facades support. In cases where one set of facades supports more than one presentation, this may not quite hold. A new presentation might combine information from associated facades in the same presentation. This is perfectly reasonable. Although it is useful to base facade structure on presentation structure, it is also wise to let one set of facades support multiple similar presentations. In this case, breaking the tie between presentation and facade structure is a justified sacrifice.

References

1.   Cairns, T., A. Casey, M. Fowler, M. Thursz, and H. Timimi. *The Cosmos Clinical Process Model.* National Health Service, Information Management Centre, 15 Frederick Rd, Birmingham, B15 1JD, England., Report ECBS20A & ECBS20B <http://www.sm.ic.ac.uk/medicine/cpm>, 1992.

14

Patterns for Type Model Design Templates

This book uses very conceptual models, thus it is important for me to explain how these models turn into software. This chapter provides transformation patterns that can be used to construct design templates for type models. Transformation patterns describe principles for transforming an artifact from one form into another. Design templates describe how to turn an implicit specification model into an explicit specification model and an implementation. Since implicit interface models and conceptual models are almost identical, they are valuable tools for understanding how conceptual models relate to implementations.

The chapter does not attempt to give a full set of design templates for any particular implementation environment. Implementation environments are too different, each requiring different trade-offs. It is not simply a matter of Smalltalk or C++. Many factors—hardware, databases, networks, class libraries—affect the templates that are actually used on a project. Thus I concentrate on the patterns that are found in design templates—the general principles and issues that should be considered when carrying out the transformations.

Design templates vary based on the modeling method used, the exact implementation environment, corporate standards, and the performance requirements of the final system. They can be used in a prescriptive manner or in an advisory manner. They can (at least in theory) be automated by a code generator, or they can be used by hand (as coding standards, for instance).

Not all methods need design templates. If all modeling is done using a method that is deeply rooted in the implementation environment, then little if any transformation is needed. This is the principal advantage of using an implementation-based technique. The problem with such an approach is

---

* This chapter was written in conjunction with James Odell.

that there is a greater distance between how people think about the world and an implementation-based model. Also there often are problems in moving that model to another implementation environment.

Design templates have the following goals:

- To ensure that the software is structured in the same way as the conceptual models, as far as practically possible

- To provide consistency within the software

- To provide guidelines on constructing software so that knowledge is effectively propagated around the organization

These goals lead us to an important principle: Design templates should *define the interface* of software components and *suggest the implementation* of those components. A goal in the process should be that a programmer, new to the domain but familiar with the templates, should know what the interface of all the components is simply by looking at the analysis model. In practice it may not be possible to achieve this goal completely, but we should aim to get as close as we can.

Modeling Principle   *Design templates define the interface of software components and suggest the implementation of those components.*

Design templates should thus provide a statement of the required interface and can provide a number of suggested implementations. Programmers must accept the mandatory interface, but they can make any implementation, either taking from the suggested list or coming up with their own alternatives. The user of the class should not need to know, or care, what implementation is chosen. In particular the class implementor should be able to change implementation without altering the interface.

It can be difficult to keep a purely conceptual model. To ensure that the interface can be fully defined, the model needs to be a specification model. It does not need to be a very explicit specification model, since the templates transform the model to a truly explicit specification model. There are a number of cases where interface issues alter the model from a purely conceptual point of view. These alterations are not serious, and it is usually better to put up with these than to build separate models and try to keep them in sync. These issues will be discussed as the chapter proceeds.

Each section in this chapter discusses a number of patterns for transforming conceptual models. We begin by discussing a pattern for *implementing associations (14.1)*. There are three implementations: pointers in both directions, pointers in one direction, and association objects. Following the basic principle, all have the same interface. Fundamental types have some special considerations. Associations are common to almost all techniques, so this pattern is widely applicable.

The second pattern discusses *implementing generalization (14.2)*. Many methods treat generalization the same as implementation inheritance. This book uses multiple and dynamic classification (see Section A.1.3), which make the transformation less direct. We consider five implementations: inheritance, multiple inheritance combination classes, flags, delegation to a hidden class, and creating a replacement. Again we define a common interface, which includes an operation to test the type of an object—a test that should be used with caution.

The remaining patterns are shorter and include patterns for *object creation (14.3), object destruction (14.4)*, finding objects with an *entry point (14.5)*, and *implementing constraints (14.6)*. We will briefly mention *design templates for other techniques (14.7)*, but there is no detailed discussion.

If you don't use design templates, then you might treat this chapter as an indication of how programmers should interpret conceptual models. The techniques in the chapter are valuable in transforming the models from this book to more implementation-based methods, as well as transforming to OO languages. Anyone wishing to use the analysis patterns in this book with Booch's method (for example) will need to use these patterns, particularly when dealing with generalization.

Different languages have different names for various elements. I use the term *field* to represent a data value of the class (a Smalltalk instance variable or a C++ data member). I use the term *operation* to refer to a message that a class will recognize (a Smalltalk method, or selector, or a C++ member function). I distinguish between operation (the declaration) and method (the body); thus a polymorphic operation has many methods. I use the term *feature* to represent either a field or an operation.

This chapter assumes that you have access to a class library of collection classes. Collections, also known as containers, are classes that hold a group of objects. In conventional programming languages the most common, and usually only, provided collection is the array. Object environments can provide many collections. Lewis [5] gives an excellent overview of the most common Smalltalk collections. Many C++ versions use similar approaches, although these will be superseded by the Standard Template Library (STL) [7]. Such collections include sets (not ordered, no duplicates), lists (orderedCollections in Smalltalk, vectors and deques in STL), bags (like sets but with duplicates, multisets in STL), and dictionaries (maps in STL). A dictionary is a lookup table or associative array that allows you to look up an object using another object as a key. So we could have a dictionary of people indexed by name. You would find me by sending a message of the form `PeopleDictionary at` (`"Martin Fowler"`).

These collections greatly simplify programming, and having these available is one of the great boons of an object-oriented environment. Many environments, including all Smalltalks, come with such a class library. Most C++

environments do not come with collection classes, although they can easily be bought from a number of vendors. *I strongly encourage you to familiarize yourself with and use collection classes.* To work in an object-oriented environment and not use collection classes is like programming with one hand behind your back.

14.1 Implementing Associations

The chapter begins with associations because they provide a simple yet important example of how templates work. For the purposes of this section, we will assume that all object types are implemented as classes; this assumption will be modified later on.

A number of object-oriented practitioners are uncomfortable with using associations in OO analysis. They see associations as violating the OO programming principle of encapsulation. With encapsulation the data structure of a class is hidden behind an interface of operations. Some practitioners believe that associations make the data structure public. The way out of this dilemma is to understand how associations are interpreted in the context of OO languages. Associations are present because they are useful in conceptual modeling. They do not clash with encapsulation if they are seen as a way of describing that one object type has a responsibility to keep track of and alter its relationship with another. Thus the example in Figure 14.1 shows that the employee has responsibility to know its employer and to be able to change his employer. Conversely the organization has a responsibility to know its employees and to be able to change them. In most OO languages this responsibility is implemented by accessor and modifier (get and set) operations. A data structure may be present of course, and in most cases it will be, but a data structure is not specified by the conceptual model.

Figure 14.1 An example association.

Attributes can be represented as single-valued mappings, usually to fundamental types. Thus the discussion of single-valued mapping also applies to attributes for those methods that use them.

14.1.1 Bidirectional and Unidirectional Associations

One of the first questions we need to consider is whether to use a bidirectional or a unidirectional association. There is a lot of controversy on this subject. Unidirectional associations are easier to implement and cause less coupling in the software. But they do make it harder to find our way around. The patterns in this book use bidirectional associations. We can choose to implement all associations as bidirectional, all as unidirectional, or to use a mixture. Using a mixture is less consistent but does have advantages. If we use all bidirectional associations, we can get into coupling problems. If we use all unidirectional associations, we may find some associations that really do need to be bidirectional and may be worth making an exception for.

If we want to use a unidirectional association, we need to decide which direction to support and which to drop. This will be suggested by the application. A good rule of thumb is to see what the clients of the association want to do and follow the direction that they need. I don't believe in detailed analysis of access paths, in the style of many methodologies. We should do the simplest thing first but be prepared to change it should our needs change later. If we keep a model, we should update it to show which direction we are using.

If we use bidirectional associations, we must be very wary of those that cross packages. If we maintain bidirectionality, we will cause a mutual visibility between the categories, as discussed in Section 11.2. When I use bidirectional associations, I use them freely within a category but try to avoid them between categories because it is more important to reduce visibilities between categories.

14.1.2   Interface for Associations

The interface for associations in an OO language is a series of operations to access and update the association. The exact terms and structure of these operations depend on the cardinalities of the mappings involved.

In general a single-valued mapping requires two operations: an accessor and a modifier. The accessor takes no arguments and returns the object to which the receiver is mapped to. The modifier takes one argument and changes the mapping of the receiver to that argument. Various naming conventions are possible. In Smalltalk it is conventional to name both operations `mappingName`, and the modifier is distinguished from the accessor by the presence of an argument. Thus for Figure 14.1 the employee class would have two operations: `employer` and `employer: anOrganization`. In C++ no standard convention exists, but frequently names such as `getEmployer()` and `setEmployer (Organization org)` are common. Using `getEmployer()` and `setEmployer()` is the most natural, but some prefer to use `employerSet` and `employerGet()` (or `employerOf()` and `employerIs()`) so that both operations appear together in an alphabetically sorted browser.

A multivalued mapping requires three operations. Again there is an accessor, but this one returns a set of objects. All multivalued mappings are assumed to be sets unless otherwise indicated. The interface for nonsets is different and is beyond the scope of this section. Two modifiers are required, one to add an object and one to remove an object. The accessor is usually named in the same way as for single-valued mappings, except I prefer a plural form to further reinforce its multivalued nature (for example, `employees` or `getEmployees()`). Modifiers take the form of `addEmployee (Employee emp)`, `removeEmployee (Employee emp)` or `employeesAdd: anEmployee`, `employeesRemove: anEmployee`.

It is not necessary to provide modifiers on both sides of a bidirectional association. Frequently it seems that modifiers are only likely to be used in one direction, usually the one that is most constrained (such as `Employee::employer`). Accessors should always be provided in both directions of a bidirectional association; that is what makes it bidirectional.

In a bidirectional association the modifiers must always ensure that both mappings are updated. Thus changing the employer of an employee changes not only the link from the employee to the organization but also the reverse links. We discuss the implementations in Sections 14.1.5 to 14.1.8.

The modifiers should also ensure that constraints are checked. In practice the upper bound is covered by the nature of the interface if it is one or many and only needs to be checked for other numbers. The lower bound is the one that usually needs explicit checking if it is nonzero. In single-valued mappings the lower bound indicates whether a null can be provided as an argument. For multivalued mappings a lower bound implies a check in the remove operation. The cardinality of one mapping can affect operations implementing the other. For instance, in Figure 14.1 there should not be a remove employee operation on organization since that could not be done without breaking the constraint on employee. For the same reason no modifier should be provided for an immutable association.

Type checking can be performed in the modifiers if it is not built into the language. This is a moot point in Smalltalk, which is by nature untyped. To do type checking you need some type test capability, such as that discussed in Section 14.2.6. I like to put type checks into a special precondition block. All objects have an operation called `require: aBlock`. The operation evaluates the block and raises an exception if it results in false. I then test the type within this clause with a statement such as `self require: [aCustomer hasType: #Customer]`. This allows me to easily take out the type checking for performance reasons, rather like precondition checks in Eiffel. (Indeed I use this structure for precondition checking in general.)

The set returned by the accessor of a multivalued operation can be used for further manipulation using the facilities of whatever set class is present in the environment. However, you must ensure that modifying the membership of the set by adding or removing objects does not change the mapping from which the set was formed. Modification of the mapping can only come from modifier operations that are part of the explicit interface (see Section 6.9).

In some cases the return of a set by a multivalued accessor may be a performance hit. In these cases the interface can be extended to include common set operations (such as select, do, and collect) and an iterator [4]. Such extensions should follow the naming conventions of whichever set class you are using. These interface extensions can cause the interface to become bloated, however.

In C++ there is often an issue about what should be returned by accessors: the object or a pointer to the object. Whatever is returned should be made explicit by the design templates. A common convention is to return the value for all built-in data types, the object for all fundamental classes, and a pointer for all other classes. In Smalltalk this does not apply since you always work with objects, or at least it seems that way! In the discussion below I always refer to returning references; the actual templates should make clear exactly what is being returned for C++ and similarly pointer-explicit languages.

14.1.3   Fundamental Types

Some object types are fairly simple and prevalent throughout all parts of a model. As such they require slightly different treatment than most object types, particularly with respect to associations. Examples of such object types are the classic built-in data types of programming environments: integer, real, string, and date. Good OO analysis, however, typically uncovers other examples: Quantity, money, time period, and currency are typical examples. It is hard to give rules for what makes a type fundamental—primarily it comes from its presence all over the model and a certain internal simplicity. This means that if the fundamental type's associations are implemented in the standard way, it will be burdened with a large number of operations linking the fundamental types to other types all over the model. Thus with fundamental types, mappings to nonfundamental types should not be implemented; that is, there should be no operations. In addition, associations to other fundamental types should be handled on a case-by-case basis.

It is useful to indicate fundamental types in some way on a model. One way is to mark the object type as fundamental in the glossary. Another is to use one-way associations. The problem with one-way associations is that they are essentially an implementation feature and may confuse non-IT analysts.

A common feature of fundamental types is that their key features are immutable: You cannot change any property of the type. Consider the object $5. You cannot change either the number (5) or the currency ($) without describing a separate object. Not all properties are immutable, however. Currency can be considered a fundamental type yet may have mutable properties such as its holiday list (for trading purposes). It is particularly important with fundamental types to ensure that the immutable properties are properly enforced.

14.1.4 Implementing a Unidirectional Association

Implementing a unidirectional association is pretty straightforward. You have a field in the class that is the source of the single mapping, and this field contains a reference to the target object. The accessor returns the reference and the modifier changes the reference.

14.1.5 Bidirectional Implementation by Pointers in Both Directions

In this implementation the association is implemented by pointers from both participating classes. If a mapping is single-valued, then there is a simple pointer from one object to another, such as the pointer from Peter to NASA shown in Figure 14.2. If a mapping is multivalued, then the object will have a set of pointers to the other objects (for example, in Figure 14.2 NASA points to a set of pointers that contains pointers to Peter, Jasper, and Paul). For languages that support containment, it may be useful to contain the set of pointers rather than to point to it. There may be space implications, however, since sets are able to grow at will. Similarly if a single-valued mapping points to a built-in data type or to another fundamental type, then containment can be used instead of a pointer.

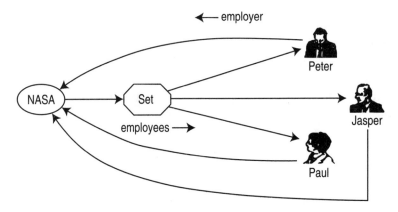

Figure 14.2   Implementing by pointers in both directions.

The accessor operations are relatively straightforward. For a single-valued mapping the accessor merely returns the reference. For a multivalued mapping the accessor returns a set of references; however, it must not return *the* set of references because the user of the set would then be able to change its membership and break the encapsulation. The encapsulation boundary should include all sets implementing multivalued mappings. One way out of this is to return a copy of the set so if any alterations are made, they do not affect the actual mapping. However, this may incur a significant time over-head for large sets. Alternatives are to return a protection proxy or an external iterator [3]. A protection proxy is a simple class that has a single field containing the set. All permitted operations are defined on the protection proxy, which it implements by passing the call onto the contained set. This way updates can be blocked. An external iterator is rather like a cursor into the collection. The iterator can return the object that it is pointing to and can be advanced through the collection.

Since there are two pointers implementing each link between two objects, it is important that modifiers keep them in sync. Thus a modifier called to change Peter's organization to IBM must not only replace the pointer from Peter with one that points to IBM but also delete the pointer to Peter in NASA's employees set and create one in IBM's employees set. But doing this gets us into an OO conundrum. Employee needs to use some operation that will manipulate the set pointer alone without returning a call to Peter (otherwise, we get in an endless loop). However, this operation must not be part of organization's interface. In C++ this is a classic use of the friend construct. In Smalltalk we have to create such an operation but mark it as private (which of course does not stop employee from using it). In these cases a useful move is to have only one modifier do actual work that manipulates the data and/or the private operations. The other modifier should then just call that one modifier. This ensures that there is only one copy of the update code.

This implementation works well. It is fast in navigation in both directions. Although ensuring all pointers get updated together is a little tricky, once it has been sorted out, the solution is easy to replicate. Its principal disadvantages are the size of the sets required for multivalued mappings and a slower speed for updates.

14.1.6   Bidirectional Implementation by Pointers in One Direction

This implementation uses pointers in one direction only. To navigate in the other direction, we need to look at all instances of the class and select ones that point back to the source object. In Figure 14.3 the employees mapping would require getting all instances of employee and selecting those whose employer is NASA.

Modifiers are straightforward. The modifier on the class with the pointer merely changes the pointer, and that public routine can be called directly by a modifier on the other class. There is no danger of multiple pointers getting out of step.

This scheme is space efficient because it stores only one pointer per link, but it will be slow when navigating against the direction of the pointers. Its update speed is fast.

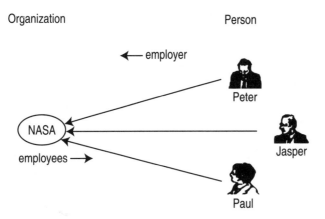

Figure 14.3   Implementation with pointers in one direction.

14.1.7   Bidirectional Implementation by Association Objects

Association objects are simple objects with two pointers that can be used to link two other objects, as shown in Figure 14.4. Typically a table of such objects is provided for each association. Accessors work by getting all objects within that table, selecting those that point to the source, and then following each pointer to the mapped objects. Modifiers are simple, merely creating or deleting the association object. Special association classes can be built; or dictionary classes with their hash table lookups can be used to implement them.

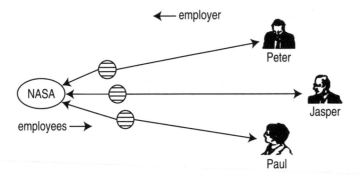

Figure 14.4   Implementation with association objects.

Association objects are not very fast in either direction but can usually be indexed (by using a dictionary), which can improve speed. They are space efficient if most objects are not related in the mapping, in which case space is only used if needed. They are also useful if it is not possible to alter the data structure of either participating class.

14.1.8   Comparison of Bidirectional Implementations

In most cases the choice will be between pointers in both directions and pointers in one direction. The former provides speed of access in both directions, while the latter is much more space efficient and faster on update. The cardinalities and the actual number of links affect the trade-off.

Association objects are useful in special cases, but on the whole they are not the first place to look.

14.1.9   Derived Mappings

On the whole, derived mappings look no different than any other kind of mapping. Accessors are provided just the same as base mappings; they should be indistinguishable. Often, however, it is not possible to provide a modifier. The important thing about derived mappings is the constraint they imply between the derived mapping and the combination of other mappings that make up the derivation.

14.1.10 Nonset Mappings

Although the majority of multivalued mappings are sets, there are exceptions. In this book they are indicated by short semantic statements such as [list], [hierarchy], and [key: mappingName]. These kinds of statements imply a different interface. Mappings marked with [list] will return a list rather than a set and will have modifiers such as `addFirst`, `addLast`, `addBefore (Object)`, and `indexOf (anObject)`. I have not attempted to provide all the interfaces for these cases in this book. If we use such constructs, however, we should ensure we work out the design templates for them. Usually we should base the interface on that of the underlying collection. We can also think of these constructs as association patterns (see Chapter 15).

14.2   Implementing Generalization

One of the most noticeable differences between OO type modeling and most conventional data modeling practices is the great use of generalization. Although generalization has long been part of many data modeling approaches, it is often seen as an advanced or specialized technique. The close relationship between generalization and OO's inheritance ensures a central place for it in OO analysis.

Many OO methods use generalization as an analysis equivalent to inheritance. Methods that use dynamic and multiple classification, however, require more thought because mainstream OO languages only support single static classification. The approaches to implementing multiple dynamic classification can also be used to reorganize inheritance structures and implement generalization in environments that do not support inheritance.

For generalization, I describe the implementations first and then the interface, since this makes it easier to understand the variations the interface needs to support.

14.2.1 Implementation by Inheritance

In most methods subtyping and subclasses are synonymous, thus providing the best possible form of implementation. The interfaces for each type are placed on corresponding classes, and method selection is properly supported by the language. Thus this approach is always preferred if possible. Its disadvantages are that it does not support multiple or dynamic classification.

14.2.2 Implementation by Multiple Inheritance Combination Classes

Figure 14.5 shows an example of multiple classification, which we can deal with by multiple inheritance combination classes. In this example we would create classes for priority corporation and priority personal customer in addition to classes for each of the four object types on the diagram. By using multiple inheritance the classes can neatly capture all the required interfaces and let the programming system deal with method selection in the usual way.

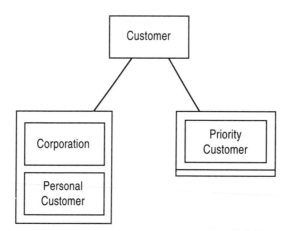

Figure 14.5   An example of multiple classification.

There are two disadvantages to this approach. The first is that an object type with many partitions can cause an unwieldy set of combination classes. Four complete partitions, each with two types, require 2^4 combination classes. The other disadvantage is that this approach only supports static classification.

14.2.3   Implementation by Flags

If a programmer who had never heard of inheritance was asked how to implement the need for customers to record whether they are a priority or not, the answer would probably be "with a status flag." This old-fashioned scheme is still effective. It provides a quick way to support multiple and dynamic classification. Flags are easily changed at will, and one flag field can be defined for each partition. Indeed this is the scheme used for state changes in OO programs not based on dynamic classification.

The main difficulty with this approach is that we cannot use the inheritance and method selection within the language. Thus all operations in the interface of the subtype have to be put on the supertype's class. In addition, all fields required to support subtypes need to be included in the supertype class. Thus the customer class implements both the customer and the priority customer object types.

If the receiving object is not an instance of the subtype, it is clearly not appropriate to use operations defined on the subtype, such as asking for the rep of a nonpriority customer, as shown in Figure 14.6. This would cause an error (a run-time error in Smalltalk and probably a compile-time error in C++) if we are using inheritance. All operations defined on a subtype must be guarded by a check to ensure that the receiver is of that subtype. If that check fails, the routine exits, yielding some sign of the problem, usually an exception. This exposes a further disadvantage of this scheme in C++—it is not possible to catch these errors until compile time.

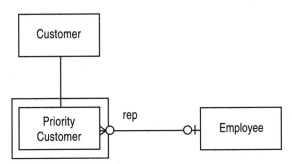

Figure 14.6   Priority customer example.

Since inheritance is lost, its partner polymorphism is also only a memory. Thus if a shipping price operation is polymorphic, then the method selection needs to be implemented by the programmer. This is done using a case statement *inside* the customer class. A single shipping price operation is provided as part of customer's interface. In the method for that operation, there is a logical test based on the subtypes of customer, with possible calls to internal private methods. If the case statement is kept within the class and a single operation is published to the outside world, all the advantages of polymorphism remain. Thus the soul remains even if the body is absent.

The final disadvantage of this implementation is that space is defined for all data structures used by the subtype. All objects that are not instances of the supertype waste this space. If there are a lot of associations on the subtype, this can cause problems.

14.2.4   Implementation by Delegation to a Hidden Class

This approach is a useful variant on using flags to implement subtyping. In this case a class is prepared for the subtype, but this class is hidden from all but the supertype class. We must provide a field in the supertype class for a reference to the subtype (which can double as a flag). Again we must move all the operations of the subtype to the supertype's interface. However, the data structure remains on the supertype. All the operations on the supertype class, which come from the subtype class, delegate the call to the subtype class, which holds the actual method.

Thus for the conceptual model shown in Figure 14.7, an instance of executive would have one instance each of employee and executive, as shown in Figure 14.8. The executive object and its class are not seen by any component other than the employee class. (In C++ all its members would be private and employee its friend.) The `giveStock` operation, defined on the executive type, would be placed on employee. When pay is sent to an employee object with an associated executive, the method on employee for pay merely calls the pay method on executive and returns any result. In this way no other part of the system knows how subtyping is implemented. Method selection for polymorphic operations are implemented in the same way as for flags (an internal case statement) with a call to the executive's method if appropriate. Another approach would be to place all methods on employee and make executive nothing but a data structure. This, however, would make executive less of a self-contained module.

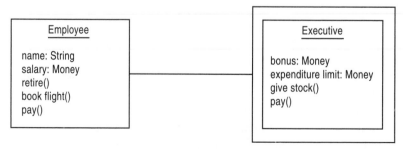

Figure 14.7   Conceptual model of employee and executive.

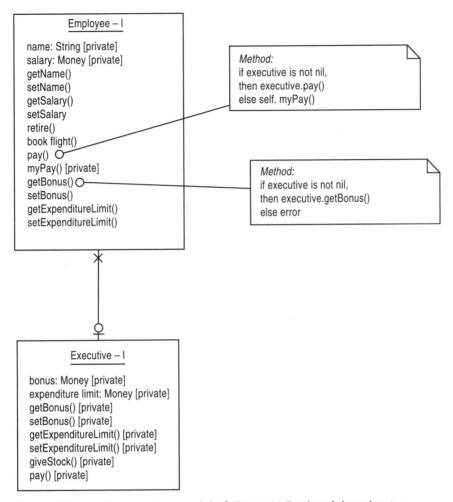

Figure 14.8   Implementation model of Figure 14.7 using delegation to a hidden class.

The logical conclusion of this approach is the state pattern [3] shown in Figure 14.9. In this case there is always a hidden class present. The different hidden classes all have a common abstract superclass, which is itself hidden. Employee simply delegates pay to its hidden class. Whichever subclass is present responds appropriately. This allows new subtypes to be added without changing the employee class, providing they do not add to the interface of employee (a similar approach is the envelope/letter idiom [3]).

The main advantages of using a hidden class over using flags alone is that it provides greater modularity for complex subtypes. It also eliminates wasted space.

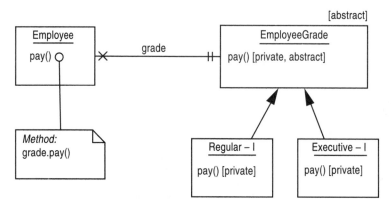

Figure 14.9   Implementation of employee and executive with the state pattern.

An instance of the abstract EmployeeGrade class is always present. Any state-dependent behavior is declared on EmployeeGrade as an abstract method and implemented by the subclasses. I have used an arrow to show subclassing (from Rational's Unified Modeling Language (UML) [1] to reinforce the difference between subclassing and subtyping.

14.2.5   Implementation by Creating a Replacement

One way to handle changes in type is to implement the subtype with a subclass and on reclassification to remove the old object and replace it with a new one of the appropriate class. This allows the programmer to retain the advantages of inheritance and method selection while still providing dynamic classification.

The procedure for carrying this out is to create the object in the new class, copy all common information from the old object to the new, change all the references pointing to the old object to point to the new one, and finally to delete the old object.

In many environments the biggest problem is finding all the references to the old object and moving them to the new one. Without memory management this can be nearly impossible. Any references that are not caught become dangling pointers and lead to a crash that is difficult to debug. Thus this approach is not recommended for C++ unless some memory management scheme is used that can reliably find all references. Languages with memory management may find this easier; Smalltalk provides a method (become) to do the swapping of references.

If all references can be found and changed this approach is plausible. Its remaining disadvantage is the time taken in copying common information and in finding and changing the references. This amount of time varies considerably among environments and determines the approach's suitability.

14.2.6   Interface for Generalization

All five implementations work well, and all are regularly used in object-oriented programming. For each implementation to be an alternative for conceptual generalization, we need to have a single interface for all of them.

A controversial question in OO programming is whether there should be an operation that returns an object's classification. Such an operation is often important—how else can we take a set of people and filter it to leave only the women? Such an operation, however, also presents the danger that programmers will use it within a case statement subvert polymorphism and the advantages that it brings. There seems little that can be done within the structure of OO programming to eliminate this dilemma. An operation to return an object's classification is often necessary and thus should be provided. However, for the sake of good programming style we should not use such an operation instead of polymorphism. As a general guideline, classification information should only be requested as a part of pure information gathering within a query or for interface display.

Some conventions currently exist for finding out the classification of an object. Both Smalltalk and C++ programmers use operations named isState-Name to determine whether an object is in a certain state. Smalltalk has a message isKindOf: aClass to determine class membership. C++ does not hold class information at run time (although that will change with the forthcoming standard). However, sometimes operations that effectively give this information are provided when a need is there.

Two broad naming schemes can be used. The first is to use the naming form isTypeName. The second is to provide a parametric operation such as hasType (TypeName). The first scheme is the normal convention used with flags and hidden classes. It works well in this guise but has a problem covering subclassing. If we want to add a new subclass to an existing class, we need to add the isTypeName operation to the superclass as well as the subclass. Otherwise, calling isTypeName on the superclass causes an error. The hasType convention is more extensible since subclasses can be added without a change to the superclass. Remember that in all cases we want *type* information, not class information.

No typical naming standard exists for type changes. Names such as make-TypeName or classifyAsTypeName are reasonable (I prefer the former). Such operations should be responsible for declassifying from any disjoint types. Thus a complete partition need only have as many modifiers as there are types in the partition. Incomplete partitions need some way to get to the incomplete state. This can either be done by providing declassifyAsTypeName methods for each object type in the partition, or by providing a single `declassifyIn-PartitionName` operation. Note that partitions that are not expected to be dynamic will not have these modifiers.

When these modifiers are used, associations will imply similar issues to those discussed under creation and deletion. Thus mandatory mappings require arguments in a classification routine, and a declassification can lead to choices akin to single and multiple deletion.

Not all subtypes are dynamic, but the decision about whether to make a partition dynamic or not depends on whether the model is a conceptual or interface model. In conceptual modeling, marking a partition as immutable is a strong constraint and is often quite rare. Although it might be argued that for most applications we would not want to change people from male to female, that type change is not a conceptual impossibility. Even before recent medical advances occurred, such a change might be required. A company might think that a person was female and only later discover that he is male. Such a discovery is conceptually handled by a type change.

The fact that most languages handle type changes poorly prompts us to reduce the amount of type changing that is going on. Thus when a partition is only dynamic in very rare cases, it is reasonable, in a specification model, to declare it as static. The rare cases, often due to error in identification or a mistake by the user, can be handled by the user creating a replacement object explicitly. This is another source of difference between a purely conceptual model and a conceptually based specification model.

14.2.7   Implementing the hasType Operation

At this point it is useful to say a few words about implementing the type accessor. Each class in the system will need a `hasType` operation. The method will check the argument against all the types implemented by the class. If flags have been used, then they are checked to test for the type. Even if no flags are present, the class will almost certainly implement a particular type, and that type must be checked. If any of these tests are true, then true is returned. If, however, none of the class types match, then the method on the superclass must be called and the result of that returned. If there is no super-type, then false is returned. Thus in practice a message sent to the bottom of a hierarchy will bubble up the hierarchy until it hits a match or it runs out at the top and comes back false. This mechanism makes it easy to extend the type hierarchy because only the class that implements the type needs to check for that type.

14.3   Object Creation

Mechanisms are required to create new objects, both those that are implemented directly by a class and those that are indirectly implemented.

14.3.1   Interface for Creation

Each class must have a way of creating instances of the types it implements. Creation implies not only forming a new instance object but also satisfying the various constraints that exist for the object so that it is a legal object.

All mandatory associations must be filled during the creation operation (a complete creation method [1]). This implies that the creation operation must have arguments for each mandatory operation. Similarly any subtypes in complete partitions implemented by the class must be chosen through arguments. Mandatory cases and immutable association or partitions that are not mandatory should also be chosen through arguments.

Sometimes it is difficult to use the default object creation mechanisms to do this, due to other assumptions in the implementation environment. Factory methods [3] should be used in these circumstances.

It is also permissible to include optional, mutable features in the creation arguments. However, it is usually better first to create the object and then to send it the necessary messages to set up these features.

14.3.2   Implementation for Creation

All object-oriented languages have their own conventions for creating new objects. Typically these provide for allocating storage and the initialization of fields. However, the initialization routine is not always an appropriate place for setting up the mandatory features passed through arguments.

In Smalltalk the usual idiom is to have each class support a creation message (often called new) that can take arguments. During creation it is often arranged for the new object to be sent an initialize message that takes no arguments. This initialize is useful for setting the instance variables of multi-valued mappings to a new set but cannot support initializing associations since it takes no arguments. The best thing is to use Kent Beck's Creation Parameter Method pattern [1] by having a special method to set these initial parameters.

C++ provides a constructor for initialization. Much can be done, here but sometimes there can be problems with constructor semantics. Often it is better to use the constructor only within another create operation; the "Gang of Four" creation patterns [4] are particularly helpful for such cases.

14.4   Object Destruction

As objects live, so may they die. Not all objects can be destroyed, some objects have to live forever (medical records, for example). Even then they may be destroyed by one system having been archived elsewhere.

The biggest problem with destroying objects is living with the consequences. For example, deleting an instance of order from Figure 14.10 causes a problem if there are any order lines connected to it. Such order lines must have an order (mandatory association), so if we simply delete the order, the order lines are in violation of their constraints.

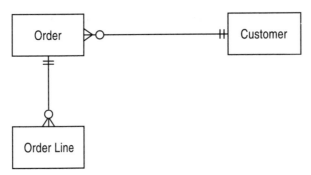

Figure 14.10   Example with customers and orders.

There are two solutions to this problem. The first is the single delete—the kinder, gentler approach. If the delete results in any object being left in violation of its constraints, then the destruction fails. On the other side is the multiple (or cascading) delete—the hard and nasty approach. If this delete leaves an order line in violation of its constraints that object is also deleted. If anything has a mandatory mapping to this object, then those dependent objects are deleted as well—causing a ripple effect throughout the information base.

In practice, deletes can have varying degrees of cascade. A destruction operation can be multiple with respect to some mappings but single with respect to others. This is perfectly permissible, but it must be ensured that the destruction is all or nothing.

These issues are added to concerns about references in environments, like C++, that do not have memory management. Single and multiple deletes are about ensuring that objects do not break their cardinality constraints, and memory management avoids dangling pointers.

14.4.1   Interface for Destruction

Different object-oriented environments have their own approaches to destruction. All destroyable objects should have a fully single destroy operation. This is all a programmer needs, but it does put the onus on the user of the class to destroy things in the right order. Together with a fully single destroy, some harder deletes can also be provided. It must be made clear, however, for which mappings the destruction is multiple.

14.4.2   Implementation for Destruction

It is during destruction that the presence of memory management makes itself most felt. It makes little difference to the destruction method itself but does affect the consequences of error.

In both cases it is important that the object to be destroyed have all its links with associated objects broken (in both directions). The necessary checks must be made to see if the related object will be in violation of its constraints. If the delete is multiple, then the object too is destroyed. If the delete is single, then the whole destruction is abandoned and no changes are made to the information base. Any changes that were made so far must be rolled back. With a nonmemory-managed system the final step is to deallocate the storage. With a memory-managed system no explicit deallocation is made—with all its links removed the object dies of loneliness and gets garbage collected.

14.5   Entry Point

There is now a well-designed structure of connected objects. From any object it is easy to use the type model to decide how to navigate to another object. There is still one important question, however: How do we get into the object structure in the first place? This question may seem odd to those who use traditional, and in particular relational, databases because the entry points to these databases are the record types. Getting hold of the data involves starting at the record type and selecting individual records. Starting from a list of all instances of a type is not always the most appropriate method, however. Object-oriented systems, in particular, can provide different forms of access that can be more efficient and provide other useful abilities.

We don't need a list of all instances for all types. Consider the example in Figure 14.11. Since all instances of order line are connected to an instance of order, we need not hold a reference from the type order line to all its instances. If we think it will be rare for anyone to ask for all order lines, regardless of order or product, then we can neglect the reference. In the unlikely occurrence that someone does want a list of all order lines, then we could provide this by getting a list of all instances of order and navigating across the mapping to order line. Thus we can save the storage required to hold all the references to all instances of order line at the cost of one level of indirection should we ever require all instances of order line. This is purely an implementation trade-off. In a relational database the trade-off is irrelevant since the database uses fixed tables.

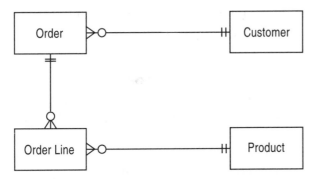

Figure 14.11   Customer, order, product example.

The same argument can be extended to order. We might consider that all instances of order are required if a person wishes to select an order by typing in an order number. Since the order number typically is a string, references from string to order are not usually held, and all instances of order are required. However, we could argue that orders are, in reality, always accessed once the customer is found. Again it is an implementation question as to whether to hold the pointers or not.

This argument cannot be extended to customer because customer lacks any mandatory relationships. Thus it is possible for a customer not to be related to any other object. A list of all instances of customer is thus necessary to ensure that such a customer is found. This necessity to hold a list is what makes customer an entry point.

Note that the decision of which object types should be entry points is purely a conceptual issue. Object types with no mandatory relationships must be entry points. Those with mandatory relationships can hold a list of instances, but that in itself does not make them conceptual entry points.

14.5.1   Interface for Finding Objects

It is useful for all types to have an operation that returns all instances of the type. Such an operation is essential for pointers in one direction to work when navigating against the grain.

It can often be useful to provide some operation to find an instance according to some criteria. An example might be findCustomer (customer-Number). Although it is difficult to provide general rules for using such an operation, in general the most natural way is to use navigation. Thus rather than asking to find all orders whose customer is ABC, it is conceptually easier to ask customer ABC for all its orders. This can cause optimization problems due to the navigational expression of the query, but these can often be resolved within customer's accessor.

When the finding is being done with respect to fundamental types, this option does not apply, so a general find routine is more useful. However, even then it should be done in as general a way as possible. The easiest approach is to ask for all instances of a class and then use the built-in select operation on the returned set. This does not work well for classes with many instances. The next move is to provide a select operation that will take any Boolean operation as an argument. This allows maximum flexibility with only one operation on the class's interface. However, it is much harder to do in some languages than in others. Only when these approaches are exhausted and it is too expensive to do it in a more generic way should we use a find with specific arguments. We must always take care not to bloat a class's interface.

Note that these instance-finding operations are as valid for non-entry points as they are for entry points. Indeed the instance accessors should fit the same pattern.

Entry points need an additional operation to make an object fit within the structure. Merely creating an object may not place it within the structure, particularly if it is not related to any other object within the structure. Thus entry point objects need an operation to insert them within the structure.

The above interface comments are true for in-memory systems. Slightly different characteristics occur when using databases. Different database management systems (either OODBMSs or relational interfaces) have their own conventions. The pragmatic thing to do is to use those conventions with the proviso that, as much as possible, interfaces should be free of database management system specifics.

14.5.2 Implementation of Find Operations

The usual way of implementing an entry point is through some collection class. This collection can be a special singleton class (such as customer list) or a static field in the class. Asking a type for its instances means that the objects of the collection are returned. As with multivalued associations, it is important that the collection be unchangeable except through the entry point's interface.

A non-entry point also typically has an operation to return all instances. This can be done by navigating from an entry point. Selects and finds work in a similar way.

14.5.3 Using Classes or Registrar Objects

Both the interface and the implementation of entry points can be done either by classes or by registrar objects. A class-based implementation of entry points results in each entry point class holding a collection of its instances as a class or static variable. The alternative is to have a separate registrar object that holds a collection for each entry point class. The main advantage of the registrar approach is that it allows separate registrars to exist, perhaps for different contexts. Thus if two clinical departments wish to maintain different instances of disease, this can be done by having a separate registrar object for each clinical department.

In the interface the difference lies in whether programmers send find messages to the class or to a registrar object. Using a registrar removes this responsibility from each class, but the registrar needs at least one find operation for each entry point class. If find operations are also used for non-entry points, then the registrar needs at least one find operation for each class. Using a registrar is useful when programmers need to understand and swap between different contexts. If only a single context is used, it can be set up as a global and the class-based operations can delegate to the appropriate registrar.

14.6 Implementing Constraints

Type models help define the constraints that a type must satisfy. Cardinalities and partitions both indicate constraints. More complex situations require more complex types. The short and long semantic statements used in this book most often indicate the more complex constraints.

Constraints do not generally affect the explicit interface of classes in programming languages. An exception is Eiffel, where constraints define the class invariant. For languages without Eiffel's features, the constraints must be taken into account by all modifiers. The programmers writing modifier operations must ensure that using the modifier leaves the object in a state that violates none of its constraints.

It is often useful to implement an explicit accessor to determine if an object fits within its constraints. An operation named something like checkInvariant should be provided for all classes to generate an exception if something is wrong and do nothing if all is well. This can be used as a health check at various points, included as part of a postcondition check during debugging and as part of system sanity checks during operation— which are particularly valuable for database systems.

Smalltalk and C++ do not have explicit capabilities for constraints and assertions in the way that Eiffel does. They can be set up with a weak, but reasonably effective, alternative. In Smalltalk you can set up an operation (called something like require: aBlock) that takes a block as an argument. The method can be written in class object to execute the block and throw an exception if it comes back false. The require method can then be used for precondition checks, invariant checks, and some postcondition checks. C++ has a macro called assert that can be used for the same purposes.

14.7   Design Templates for Other Techniques

This book is dominated by type models. Hence the design templates in this chapter are transformations from type models. Similar principles can apply with other techniques. Although such a direct mapping is not as plausible, design template patterns can be provided for event diagrams [6]. There has been quite a lot of discussion over the last few years about design templates for various kinds of state models, although we are still waiting for a solid statement on the subject. Interaction diagrams are sufficiently close to implementation to be fairly obvious in their relationship to code.

Over the last few years there has been a small but significant group of developers stressing this kind of transformation approach. Shlaer and Mellor have been at the forefront of this group [8]. I hope that as time passes more attention will be paid to this topic and that we will see more patterns and some complete design templates. I suspect that a full set of templates is more likely to be produced as either a commercial tool (probably linked to CASE tools) or as an in-house effort. I hope that patterns for such templates will become a regular part of the literature.

References

1. Beck, K. *Smalltalk Best Practice Patterns Volume 1: Coding*, Englewood Cliffs, NJ: Prentice-Hall, in press.
2. Booch, G., and J. Rumbaugh. *Unified Method for Object-Oriented Development.* Rational Software Corporation, Version 0.8, 1995.
3. Coplien, J.O. *Advanced C++ Programming Styles and Idioms.* Reading, MA: Addison-Wesley, 1992.
4. Gamma, E., R. Helm, R. Johnson, and J. Vlissides. *Design Patterns: Elements of Reusable Object-Oriented Software.* Reading, MA: Addison-Wesley, 1995.
5. Lewis, S. *The Art and Science of Smalltalk.* Hemel Hempstead, UK: Prentice-Hall International, 1995.
6. Martin, J. and J.J. Odell. *Object-Oriented Methods: Pragmatic Considerations.* Englewood Cliffs, NJ: Prentice-Hall, 1996.
7. Musser, D.R., and A. Saini. *STL Tutorial and Reference Guide.* Reading, MA: Addison-Wesley, 1996.
8. Shlaer, S., and S.J. Mellor. "A deeper look at the transition from analysis to design." *Journal of Object-Oriented Programming*, 5, 9 (1993), pp. 16–21.

15

Association Patterns

Associations are a common construct in analysis and design methods. Often a particular situation will recur with an association. A special notation may be introduced, but it is possible to model the situation without this notation. A useful way of thinking about this is to consider the situation to be a pattern. This association pattern can be represented in a base form, or a new notation can be introduced as a shorthand. Both are equivalent in meaning.

This chapter focuses on three such situations. An *associative type (15.1)* occurs when you want to treat an association as a type, typically by giving it some features. A *keyed mapping (15.2)* is used to give a lookup table, or dictionary, behavior to a mapping. Each of these patterns uses many methods with additional notations. Understanding the patterns behind the notations is valuable. A method may not support an additional notation, so it is essential to know how to work without it. This is particularly true if you are used to a method that supports a notation and are moving to one that does not, or if you are translating between methods and one method does not support a notation.

Even if your method uses a notation for an association pattern, it is important to understand how notation relates to simpler ideas. If the situation is rare, it is often better not to introduce an extra piece of notation to remember, but to use the base form.

The third association pattern is the *historic mapping (15.3)*. We can use historic mappings to keep a history of the value changes of a mapping (such as a history of salaries for an employee). This is not supported by a specific notation in any method that I am aware of. However, this is a vital pattern for many information systems. When a historic mapping is needed, it can be valuable to introduce a notation as a shorthand for the association pattern.

Particular complications arise when not only is the world changing but also our knowledge of it is changing at different places; this leads to *two-dimensional history (15.3.1)*.

Several factors affect the choice between using the notation or the base form. Conceptually the principal trade-off is between the conciseness offered by the notation and the extra notation we need to remember. In a specification model, a notation implies a different interface in the software. This interface is probably more convenient to use than that obtained by transforming from the base form. However, operations can always be added to the specification model to provide the more convenient interface. This adds extra explicit operations to the specification model but avoids the extra notation.

Whether to use the notation or the base form is a matter of choice. In this chapter I indicate my preferences, which, I should stress always take second place to the desires of a client. It is my job as a consultant to make the client's life easier.

Association patterns operate at the meta-level: They are patterns that are used in describing modeling languages rather than the models themselves. I use the term *meta-model patterns* to describe this general class of patterns. Other meta-model patterns could be used to describe meta-level concepts in generalization, state models, or any other modeling technique.

15.1 Associative Type

A common modeling situation occurs when we wish to add an attribute to a relationship. For example, an early model indicates that a person is employed by a company, as shown in Figure 15.1. Later work reveals that we should record the day that the employee started, and it must lie on the relationship. We can add the start date attribute to the relationship using a notation such as Rumbaugh's [2], shown in Figure 15.2.

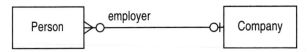

Figure 15.1 Simple relationship between person and company.

If a modeling method does not support adding an attribute to a relationship in this way, there are a number of alternatives. In our example one alternative is to add the start date to the person. Since a person has, by definition, only one company, there is no danger of ambiguity. We might think that the start date attribute is really a part of the relationship, but it is difficult to

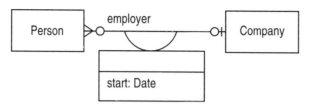

Figure 15.2   Adding a start date attribute to Figure 15.1

This diagram uses Rumbaugh's collar notation.

justify as anything other than semantic nit-picking. A more reasonable objection is that the start date should not have a value unless there is an employer. This could be resolved by a rule, although this is always a less than ideal solution, in particular since most methods do not support these kinds of rules well.

This approach cannot be used on relationships where both mappings are multivalued as in Figure 15.3. Since a person has a different competency for each skill it is impossible to put the number on person.

In methods that do not support association types, we can introduce an additional type, as shown in Figure 15.4 (note how the cardinalities have been transferred from Figure 15.1). This handles the situation quite well. The new type may be somewhat artificial, but all models contain a certain amount of artificiality since they represent a real situation with a greater degree of formality than exists in natural language. One of the most significant differences between the two models lies in the interface implications. In Figure 15.2, person has a `getEmployer` operation that returns the associated company. The Figure 15.4 model has a different interface that returns the employment

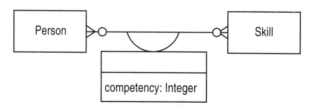

Figure 15.3   A relationship where both mappings are multivalued.

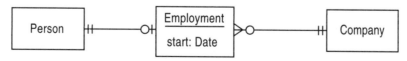

Figure 15.4   Adding an employment type as a holder for the start date.

object. The employment object then needs an additional message to get the company, so we need to make the original association a derived association, as shown in Figure 15.5.

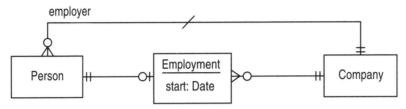

Figure 15.5   Restoring the employer mapping with a derived mapping.

We can consider a more subtle point by considering the many-many associations shown in Figure 15.3. Figure 15.6 uses the same introduction of a new type. Just adding the competency type works well on first inspection, because it allows a person to have many competencies, and thus multiple skills, each with a competency value. The problem is that that model is more permissive because it also allows multiple competencies for the same skill. To eliminate this we need the additional uniqueness rule for competency, indicating that each competency must have a unique combination of person and skill.

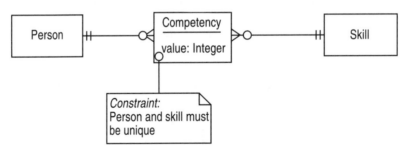

Figure 15.6   Using a new type to handle Figure 15.3.

This issue is often not noted by modelers who do use the associative type notation. Figure 15.7 is another typical use of this notation in which the relationship holds an understanding that a person can be an employee of many companies, and some of these employments may have completed, so we have

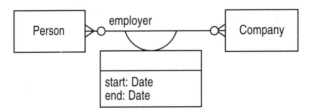

Figure 15.7   Employment associative type.

a history of employment. It is quite possible for a person to have two periods working for the same company. Hence we would not add a constraint of the style shown in Figure 15.6. The problem is that, in general, we do not know whether to interpret an associative type as having the constraint or not.

In practice, modelers use the associative type notation with both interpretations. That is not in itself a fault, but they should make clear which they mean. It is reasonable to use Figure 15.7, but in that case a rule must be used for the Figure 15.3 case along the lines of the rule in Figure 15.6. If modelers wish to use the Figure 15.3 case as the usual interpretation, then they cannot use a model of the form of Figure 15.7; they must use a new type instead.

On the whole I don't tend to use associative type notations. Unless they include a definite rule, such as that of uniqueness, then I don't think they add very much value for the extra notation. The uniqueness can be useful but is so rarely used properly that I would rather use an extra type and add the uniqueness rule to make it explicit.

15.2   Keyed Mapping

Keyed mappings represent a technique that mirrors in analysis the technique of using dictionaries (indexed lookup tables, also called maps [1] or associative arrays) to implement relationships. Examples of its use are shown in Figures 15.8 and 15.9. Our main concern is to record how many of a particular product are on a particular order. The classic data model for this is shown in Figure 15.8. The model shown in Figure 15.9 uses keyed mapping notation, which concentrates on asking an order how many of a product it has and changing this. Figure 15.8 balances this with the product being able to answer which orders it is ordered in and how much on each order.

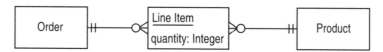

Figure 15.8   A classic order, line item model.

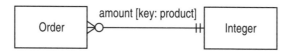

Figure 15.9   Using a dictionary to model Figure 15.8.

An important part of the interpretation of these models is how they affect the interface of the types. The Figure 15.8 model implies an interface of getLineItems on order and product. The Figure 15.9 model implies an interface of getAmount (product) on order. No interface is implied for product.

To find the use of a product in different orders would require asking all instances of order whether they have an amount for the product, which is somewhat more circuitous. Another difference lies in asking an order what products are present on it. For Figure 15.8 this merely requires asking an order for its line items and then each line item for its product. For Figure 15.9 this would require asking the order for the dictionary of amounts and then asking for its keys; order would have to provide a getAmounts operation to allow access to its dictionary (or more strictly a copy). Otherwise, we would need to test every instance of product against the order.

Keyed mapping notation can be used to handle uniqueness constraints. The Figure 15.8 model would usually come with a rule to say that only one line item can exist for a product within an order. We would not want a line item for 30 widgets and a separate line item for 20 widgets on the same order. A better proposal is to have a single line item for 50 widgets. This needs a rule for Figure 15.8 but is quite explicit in Figure 15.9, since an order can only have one quantity for a product.

We need to consider what response the order should make if it is asked for the amount of a product that is not on the order. In this example it seems reasonable to return 0, making the keyed mapping mandatory. In other cases we might wish to make a null return, which would make the mapping optional.

If both representations are valuable, then there is no reason why we can't use both of them together. We can note the redundancy by using a rule or a derivation marker, as shown in Figure 15.10. Using both representations supports the fact that the Figure 15.8 approach is more flexible in general cases while the Figure 15.9 approach adds a very useful shorthand behavior, as well as making the uniqueness explicit.

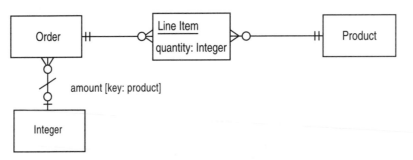

Figure 15.10   Using both representations, marking one as derived.

I find the keyed mapping notation a very useful construct. Whether I use it or an extra type depends on the situation and what I want to emphasize. Although I can certainly live without it, I often find it a handy construct. Beware not to overuse it, though. Often the extra type is important for additional information and behavior. In Figure 15.8 we could easily add a cost for the line item, which would be awkward using Figure 15.9. Naturally the "eat your cake and have it too" answer of Figure 15.10 is a frequent choice.

15.3   Historic Mapping

Objects do not just represent objects that exist in the real world; they often represent the memories of objects that once existed but have since disappeared. Using objects to represent memories is perfectly acceptable—memory of existence is often as real to people as the existence itself—but it is important to be able to tell the difference. Consider the issue of recording a person's salary. At any single moment a person has a single salary, as shown in Figure 15.11. However, as time passes that salary may change. This in itself does not invalidate Figure 15.11 as a model, unless we need to remember the history of the salary. If all we want is to remember past salaries then Figure 15.12 will do the trick, provided that we add to the modifier of salary the ability to append the old salary to an old salaries list. By using a list we cannot only record previous salaries but also preserve the order in which they were applicable.

Figure 15.11   At any point in time a person has one salary.

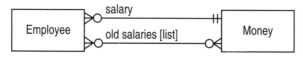

Figure 15.12   A model that remembers past salaries.

Figure 15.12 may be adequate in many situations, but it doesn't help us answer the question "What was John Smith's salary on January 2, 1997?" To answer this question we need the rather more sophisticated approach suggested by Figure 15.13. This model gives us the ability to record both salaries and their full histories. We do need an additional rule, however: Salaries for a person must not have overlapping time periods. This rule is often implicitly assumed, but is usually not shown explicitly—and is thus forgotten.

The model shown in Figure 15.13 provides the power we need, but it is rather clumsy. The important point that an employee can have only one salary at a time is lost without looking at the underlying rules. One association

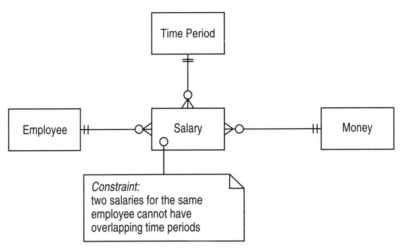

Figure 15.13   A full record of salary history.

between two types is now four types and three associations. This can add significantly to the complexity of a diagram, particularly if there are many such historical relationships. The interface suggested for this is also rather clumsy. The answer to the question in the previous paragraph involves asking John Smith for all his salaries and then selecting the one whose time period includes January 2, 1997.

I often use the model shown in Figure 15.14, which combines the flexibility of the Figure 15.13 approach with the diagrammatic economy of the Figure 15.11 snapshot. All the details are hidden behind the small but significant [history] keyword. I have introduced a new notation, which is perfectly permissible so long as I define it properly. I'll forego a mathematical definition and instead indicate the interface defined by the keyword. Figure 15.11 implies an accessor getSalary() to return the value of the salary and a modifier setSalary(Money) to change it. Figure 15.14 implies a different interface: The accessor getSalary() still exists but this time returns the current value of the salary mapping. This is supported by getSalary(Date), which returns the value of the mapping at the supplied date. getSalary() is equivalent to getSalary (Date::now).

Updating is a little bit more complex. We can use a setSalary (Money, Date) operation to append a new salary, starting at a particular date, to the history. This is a good interface for additive changes but is not sufficient if the old

Figure 15.14   Representing the power of Figure 15.13 with a simpler notation.

record needs alteration. A setSalaryHistory (Dictionary (key: TimePeriod, value:Money)) operation would be our best bet, together with a getSalary-History() operation. Then the client can get the current salary history as a dictionary, use the standard dictionary operations, and then amend the whole record in one go. This is better than updating one record at a time because of the rule that an employee must have one salary at any one date. If alterations are made one record at a time, it is awkward to keep the rule true after every change. Taking the complete record out, changing it (without the rule checking), and replacing it all at once is much easier to manage.

Clearly a dictionary implementation with time period keys is suggested here. Such an implementation easily supports all the behavior required by the interface and is a simple use of the approach. We can even go further and introduce a special class to handle historic collections.

The history notation is not currently suggested by any methodologist to my knowledge. It is very valuable because it simplifies a situation that is both common and sticky. The ideal solution is to have an object system with full "time travel" capability. Such a system is not completely farfetched, and its arrival will remove the need for any special handling of history.

This section is also a particular case of a general point. In modeling you may come across a repetitive situation that is both common and awkward to model. Don't be afraid to introduce a new notation to simplify this, but you must define it properly. The key trade-off to consider is the simplification of a new construct versus having to remember the extra notation. A good notation is a compromise, allowing elegance but without a vast notation. The trade-off is not the same for all projects, so don't be afraid to make your own decisions in these matters.

Modeling Principle *If you come across a repetitive situation that is difficult to model, then define a notation. However, define a notation only if the resulting simplification outweighs the difficulty of remembering the extra notation.*

15.3.1 Two-Dimensional History

The above discussion focuses on the problem of being able to retrieve the values of some attribute of an object at some point in the past. Many systems have a further complication that results from the fact that they do not receive knowledge of changes in a timely manner.

Imagine we have a payroll system that knows that an employee has a rate of $100/day starting on January 1. On February 25 we run the payroll with this rate. On March 15 we learn that, effective on February 15, the employee's rate changed to $110/day. What should the employee object answer when asked what its rate was for February 25? There are two answers to this question: what the employee thought the rate was at that time and what the employee thinks the rate is now. Both of these rates are important. If we need

to look back at the February 25 payroll run to see how the numbers are calculated, we need to see the old figure. If we need to process a new entitlement,
perhaps for a couple of hours overtime that were not reported previously, we
need the rate as we understand it now.

Life being what it is, things can get worse. Assume we made corresponding adjustments and made the late overtime payment, all of which gets processed in a payroll run on March 26. On April 4 we are told that the
employee's rate was changed again to $112 effective February 21. Now the
employee object can give three answers to what its rate was on February 25!

To deal with this kind of problem in general, we need a two-dimensional
history. We are asking the employee what its rate was at some point in the
past, according to our knowledge at some other point in the past. Thus two
dates are needed: the date at which the rate is applicable and the date on
which we base our knowledge, as shown in Table 15.1.

APPLICABLE DATE	KNOWLEDGE DATE	RESULT
February 25	February 25	$100/day
February 25	March 26	$110/day
February 25	April 26	$112/day

Table 15.1 Two-dimensional rates for the example.

The single dimensional example effectively has to choose between treating the applicable and knowledge dates as the same, or always considering
the knowledge date to be "now."

Adding full two-dimensional capabilities to history certainly adds a lot of
complication, and it is not always worthwhile. It is important to look at why
these different rates might be needed. In this example the only reason we
need to know anything other than our current knowledge of the past might be
to explain and post adjustments to previous payroll runs. Another way of
dealing with this would be to embed all the information about how a payroll
calculation is made into the result of the payroll calculation. If this information will only be inspected by a human and not processed, this can be done in
a textual attribute. Calculating adjustments can be done by reference to the
results of the calculation—the rate that was used is not necessarily needed.
Even if the rate is needed, making a copy may be considered safer. With all
this in place, only a one-dimensional history is required so that retroactive
entitlements (such as that late-reported two hours overtime) can be processed.

Two-dimensional history also affects timepoints that are placed on
events. Unless we are confident that we always know as soon as an event

occurs, we need two timepoints on any event: the timepoint when the event occurred and the timepoint when our system became aware of the event. (Examples of this include the two timepoints on entry discussed in Section 6.1, and the dual time records discussed in Section 3.8.)

References

1. Musser, D.R., and A. Saini. *STL Tutorial and Reference Guide.* Reading, MA: Addison-Wesley, 1996.
2. Rumbaugh, J. "OMT: The object model." *Journal of Object-Oriented Programming,* 7, 8 (1995), pp. 21–27.

16

Afterword

What do you think about this book? Have you found the patterns useful and interesting? While I hope that you have, I also hope you feel unsatisfied—that there is more to say and more to understand. This section is about where to go to next.

One thing you can do is try out some of these patterns. Reading a book of patterns really only gives you enough to get a sense of what patterns exist. When I read the "Gang of Four" [1] book, it gave me a taste of their ideas. To learn how the patterns worked, however, I needed to try them out. After reading, there are still many aspects of the "Gang of Four" patterns that I don't really appreciate and understand, but I know that practice and further readings will increase my understanding.

When you try them out, please let me know about your work. Are there parts of the patterns that are poorly explained? Are there other variations that I should consider? Please send me e-mail and let me know so that I can further spread this information. (My e-mail address is 100031.3311@ compuserve.com.) Addison-Wesley is providing a Web site at http://www.aw.com/cseng/categories/oo.html to go with this book on which I expect to publish supplemental information about analysis patterns and provide additional explanations and notes about what I, and others, have learned about using the patterns.

One of the biggest problems with this book is that there are so many gaps. I have described patterns from a few domains, but there are many other domains out there with patterns to understand. Even the domains I have covered have more patterns to find. And the patterns I have described are incomplete; there is much to learn about how to use them, what variations exist, what implementation issues appear, how they can be tested, and how to get the best performance.

This book reflects the incomplete state of my knowledge. To go further, you need to look at the growing body of work being generated by the patterns community. Other patterns books are being published, and even more will come out rapidly over the next few years. Although there isn't much yet on analysis patterns such as these, I hope this book will encourage more such books to appear. In many ways the greatest benefit of this book would be if it stops the endless succession of analysis and design books and starts a new succession of patterns books.

One of the best places to get information on patterns is the World Wide Web. Ralph Johnson's patterns home page[1] is the central source of patterns information. Ward Cunningham's Portland Pattern Repository[2] also contains much valuable on-line information.

A number of conferences are now including talks and sessions on patterns. The most focused patterns conference, however, is Pattern Language of Programming (PLoP) held each September at Allerton Park in Illinois. The conference is a unique event, most notably in the way papers are presented. Instead of a formal presentation, each paper is critiqued in a writers workshop by the other authors. The result is a fascinating discussion of each paper, in which authors learn a lot about how other people view their work.

The next step is to write some patterns of your own. This is not that daunting an experience. I have discovered that the patterns community is open to new ideas and keen to encourage more people to write patterns. PLoP is an excellent forum to submit a pattern and provides a first class venue to see the whole area of patterns developments. You can also publish patterns on the Web—the Portland Patterns Repository is expressly designed for this purpose. I also intend to publish other people's analysis patterns on this book's Web site. Indeed I hope that future editions of this book will contain patterns from other authors, and that my role will become more of an editor than an author.

I wrote this book because, when I started out, I wanted to read a book such as this. I still do. I hope that this book and those that follow it will mean that future generations of software projects will not start from blank sheets of paper.

References

1. Gamma, E., R. Helm, R. Johnson, and J. Vlissides. *Design Patterns: Elements of Reusable Object-Oriented Software.* Reading, MA: Addison-Wesley, 1995.

---

[1] http://st-www.cs.uiuc.edu/users/patterns/patterns.html

[2] http://c2.com/ppr/index.html

Appendix

Techniques and Notations

To write a book like this, I need to use some modeling techniques, but I don't want to spend too much time discussing them. After all, this is a book about patterns, not a book about modeling techniques (there are plenty of books on that subject). There are, as yet, no standards for techniques, so I am forced to choose something that I feel is appropriate and not too alien. I find that no method has everything and that I like to mix techniques from different methods. In this appendix I will discuss the techniques I use and the notation for them.

A.1 Type Diagrams

The type diagram shows a structural view of a system. It concentrates on describing the types of objects in the system and various kinds of static relationships that exist among them. The two most important kinds of relationships are associations (a customer rents a number of videos) and subtypes (a nurse is a kind of person).

In this area lie the most contentious arguments about notation. Everybody chooses their own, very different, notations. There are thus many techniques to choose from for this book, all of which are broadly similar. Picking one is not easy.

One strong contender is Rational Software's Unified Modeling Language (UML) [2]. But there are two problems with using this method for the book. First there is the matter of timing. This book was written during 1994 and 1995, and the Unified Modeling Language was only published after the book was fully drafted. Even as I write this, the notation is only available in a pre-release form, and Rational is discussing significant changes before making a formal release available. The second problem is that the Unified Modeling Language concentrates on implementation modeling rather than conceptual modeling—and this book focuses on conceptual patterns.

I chose Odell's [5] notation for the type diagrams primarily because his approach is the most conceptual of the major OO methods. I have adapted it in a number of places, however, to better fit my needs.

Most methods have some form of structural modeling technique. For a tutorial on the subject, Odell [5] is the most suitable for this book as he uses a very conceptual approach. A developer should also read a more implementation-oriented book, such as Booch [1], to provide the implementation perspective. Cook and Daniels [4] provide the most rigorously defined description of structural modeling and are worth reading for that.

A.1.1   Type and Class

The starting point is the notion of a type, represented by a rectangle. It is significant that I use the word *type* rather than *class*. It is very important to understand the difference between the two. A type describes the *interface* of a class. A type can be implemented by many classes, and a class can implement many types. A type can be implemented by many classes with different languages, performance trade-offs, and so forth. A single class can also implement many types, particularly where subtyping is involved. The distinction between type and class is very important in a number of design techniques based on delegation, as discussed in the "Gang of Four" book [3]. The two terms are often confused because most languages do not make an explicit distinction. Indeed most analysis and design methods do not make an explicit distinction.

I find it useful to think about building type diagrams[1] from three perspectives: conceptual, specification, and implementation [4]. Conceptual models model the way people think about the world. They are entirely mental pictures that ignore any technological issues. Conceptual models can vary, depending on whether they represent the real world or what we know about the world. An example of this is a person and a birth date. In the real world all people have birth dates, so it is reasonable to model birth date as a mandatory attribute of person. However, we can know about a person without knowing their birth date. Thus for many domains birth date can be optional in a conceptual model that reflects what we know of the world. This distinction can be very important for historical information. A model that represents the structure of the world as it is often can be best drawn as a snapshot of a moment in time. If it represents what we know, however, it often needs to reflect our memories, too. The models in this book take the perspective of

---

[1] This distinction can also apply to other techniques, but it is most pronounced with structural models.

capturing a model of what we know about the world, since that is the perspective most useful in information systems.

Specification models are models that can be used to define the interface of the software components in the system. Specification models can be implicit or explicit. An example of an explicit specification model is a C++ header file, which details exactly what operations exist, their parameters, and their return types. Implicit specification models need to be combined with some conventions that show how they resolve to an explicit interface. For example, an attribute of birthdate on an implicit specification model resolves to the operations `birthdate` and `birthdate: aDate` for Smalltalk, and the operations `Date getBirthdate() const` and `void setBirthDate(Date)` for C++.

Implicit specification models can be closer to conceptual models than explicit models, and they can also carry more information than many explicit interfaces. C++ and Smalltalk interfaces miss a great deal of information about the rules for using parts of the interface. Eiffel, which has assertions, can be more complete, but less comprehensible than an implicit model, which closely follows the conceptual model.

Implementation models lay bare the internals of a class.[2] They are useful as documentation and for designers of that class. They should not be used by any of the class's clients, except when they illustrate general implementation principles used throughout the project.

Conceptual models and implicit specification models are almost identical. Thus you can consider the type diagrams in this book to be both conceptual models and implicit specification models. If a distinction does surface between these two, I point it out in the text. The few implementation models in the book are clearly labeled as such, but I use the same notation.

Chapter 14 discusses how type models relate to implementation models. On those occasions where implementing a pattern introduces something beyond the bounds of Chapter 14, the implementation is discussed with the pattern.

A.1.2   Associations, Attributes, and Aggregation

Associations represent relationships among instances of types (a person works for a company, a company has a number of offices, and so on). A precise interpretation of associations depends on whether they are part of a conceptual, specification, or implementation model. A conceptual interpretation merely states that there exists a conceptual relationship among the objects. In terms of responsibility, they have responsibilities for knowing about each other. Thus an association between an order and customer is interpreted as meaning that an order knows its customer and vice versa. In a

---

[2] An implementation model would be more correctly called a class diagram.

specification model, operations exist for accessing and updating the relationship; an explicit specification model shows the operations and their names on the model. An implementation model interprets an association as the existence of a pointer or other reference. It is important to note that in conceptual and specification models, associations do *not* indicate data structure. Encapsulation is thus preserved.

I like to make a distinction between an association and a mapping. A mapping (sometimes called role) is a directed link from one type to another. An association contains one or two mappings. A unidirectional association is just one mapping and can be seen as the same as a mapping. A bidirectional association contains two mappings, which are said to be inverses of each other. This inverse is not quite the same as that of inverse functions in mathematics. Essentially it means that if you navigate a mapping and its inverse, you will get a collection of objects that include the one you started from. Thus if a customer navigates through the set of orders it has made, each of those orders points back to that customer. The term source (or domain) indicates the type the mapping maps from, and the term target (or range) indicates the type the mapping maps to. (For example, in a mapping from customer to order, customer is the source and order is the target.) When a name appears with an association, the name is that of one of the mappings. You can tell which mapping it is by the position of the name to the association line: With the target at the front and the source at the back, the name is on the left.

There is some controversy about the value of bidirectional associations. Conceptually all relationships are bidirectional. Consider an association between a person and their birthdate. It makes perfect *conceptual* sense to say there is a relationship between a date and the people born on that date. In a specification model this is not true. To give date a set of operations to all the things that reference it would bloat the birth date's interface to an unreasonable degree. The other problem with bidirectional associations is that they increase the coupling among types. This can make reuse more difficult. Many people use unidirectional associations to reduce the dependencies among types. The counterargument is that in information systems much of the work is navigating through the links among types. When these links are mainly one-way, it is more difficult to find your way around. An analogy is that of trying to find yourself around a city: One-way streets make the whole thing much more difficult, even if you know the city.

The patterns in this book indicate bidirectional associations. When you use the patterns you can choose to use either bidirectional associations or unidirectional associations. The application you are working on should suggest which direction to use and which to discard. Your choice does not really affect the pattern. If you use bidirectional associations you can use the patterns in Section 14.1 to help you implement them.

A key aspect of associations is cardinality (sometimes called multiplicity). This specifies such things as how many companies a person can work for and how many children a mother can have. Cardinality is a feature of the mapping rather than the association: Each mapping has its own cardinality. There are many symbols for cardinality; Figure A.1 shows the ones I use in

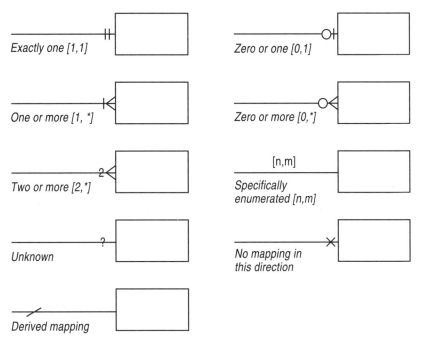

Exactly one [1,1]

Zero or one [0,1]

One or more [1, *]

Zero or more [0,*]

Two or more [2,*]

[n,m]

Specifically enumerated [n,m]

Unknown

No mapping in this direction

Derived mapping

Figure A.1   Symbols for cardinality used in this book.

this book. Mappings with an upper bound of one are called single-valued, and those with an upper bound of more than one are called multivalued. Multivalued mappings are assumed to represent a set unless otherwise indicated (by a short semantic statement).

In this book I consider an attribute to be the same as a single-valued mapping. Sometimes I show an attribute inside a type's rectangle, sometimes with an association. The difference is merely that of notational convenience.

Some methods use aggregation relationships, which are part/whole relationships (for example, a hammer is made up of a head and a haft). I don't use aggregation very much in this book. I don't find the concept terribly useful for domain models, because most of its semantics are on any association. It thus becomes another piece of notation to remember and argue over, and the result of the argument is usually not very important either way. I do, however, use it in the application tier (see Section 13.6).

Derived (or computed) associations describe how associations can be defined based on other base associations (thus grandfather is an association defined by using the parent association followed by the father association.) Derived mappings on a conceptual model indicate that a mapping is based on other mappings present on the model. On a specification model it indicates that the result of the accessor for a derived mapping is the same as using the combination of underlying mappings. In this way the derived mapping can also be seen as a constraint between the derived and the base mappings. Marking a mapping as derived has no significance for the underlying data structure other than this constraint. The implementor can choose any data structure as long as the user of the type is given the impression that the derived mapping is derived according to the model. On an implementation model derived mappings indicate the difference between stored data and a method over that data.

There are many other variations on the association theme. I try to keep things as simple as possible. Some useful variations are discussed in Chapter 15 as association patterns.

A.1.3   Generalization

Let's consider personal and corporate customers of a business as a typical example of generalization. These two types of customers have differences but also many similarities. The similarities can be placed in a general customer type, with personal and corporate customer as subtypes.

Again this phenomenon has different interpretations at the different levels of modeling. Conceptually we can say that corporate customer is a subtype of customer if all instances of corporate customer are also, by definition, instances of customer. In a specification model the interface of corporate customer must conform to the interface of customer. That is, an instance of corporate customer can be used in any situation where a customer is used, and the caller need not be aware that a subtype is actually present (the principle of substitutability). The corporate customer can respond to certain commands differently than another customer (polymorphism), but the caller need not worry about the difference.

Inheritance and subclassing in OO languages is an implementation approach in which the subclass inherits the data and operations of the superclass. It has a lot in common with subtyping, but there are important differences. Subclassing is only one way of implementing subtyping (see Section 14.2). Subclassing can also be used without subtyping—but most authors rightly frown on this practice. Newer languages and standards increasingly try to emphasize the difference between interface-inheritance (subtyping) and implementation-inheritance (subclassing).

Two questions arise concerning the relationship between an object and a type. First, does an object have a single type that can inherit from supertypes (single classification), or does it have several types (multiple classification)? Multiple classification is different than multiple inheritance. With multiple inheritance a type can have many supertypes, but each instance is of a single type that may have supertypes. Multiple classification allows multiple types for an object without defining a specific type for the purpose. We might have personal, corporate, and important customers as subtypes of customer. A customer might be both personal and important. With multiple classification we can give an object both the personal and important customer types (with customer inherited from them). Without multiple classification we must explicitly define an important personal customer type. If there are many subtypes, we can end up with a very large number of combinations, which is difficult to manage.

Conceptually speaking, multiple classification is a more natural way of thinking. However, most OO languages, and certainly mainstream C++ and Smalltalk, use a single-classification approach. Many methods also use single classification. The trade-off is between a conceptually more natural approach that requires more effort in transforming to code, or a more implementation-bound approach that is easier to transform. I prefer the more conceptual approach and use multiple classification in this book.

When using multiple classification we must show which combinations are legal by grouping subtypes into partitions, as shown in Figure A.2. Types within the same partition are disjoint; that is, no object can be an instance of more than one type within a single partition. Thus it is impossible for the supertype to be both subtype-1 and subtype-2. An incomplete partition indicates that an instance of the supertype need not be an instance of a subtype within that partition. A complete partition indicates that every instance of the supertype must also be an instance of a subtype within the partition.

The second question is whether an object can change its type. For example, when a bank account is overdrawn, it substantially changes its behavior, with several operations (withdraw, close) overridden. Dynamic classification allows objects to change type within the subtyping structure, while static classification does not. Again the principal OO languages, and most OO methods, are static, and the same trade-offs apply as for single/multiple classification. This book takes the more conceptual dynamic classification approach.

One way of looking at dynamic classification is that it unifies the notions of state and type. When using static classification we must pay attention to state-dependent behavior separately from subtyping. Dynamic classification treats them both the same.

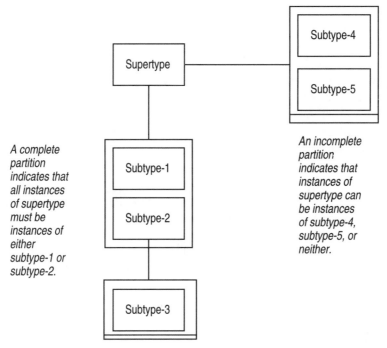

A complete partition indicates that all instances of supertype must be instances of either subtype-1 or subtype-2.

An incomplete partition indicates that instances of supertype can be instances of subtype-4, subtype-5, or neither.

Figure A.2   Generalization notation.

An instance of the supertype may be subtype-1 and subtype-4, but not subtype-1 and subtype-2.

The use of dynamic classification brings to light a subtle difference between conceptual and implementation models. In a conceptual model all subtyping is considered dynamic, unless explicitly denied by the short semantic statement [immutable]. This reflects not only the changes that can occur in the world but also our changing knowledge of them. For some businesses it might be true that a personal customer cannot change into a corporate customer. It may also be true that a customer whom we thought was personal is actually corporate. Here our knowledge of the world implies a dynamic classification, even if the world itself is static. Information systems are usually built on our knowledge of the world, thus conceptually the subtyping is dynamic.

However, the extra complexity of handling dynamic classification cannot be ignored. Thus conceptually dynamic subtypes are often declared static in a specification model. This effectively says that although we know that the classification can change, it happens rarely enough that we don't wish to go to the extra effort (and cost) of supporting it. If it ever does happen, the users will have to sort it out by copy and replace. For many situations the dynamism is sufficiently rare to make this approach worthwhile. Flexibility in the long term can be maintained by ensuring that the accessor interface is the same in either case (see Section 14.2.6).

In the end the decision to make a partition static or dynamic depends on the application, so I have tried not to make any general statements in the patterns. For simplicity I recommend using static partitions whenever you can when you are working in a statically classified language.

If you are using a method that does not use multiple dynamic classification, then you will need to transform the models using the patterns developed in Section 14.2.

A.1.4   Rules and Semantic Statements

Associations and subtypes allow us to say much about types, but not all. I may have a life insurance policy object with mappings for policyholder and beneficiaries. I can use the cardinality constraints to capture statements such as there is only one policyholder but there may be many beneficiaries; however, the constraints do not allow us to say the policyholder must not be a beneficiary. To do this we need a more flexible constraint. A constraint is a logical expression about a type that must always be true. Constraints are often missing from OO methods although they have been present in Eiffel (where they are called invariants) for a long time.

I express constraints using semantic statements, as shown in Figure A.3. Short semantic statements refer to common situations that can be summed up in a couple of words and are added in square brackets. Table A.1 lists the short semantic statements used in this book.

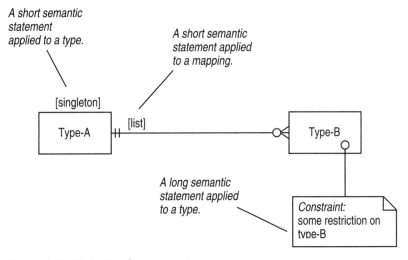

Figure A.3   Notation for semantic statements.

MARKER	ATTACHED TO	MEANING
[abstract]	Type	Type may not have any instances that are not instances of some subtype.
[abstract]	Mapping	Should be overridden by subtypes of the domain. The source is also abstract.
[class]	Mapping	Mapping is from the class rather than from instances. This is the equivalent to class variables or static members.
[Dag]	Recursive association	Objects connected by this association form a directed acyclic graph.
[Dag]	Mapping	Mapping returns a directed acyclic graph of objects.
[global]	Package	Package is visible to all other packages.
[hierarchy]	Recursive association	Objects connected by this association form a hierarchy.
[hierarchy]	Multivalued mapping	Mapping returns a hierarchy of objects.
[historic]	Historic mapping	Keeps a history of previous connections (see Section 15.3).
[immutable] or [imm]	Mapping	Mapping cannot be altered after creation of an instance.
[immutable] or [imm]	Partition	Subtypes are static. Objects cannot change type within this partition.
[key: *a type*]	Mapping	A keyed mapping (see Section 15.2).
[list]	Multivalued mapping	Mapping returns an ordered collection (list) of objects.
[multiple hierarchies]	Recursive association	Objects connected by this association form several hierarchies.
[singleton]	Type	Type can only have one instance.
[*number1, number2*]	Mapping	*number1* is the lower bound and *number2* the upper bound of the mapping.

Table A.1 Short semantic statements.

Not everything can be expressed as a short semantic statement. When more room is needed, I use a long semantic statement, which contains more text in a dog-eared box. A long semantic statement has a heading indicating what it describes. These headings are listed in Table A.2.

HEADING	ATTACHED TO	MEANING
Constraint	Type	Statement that must be true for all instances of the type.
Derivation	Derived mapping	A way of deriving the mapping. Implementations can choose another equivalent way.
Instances	Type	A list of all allowed instances of the type.
Method	Operation	Indicates the method for the operation.
Note	Anything	An informal comment.
Overload	Type	Indicates how the type overloads some feature of the supertype.

Table A.2   Headings for long semantic statements.

Not all methods provide a way of capturing the kind of information shown in semantic statements. It is important, however, that much of this information not be lost. Increasingly methods are providing some kind of visual note, similar to the long semantic statement, that can be used in this way.

A.1.5   Fundamental Types

In traditional data modeling the world is often divided into entities and attributes. The division is somewhat arbitrary. In practice it often boils down to attributes being the fundamental data types supported by the environment—usually integer, real, string, date, and perhaps a couple of others.

With object systems we can easily define new types that have many of the same features as these built-in types. A classic example from Smalltalk is the fraction. In Smalltalk a fraction works just like any other number; indeed if we execute $\frac{1}{3}$ in Smalltalk the answer is the fraction $\frac{1}{3}$, not some pseudo-infinitely recurring decimal.

When developing systems we must make use of these types. A classic example is handling monetary values. The value of a car in a database is typically held as a number, yet it is nonsense to say that a car costs 10,000. The currency is all important. With objects we can actually define a money type that knows both the number and the currency. It can perform addition (checking that the currencies match) and create a printout formatted the correct way.

Table A.3 lists the fundamental types used in this book.

An important point about fundamental types is that mappings from a fundamental type to a nonfundamental type are never implemented. Otherwise, the fundamental type would get a huge interface crowded with accessors to

TYPE	DESCRIPTION
Boolean	True or false, with the usual operations.
Currency	Subtypes of unit representing monetary currencies (e.g., US dollars, sterling, yen).
Date	The usual dates (e.g., 1-Apr-1995).
Duration	A subtype of quantity whose units are time (e.g., 5 days, 3 hours). Note that we cannot convert from days to months.
Integer	The usual integers (...-1, 0, 1, 2...).
Magnitude	A type that supports the comparative operations, such as <, >, =, ≥, ≤.
Money	A subtype of quantity whose units are currencies (e.g., $5, 250 FFR).
Number	The supertype of integer, real, and fraction.
Quantity	A type with a number and units (e.g., 4 inches) (see Section 3.1).
Range	A range between two magnitudes (see Section 4.3).
Real	The usual real numbers.
String	A short piece of text. There is no fixed limit, but I usually interpret it as a short one-line text item. Longer items use the type text.
Text	A long piece of text, usually with formatting.
Time	Time of day (e.g., 1:20 p.m.). Not fixed to a specific date (see Timepoint).
Timepoint	A point in time. It may be only a date, or it may be a combination of date and time.
Time Period	A period with a start and end timepoint. A time period can tell if it overlaps with another, or if a timepoint lies within it. It is a Range of Timepoints.
Time Reference	The supertype of time period and timepoint.
Unit	The unit for a quantity (e.g., inches, newtons).

Table A.3   Fundamental types used in this book.

every type that used it. This would be both unwieldy and not reusable. A conceptual model can show that a mapping exists, since conceptually the mapping does exist, but a corresponding specification model cannot.

Some authors refer to these kinds of types as literals; however, other authors use the term *literal* to stand for nonobject types (such as the type real in C++), which is why I use the term *fundamental type*.

I have not attempted to make a complete specification of fundamental types in this book. Consider this an exercise for the reader (or a future edition). Some of these types are given a specification in Cook and Daniels [4].

A.2   Interaction Diagrams

Interaction diagrams show how several objects collaborate to get something done. An interaction diagram has a number of vertical lines that represent objects. Arrows between the lines represent messages sent between objects, with sequence indicated by progression down the paper, as shown in Figure A.4. Interaction diagrams are widely used and simple to follow. One unusual thing I do is use a double-headed arrow to show where the same message is sent to many objects, as occurs in a loop or iterating over a collection. I also occasionally use a dashed line to show a return value; this is not something I do all the time, but it is sometimes useful when things are getting hairy.

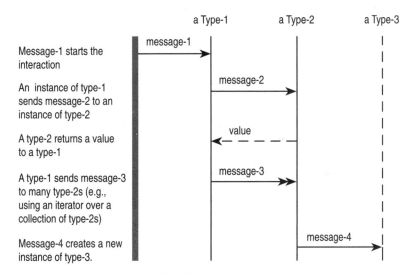

Figure A.4   Notation used for interaction diagrams.

I use interactions quite a lot in this book to show behavior. Often I use them in conjunction with an event diagram (see Section A.3) because the two approaches complement each other well. Event diagrams define behavior in a manner that encourages parallelism, yet they do not indicate which objects do what. Interaction diagrams show how this behavior can be allocated between objects while suppressing the parallelism and the precise behavioral logic.

You may be more familiar with seeing interaction diagrams expressed as numbered messages between boxes, which are equivalent to the lines down page. I prefer the lines-down-the-page-form because I think it makes it easier to see the sequence of messages.

Since interaction diagrams are so simple, you don't need much of a tutorial on them if you have not used them before. A good source for more details is Booch [1].

A.3   Event Diagrams

Event diagrams are another form of behavioral model that I use. Although they are more complex than interaction diagrams, they do allow complete control to be specified. They also are able to express parallel behavior, which is very useful in business modeling.

The boxes on an event diagram represent operations that complete by signalling an event. A trigger rule indicates that an event triggers an operation. Parallelism appears when an event type has more than one trigger rule defined on it. Hence in Figure A.5 the event type signaling the end of operation-1 triggers both operation-2 and operation-3 in parallel. This means that operation-2 and operation-3 can occur in any order or simultaneously. Parallelism can also occur with a multiple trigger, which is shown by a double-headed arrow. This indicates that the event triggers the operation many times, such as when iterating over a collection. A label on the line indicates what collection is being iterated over.

If a trigger rule leads into an operation via a control condition, the operation is only invoked if the control condition (a Boolean expression) evaluates to true. The control condition is often used to synchronize parallel threads. Each thread triggers the condition, which is designed to be true only at the appropriate synchronization point.

Two common control conditions are the and condition and the z condition. The and condition is true only when all incoming trigger rules have fired once. It is shown by a & in the diamond. The z condition is true whenever there are no operations on the diagram that are triggered to run, that is, when all is quiet and the diagram has gone to sleep. It is shown by a z in the diamond (as in zzzzzz). A z condition is often used at the end of the diagram to synchronize the end of the diagram.

The other conditional logic is that of the partition, as on operation-3. The event is subtyped depending on the outcome of the operation. A trigger rule can be placed on the supertype event to indicate a trigger that is fired whatever the outcome. The partition works the same way as in structural models. An event can have many partitions defined on it, a partition can have any number of events within it, and partitions can be defined on top of each other to any desired depth. Any event will be an instance of only one event type from each partition.

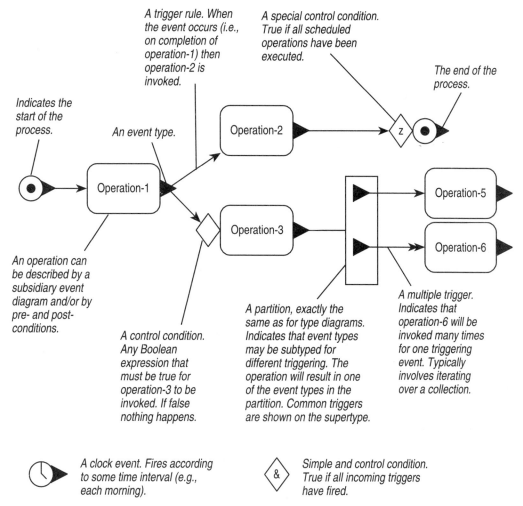

Figure A.5   Notation for event diagrams.

Event diagrams are conceptual in that they only say how some process works, not which objects carry out the process. Thus they complement interaction diagrams very well. For a tutorial on them see Odell [5].

A.4   State Diagrams

State diagrams define the behavior of a single object by describing the various states the object can get into and how the object changes state. The most widely used form of state diagram in OO methods is that of the Harel state chart. I use a subset of this form in this book. A state diagram is drawn for a single type and represents the behavior of each instance of that type.

Each state is shown by a box, as shown in Figure A.6. The boxes are linked by transitions that show how an object can move from one state to another. The transition is labeled with the event that causes the transition. If a transition has a guard, then the transition only occurs when the event occurs, and the guard evaluates to true. The guard is a Boolean expression. If a transition has an action, then this action is executed during the transition to the new state. States can be generalized into superstates. A superstate can be used to define transitions that then apply to all substates.

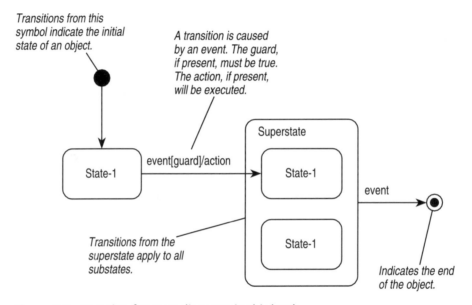

Figure A.6   Notation for state diagrams in this book.

For a simple tutorial on Harel state charts, see Booch [1]. For a more comprehensive treatment, the best source is Cook and Daniels [4]. In this book I do not use state diagrams that much, and certainly none with the power of Harel state charts, but they do pop up occasionally.

A.5   Package Diagrams

On large models we need a way to organize the mass of types that appear on the type diagram. A single large type diagram is both too complex for humans to comprehend and too difficult for software to manage. A large diagram can be broken down into pages for a human, but an arbitrary choice of pages does little to control the software. Package diagrams, as shown in Figure A.7, provide a more controlled mechanism.

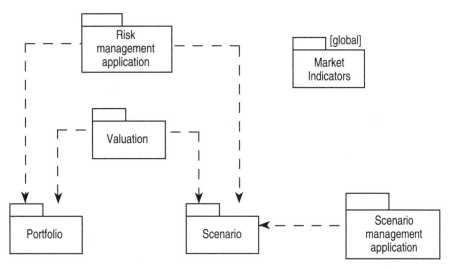

Figure A.7   Notation for describing packages.

This diagram is taken from Figure 11.3. I'm using the Rational Software's Unified Modeling Language notation [2] for packages, as I find it clearer than Booch's original notation.

A package (also called category domain, cluster, or subsystem) is a group of types (or classes). A type can belong to only one package. Usually types are assigned to packages so that types that collaborate often are put in the same package. Any type in the package can access any feature of any other type in the same package.

Packages are linked by visibility relationships. If a client type wishes to make use of a server type in another package, a visibility relationship must exist between the client type and the server type. This is required for any service: calling an operation, holding in an attribute, or passing as a parameter.

Visibility is different from a prerequisite. A prerequisite implies that one package needs the presence of another package to function. Prerequisites are transitive: If package C is a prerequisite of package B, and package B is a prerequisite of package A, then package C is a prerequisite of package A. This transitivity is not true for visibilities. Package A may not have visibility to package C; indeed package B may be specifically designed to hide package C from package A—this is the essence of a layered architecture. Prerequisites and visibilities are often confused because programming languages often merge the two together. C++ header files and Envy prerequisites define prerequisites and allow visibility to all prerequisites, which defeats the use of one package to hide another. All visibilities must be explicitly declared in a package. Hence in Figure A.7 the risk management application package must have an explicit visibility to the portfolio package to be able to use its services. If that visibility were not present, the portfolio package would still be a prerequisite (via the valuation package), but there would be no visibility. Visibilities imply prerequisites but not the reverse.

Within a package, types can be public or private. Public types are seen by packages that have visibility; private types can only be used by types within the same package. Packages can be made global, in which case all other packages have visibility to them. This is necessary for general components such as integers, strings, and collections.

When developing a large system, we try to minimize the visibilities between packages so that the system has less dependencies and is thus easier to manage. In this book I discuss packages primarily in Chapters 11 and 12.

Although this kind of model is essential for larger systems, it is not much discussed in methods. Booch [1] introduced the basic ideas that I use here, but his description is very brief, largely because it is difficult to discuss this subject without a substantial example. This lack has been rectified by Robert Martin, who gives a number of examples of the use of package models [6].

References

1. Booch, G. *Object-Oriented Analysis and Design with Applications* (Second Edition). Redwood City, CA: Benjamin/Cummings, 1993.
2. Booch, G. and J. Rumbaugh. *Unified Method for Object-Oriented Development.* Rational Software Corporation, Version 0.8, 1995.
3. Gamma, E., R. Helm, R. Johnson, and J. Vlissides. *Design Patterns: Elements of Reusable Object-Oriented Software.* Reading, MA: Addison-Wesley, 1995.
4. Cook, S. and J. Daniels. *Designing Object Systems: Object-Oriented Modelling with Syntropy.* Hemel Hempstead, UK: Prentice-Hall International, 1994.
5. Martin, J. and J. Odell. *Object-Oriented Methods: A Foundation.* Englewood Cliffs, NJ: Prentice-Hall, 1995.
6. Martin, R.C. *Designing Object-Oriented C++ Applications Using the Booch Method.* Englewood Cliffs, NJ: Prentice-Hall, 1995.

Table of Patterns

TEXT SECTION	NAME	PROBLEM	SOLUTION
2.1	Party	People and organizational units have similar responsibilities.	Create a type party as a supertype of person and organization.
2.2	Organization Hierarchies	Representing a hierarchical organization structure.	Create a recursive association on organization.
2.3	Organization Structure	An organization structure has hierarchies or more complex links.	Create organization structure as a directed relationship between two parties. Give it an organization structure type to represent the kind of relationship.
		New kinds of links appearing.	
		Keeping a history of changes to the structure.	
2.4	Accountability	Representing organization structures, employment, management, professional registration, and contracts with a similar structure.	Create accountability as a directed relationship between two parties. Give it an accountability type to represent the kind of relationship.

TEXT SECTION	NAME	PROBLEM	SOLUTION
2.5	Accountability Knowledge Level	Recording the rules that describe how accountabilities can be formed in a way that is easy to change.	Create a knowledge level for accountability by associations between accountability type and party type. This knowledge level constrains the operational level of accountability and party.
2.6	Party Type Generalizations	Of many party types in a model, most are similar to some other party type.	Allow party types to be subtyped so they inherit accountability types.
2.7	Hierarchic Accountability	Constraining some accountability types into a hierarchy.	Define a subtype of accountability type that includes the hierarchy constraint. A list of levels allows you to name each level in the hierarchy.
2.8	Operating Scope	Describing what responsibilities are implied by an accountability.	Add a number of operating scopes to the accountability. The type of operating scope depends on the type of accountability.
2.9	Post	Accountabilities are due to the job rather than the person doing it.	Create a post as another subtype of party. Appoint a person to a post with an accountability. The holder of the post then gets the responsibilities of the post while they hold it.
3.1	Quantity	Representing a value such as 6 feet or $5.	Use a quantity type that includes both the amount and the unit. Currencies are a kind of unit.
3.2	Conversion Ratio	Converting between quantities in different units.	Record conversion ratios between units.
3.3	Compound Units	Representing units such as kg/m^2.	Use a unit that is a combination of other units.

TEXT SECTION	NAME	PROBLEM	SOLUTION
3.4	**Measurement**	An object has a large number of quantity attributes.	Create an object to represent the individual measurement. This is linked to the object being measured and to a phenomenon type that describes the kind of measurement being made.
		Recording information about an individual measurement of an attribute.	
		Tracking changes in a value to an attribute over time.	
3.5	**Observation**	Attributes are qualitiative and thus cannot be measured with numbers.	Create an observation type that links the object to a phenomenon. Each phenomenon is a value for some phenomenon type.
3.6	**Subtyping Observation Concepts**	Phenomena are special cases of another phenomenon.	Allow phenomena to be subtyped with an association in the knowledge level.
3.7	**Protocol**	Dealing with similar phenomena when the method of observing can occasionally cause different interpretation.	Record the protocol used for determining the observation.
		Recording the accuracy and sensitivity of a measurement.	
3.8	**Dual Time Record**	Differences arise between when an observation is true and when you noticed it, and between when an event occurs and when you noticed it.	Record both times separately for all such objects.
3.9	**Rejected Observation**	Observations were made in error but cannot be erased.	Keep them, mark them as rejected, and record what observation rejected them.
3.10	**Active Observation, Hypothesis, and Projection**	Certainty in observations.	Subtype observations into active observations (I'm going to treat this), hypothesis (I'm going to investigate further), and projection (I think this may happen).
		Representing observations that you think may come to pass when you have to base treatment on that possibility.	

TEXT SECTION	NAME	PROBLEM	SOLUTION
3.11	Associated Observation	Recording the evidence for a diagnosis.	Treat the diagnosis as an observation with an association to the observations used as evidence.
3.12	Process of Observation	Determining the process of observation and diagnosis.	Each observation may lead to suggestions for further observations and interventions to be proposed, and to re-evaluation of contradictory observations. As these steps produce further observations, this leads to a continuous process of observation.
4.1	Enterprise Segment	Breaking down a large enterprise into pieces using different criteria and varying degrees of granularity.	Define each criteria for breakdown as a dimension, and represent it as a hierarchy of elements. Define an enterprise segment as the combination of one element from each dimension.
4.2	Measurement Protocol	Indicating that measurements are calculated or read from a database. Recording the formulas for calculations. The same phenomenon type can be determined in different ways depending on context.	Define a measurement protocol that describes how to create a measurement for a phenomenon type. Measurement protocols can be sourced or calculated, calculations can be causal, comparative, or dimension combination.
4.3	Range	Describing a range between two values.	Define a range type with upper and lower bounds and suitable operations.
4.4	Phenomenon with Range	Describing a phenomenon defined as a range on a phenomenon type.	Give the phenomenon an attribute of range. Create a range function that links the range to the phenomenon under conditions described by other phenomena.

TEXT SECTION	NAME	PROBLEM	SOLUTION
5.1	Name	Refering to an object.	Give the object a string as its name.
5.2	Identification Scheme	Ensuring an identification refers to only one object but different parties can refer to the object differently.	Create identification schemes that contain identifiers, where each identifier refers to only one unit. A party can use any identification scheme.
5.3	Object Merge	Two objects are in fact the same.	Copy the attributes of one over to the other, switch all references from the first to the other, and delete the first.
			Mark one as superseded and give it a link to the other.
			Link the two object appearances with an essence that indicates they are the same.
5.4	Object Equivalence	Some people think two objects are the same, but others think they are different.	Create an equivalence for the objects.
6.1	Account	Recording a history of changes to some quantity.	Create an account. Each change is recorded as an entry against the account. The balance of the account gives its current value.
6.2	Transaction	Ensuring that nothing gets lost from an account.	Use transactions to transfer items between accounts.
6.3	Summary Account	Looking at a group of accounts as if they were a single account.	Create a summary account with the other account as children.
6.4	Memo Account	Noting some quantity in a side account without using a transaction.	Create a memo account that does not affect real transactions and does not hold real items.
6.5	Posting Rules	Automating transfers between accounts.	Define a posting rule between the accounts.

TEXT SECTION	NAME	PROBLEM	SOLUTION
6.6	Individual Instance Method	Giving each instance of a type its own method for some operation.	Define a singleton subclass for each method.
			Use the strategy pattern.
			Create a case statement hidden inside the object.
			Separate the different behaviors into parameters.
			Build a simple interpreter.
6.7	Posting Rule Execution	Ensuring that the posting rules are all executed at the right time.	Fire all outbound rules when a entry is put into an account.
			Explicitly ask a posting rule to fire.
			Ask an account to fire its outbound posting rules.
			Backward chain the posting rules when an account is queried.
6.8	Posting Rules for Many Accounts	Defining the same posting rules for many accounts.	Define the rules on an account type.
			Define the rules on a summary account.
6.9	Choosing Entries	Asking an account for a subset of its entries. Asking an object for a selection of objects in one of its collections.	The account returns all entries, and the caller selects the ones it wants.
			The account provides an operation for each possible subset.
			The caller passes a filter object to the account.
6.10	Accounting Practice	Assigning several posting rules as a group.	Create an accounting practice to group them together.
6.11	Sources of an Entry	Seeing how a transaction was calculated.	Record the creating posting rule, and the entries that it used in the calculation, with the new transaction.

TEXT SECTION	NAME	PROBLEM	SOLUTION
6.12	Balance Sheet and Income Statement	Representing balance sheet and income statements.	Create subtypes of account.
6.13	Corresponding Account	Reconciling two parties' views of the same account.	Treat each view as separate accounts that correspond to each other.
6.14	Specialized Account Model	Using the general accounting patterns in a specific case.	Subtype the pattern's types to support the specialized needs.
6.15	Booking Entries to Multiple Accounts	Putting an entry in more than one account.	Treat one account as the real account and use a memo account for the other.
			Treat one account as the real account and use a derived account for the other.
8.1	Proposed and Implemented Action	Representing both what you intended to do and what you did.	Use separate objects for the proposed and implemented actions.
8.2	Completed and Abandoned Actions	Indicating how an action ended.	An action is completed if it was carried out as intended, abandoned if not.
8.3	Suspension	Putting an action on a temporary hold.	Put a suspension on the action. Use a time range to show how long it lasts.
8.4	Plan	Recording a group of proposed actions that you intend to perform together.	A plan is a collection of proposed actions linked by dependencies. Several parties can have different plans that refer to the same proposed action.
		Representing the dependencies among actions.	
		Allowing different people to coordinate each other's plans.	
8.5	Protocol	Performing standard procedures many times the same way.	An action can be done according to a protocol. A protocol can be divided into subprotocols linked by dependencies.

TEXT SECTION	NAME	PROBLEM	SOLUTION
8.6	Resource Allocation	Allocating resources to plans, protocols, and actions.	General resource allocations allocate a quantity of a resource type. Specific resource allocations allocate specific resources.
8.7	Outcome and Start Functions	Knowing when to carry out a protocol and what the outcome of the protocol, and any actions, will be.	Start functions and outcome functions link a protocol to the observation concepts that trigger it and may be the result of it.
9.1	Contract	Recording deals from the perspective of both the buyer and the seller.	Use a contractor with both buying and selling parties.
9.2	Portfolio	Dynamically selecting contracts for different purposes. Dynamically selecting objects.	Define a portfolio as a collection of contracts. The contracts are selected by a filter—a Boolean expression used to determine which contracts fit the portfolio.
9.3	Quote	Separate prices are given for buying and selling.	Combine both prices into a single quote.
9.4	Scenario	Prices of instruments change over time. Considering hypothetical combinations of prices. Prices of one instrument can affect prices of another.	Create a scenario to capture the real or hypothetical state of the market. A scenario gives the price of any instrument in that state and includes rules to derive prices for hypothetical market states.
10.1	Forward Contracts	A contract may be delivered in the future at today's prices.	Use a contract with separate trade and delivery dates.
10.2	Options	A party may choose to buy or sell something at a set price at some point in the future.	An option is a subtype of contract with the additional behavior. An option is a separate object with a contract as an attribute.

TEXT SECTION	NAME	PROBLEM	SOLUTION
10.3	Product	A combination option is seen as one item by the salesperson but as a collection of simpler contracts by the dealers.<hr>A salesperson sees one package, but only the items in the package are seen internally.	Treat what the salesperson sells as a product and what is internally valued as a contract.
10.4	Subtype State Machines	A barrier option has different behavior to an option, but seems like a subtype. Dealing with subtypes and state machines.	Ensure both sub- and supertype objects respond to the same events.
10.5	Parallel Application and Domain Hierarchies	You are displaying a list of objects in a user interface. These objects are various subtypes, and some subtype properties need to be displayed. Your user interface objects must not fail by sending a message to an inappropriate object.	The application object checks the type of the domain object to ensure it will understand the message.<hr>Give the supertype an interface that encompasses all subtype behaviors.<hr>Treat the properties as a run time attribute.<hr>Use an intermediate object loaded by the domain object.<hr>Use exception handling package.
11.1	Multiple Access Levels to a Package	Different clients of a package need different amounts of behavior.	Split the package into separate packages for each level of access.<hr>Allow packages to have more than one interface.

TEXT SECTION	NAME	PROBLEM	SOLUTION
11.2	Mutual Visibility	Types in two packages need to see each other.	Combine the two packages.
			Have two mutually visible packages.
			Decide that one type cannot see the other.
11.3	Subtyping Packages	Using subtypes with packages.	The subtype can be put in a separate package. Visibility to the package is with the supertype, but not vice versa.
12.1	Two-Tier Architecture	Partitioning software on a client/server system.	Put the user interface on the client and the database on the server. The user interface classes access the database directly.
12.2	Three-Tier Architecture	The two-tier architecture couples the user interface too tightly to the database design.	Have three logical tiers: application, domain, and database.
		The database interface cannot support a rich model of the domain.	
12.3	Presentation and Application Logic	Application software handles both interpretation of the domain model and driving the user interface.	Separate the application tier into presentation (user interface) and application logic (dealing with the domain model). Structure the application logic as a set of facades for the presentation.
12.4	Database Interaction	Working with a database.	Let the domain classes be responsible for saving themselves in the database.
			Create a separate layer to handle the interactions between database and domain objects.

TEXT SECTION	NAME	PROBLEM	SOLUTION
14.1	Implementing Associations	Implementing a conceptual association.	Choose one direction to implement, and use an operation and a pointer.
			Put operations and pointers in both directions.
			Put operations in both directions but a pointer only in one. Use lookup for the other direction.
			Put operations in both directions, and use a table and lookup for the pointers.
14.2	Implementing Generalizations	Implementing generalization, especially if multiple and dynamic classification is involved.	Use inheritance.
			Use classes for each combination of subtypes with multiple inheritance.
			Use an internal flag.
			Delegate to a hidden class (state pattern).
			Copy and replace.
14.3	Object Creation	Creating an object.	Use a creation method with arguments for all mandatory and immutable mappings.
14.4	Object Destruction	Destroying an object.	Have a specific destruction method. Define how much the delete should cascade.
14.5	Entry Point	Starting to look for objects.	Let the class be responsible for storing and finding its instances.
			Have a registrar find and store objects.
14.6	Implementing Constraints	Implementing constraints.	Give each object an operation to check its constraint. Call it at the end of modifiers when debugging.

TEXT SECTION	NAME	PROBLEM	SOLUTION
15.1	Associative Type	Adding features to an association.	Create a type for the association.
			Use a special notation.
15.2	Keyed Mapping	Representing values in a mapping that are keyed off another type.	Use a keyed mapping.
15.3	Historic Mapping	Recording previous values of a mapping.	Use a historic mapping.

Index

Abandoned actions, 157, 160–161, 337

Absence
  category observation, 46
  observation concepts, 47

Abstract
  mapping, 136, 322
  posting rule, 151
  type, 322

Accessors, 275–277, 278, 280

Account. *See also* Summary account
  booking entries to multiple accounts, 97,
    127–132, 337
  corresponding, 96, 124–125, 337
  derived, 130–131
  filter, 119, 120
  generally, 95, 97–98
  memo, 96, 103–104, 336
  pattern, 335
  posting, 141
  sign, 97
  specialized model, 96, 125–127, 337
  statement, 97

Account-based firing, 112–113, 143

Accountability
  abstraction, 23
  generally, 17–18, 22–24
  hierarchic, 17, 28–30, 332
  knowledge level, 17, 24–27, 332
  operating scopes, 30–32
  organization hierarchies, 17, 19–21, 331
  organization structure, 17, 21–22, 331
  party, 17, 18–19
  party type generalizations, 17, 27–28, 332
  pattern, 331
  post, 17, 32–33

Accounting and inventory. *See also* Account;
    Entry; Individual instance method
  balance sheets and income statements, 96,
    123–124, 337
  patterns, 134
  posting rule execution, 96, 111–115, 336
  posting rules, 96, 104–105, 336

Accounting and inventory *(continued)*
  posting rules for many accounts, 116–118,
    336
  practice, 119–122
  practice pattern, 96, 337
  specialized account model, 96
  Total Telecommunications example, use
    in, 133–134
  transactions, 95–96, 98–101

Accounting framework, 132

ACM. *See* Aroma Coffee Makers (ACM)

Action
  abandoned, 157, 160–161, 337
  completed, 157, 160–161, 337
  implemented, 157, 158–160, 168, 337
  proposed, 157, 158–160, 168, 337

Active observation, 36, 49–50, 334

Actual status, 69–71

Acyclic graph structure, 28. *See also* DAG
  (directed acyclic graph)

Aggregation in type diagrams, 315–318

Alexander, Christopher, 5, 6

Analysis
  design techniques, 3
  generally, 1
  pattern, 310

Anderson, Bruce, 5

Application. *See* Parallel application

Application facade
  common methods, 257, 262–264
  contents of a facade, 257, 259–262
  domain model, visibility to, 221
  generally, 257–258
  health care example, 257–259
  methods for facade attributes, 260–262
  multiple facades, 257, 267–269
  operations, 257, 264–265
  type conversion, 257, 265–267

Application logic. *See* Presentation and
  application logic

Notation for state diagrams

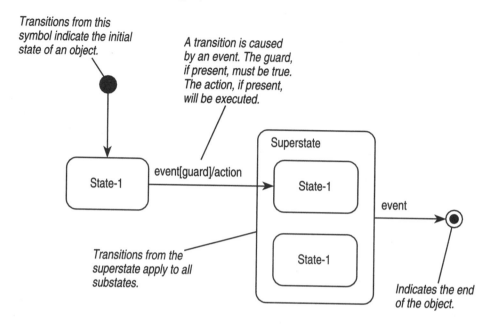

Transitions from this symbol indicate the initial state of an object.

A transition is caused by an event. The guard, if present, must be true. The action, if present, will be executed.

State-1

event[guard]/action

Superstate

State-1

State-1

event

Transitions from the superstate apply to all substates.

Indicates the end of the object.

Notation for interaction diagrams

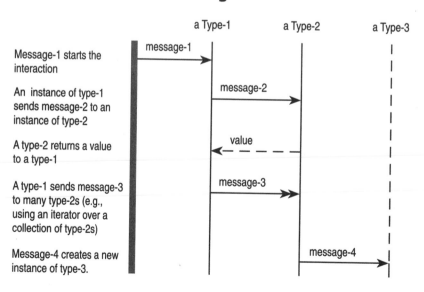

a Type-1   a Type-2   a Type-3

Message-1 starts the interaction

message-1

An instance of type-1 sends message-2 to an instance of type-2

message-2

A type-2 returns a value to a type-1

value

A type-1 sends message-3 to many type-2s (e.g., using an iterator over a collection of type-2s)

message-3

Message-4 creates a new instance of type-3.

message-4